ENEMY NUMBER ONE

ENEMY NUMBER ONE

The United States of America in Soviet
Ideology and Propaganda, 1945–1959

Rósa Magnúsdóttir

OXFORD
UNIVERSITY PRESS

Oxford University Press is a department of the University of Oxford. It furthers
the University's objective of excellence in research, scholarship, and education
by publishing worldwide. Oxford is a registered trade mark of Oxford University
Press in the UK and certain other countries.

Published in the United States of America by Oxford University Press
198 Madison Avenue, New York, NY 10016, United States of America.

© Oxford University Press 2019

Library of Congress Cataloging-in-Publication Data
Names: Magnúsdóttir, Rósa, author.
Title: Enemy Number One : The United States of America in Soviet Ideology and
Propaganda, 1945–1959 / Rósa Magnúsdóttir.
Description: New York : Oxford University Press, 2019. |
Includes bibliographical references and index.
Identifiers: LCCN 2018022788 (print) | LCCN 2018023496 (ebook) |
ISBN 978-0-19-068147-0 (updf) | ISBN 978-0-19-068148-7 (epub) |
ISBN 978-0-19-068149-4 (online component) |
ISBN 978-0-19-068146-3 (hardback : alk. paper)
Subjects: LCSH: United States—Relations—Soviet Union. |
Soviet Union—Relations—United States. | Propaganda, Soviet. |
Propaganda, Anti-American. | Cold War. | United States—Foreign public
opinion, Soviet. | Public opinion—Soviet Union.
Classification: LCC E183.8.S65 (ebook) | LCC E183.8.S65 M325 2019 (print) |
DDC 327.73047—dc23
LC record available at https://lccn.loc.gov/2018022788

9 8 7 6 5 4 3 2 1

Printed by Sheridan Books, Inc., United States of America

CONTENTS

ACKNOWLEDGMENTS

It has taken a long time to finish this project, and I feel indebted to countless people and institutions for their support. I take great pleasure in finally being able to acknowledge them all here, starting with the numerous organizations that provided funding. This project started out as a Ph.D. dissertation at the University of North Carolina at Chapel Hill, and several grants from the History Department, the Graduate School, and the University Center for International Studies (now UNC Center for Global Initiatives) funded my research stays in Moscow.

A DAAD Fellowship at the Institute for European History in Mainz, Germany, gave me time, space, and resources to start writing the dissertation. A Doric C. Quinn Fellowship from the History Department at UNC–Chapel Hill allowed me to finish it. A Fulbright Fellowship and an American Scandinavian Foundation Fellowship permitted me to study in the United States in the first place. Later, I was a visiting fellow at the Aleksanteri Institute in Helsinki, where the first steps in turning a dissertation into a book took place. As a faculty member at Aarhus University in Denmark, I twice received the most valuable gift of time in the form of sabbaticals to finish this manuscript. Aarhus University Research Foundation (AUFF) provided funding for the photo licenses, the index, as well as several writing retreats in the beautiful Mill House (Møllehuset).

At UNC, I had the great fortune to study under the direction of Donald J. Raleigh, a remarkable scholar, adviser, mentor, and friend. Always engaged in my work, Don Raleigh came up with the title for this book in 2011, and as we were celebrating the near completion of it, he came up with the title of my next (still unwritten) book. I remain eternally grateful for his continued support and encouragement.

Thinking back to my years as a scholar in training, I would especially like to thank Michael H. Hunt, who sadly passed away only recently, Robert M. Jenkins, Jeffrey W. Jones, Willis E. Brooks, and the now late David M. Griffiths for their support and guidance during my time at UNC. They all read and commented on the dissertation, offering helpful advice on how to proceed. Also, I would not have embarked upon a university career in history had it not been for the encouragement of my undergraduate adviser at the University of Iceland, Valur Ingimundarson, who has since become a collaborator and friend.

Don Raleigh has advised dozens of graduate students and passed on both his endless wisdom and wit to a large group of wonderful people who support each other all around the globe. Thank you Jackie Olich, Sharon Kowalsky, Jon Wallace, Chris Ward, Paula Michaels, Marco Dumančić, Jenifer Parks, Nick Ganson, Jeff Jones, Betsy Jones Hemenway, Kate Tranchel, Mike Paulauskas, Emily Baran, Gleb Tsipursky, Aaron Hale-Dorrell, and Annie Bland. In addition, I would like to thank Igor Fedyukin for his continued help and friendship, most recently as an ally in the book writing process. Outside of Hamilton Hall, Anne Langley was a model in work-life balance in Chapel Hill, and fellow Tar Heels Katie Gunter and the late Maria Stalnaker made my first extended stay in Moscow a true adventure.

In Moscow, many archivists and scholars helped me navigate the labyrinth of Russian archives, but I am most indebted to Vladimir Kozlov, historian and then deputy director of the State Archive of the Russian Federation, and Vladimir Pechatnov, professor at the Moscow State Institute of International Relations. Versions of the manuscript were presented at numerous conferences and workshops in the United States, Russia, Germany, the United Kingdom, the Netherlands, Denmark, and Finland. I am appreciative of all these opportunities to receive feedback on my work and have gained much from interactions with colleagues in the field, especially Sari Autio-Sarasmo, Kate Brown, Natalya Chernyshova, Dina Fainberg, Beate Fieseler, Juliane Fürst, Jessica Gienow-Hecht, Pia Koivunen, Maike Lehmann, Eva Maurer, Katalin Miklossy, Susanne Schattenberg, and Ben Tromly.

A few earlier publications included materials that appear in the book, now in revised and updated form: "The Myth of 'Amerika' and Soviet Socialism: Perceptions and Realities in the Postwar Soviet Union," *Soviet and Post-Soviet Review* 31, no. 3 (2004): 291–307; "Be Careful in America, Premier Khrushchev! Soviet Perceptions of Peaceful Coexistence with the United States in 1959," *Cahiers du monde russe* 47, nos. 1–2 (2006): 109–30; and "Mission Impossible? Selling Soviet Socialism to Americans, 1955–1958," *Searching for a Cultural Diplomacy*, ed. Jessica Gienow-Hecht and Mark C. Donfried, Culture and International History Series (New York: Berghahn Books, 2010), 50–72. I am thankful for permission to draw upon these publications.

The following people took time from their very busy schedules to read and comment on parts of the manuscript at various stages, for which I am very grateful. Almost a decade ago, David Engerman read the whole dissertation and offered advice on how to turn it into a book. Peter Bugge and Christian Axboe Nielsen read an early draft of the introduction and Stefan Blank a late version of the epilogue. Andreï Kozovoï, Paula Michaels, Erik Van Ree, and Victoria Zhuravleva read large parts of the revised manuscript at various stages and offered sound advice and constructive criticism. I am also very pleased to acknowledge the invaluable insights of my editor, Nancy Toff, who along with her assistants Elda Granata and Elizabeth Vaziri helped me navigate the publishing process. The whole production team at Oxford University Press has been extremely professional and I remain very grateful for everyone's help. I alone am to blame for any shortcomings in the book.

In the spirit of Soviet propagandists, I toast to friendship and peace among the nations and thank collectively my family and friends in Iceland, Germany, France, Denmark, Sweden, Norway, Finland, the United States, and Russia. In all these countries, there are people who helped me more than they realize. They showed interest in what I was doing, strived to understand why I was doing it, and motivated me with their own accomplishments.

The best decision I ever made was to get married to a fellow academic. Even if he also always had more than enough to see to in his own career, David Reimer never blinked an eye when I had to work evenings and weekends to finish this book and he was left alone with the responsibilities of a busy household. His support and effortless belief in equality and social justice are a continued inspiration and I could not imagine a better father to our three girls: Ella Steinunn, Hanna Régine, and Karen Þóra. They provide a most happy distraction from academia and remind me every day of what is truly important in life.

Entangled with the joy of finally seeing this book in print is deep sadness. My father, Magnús Ágúst Torfason, passed away suddenly on the eve of my doctoral defense in May 2006 and it was difficult to separate this project from his untimely death. It took much effort, but my greatest motivation continued to be the unconditional love and support I grew up with from both my parents. Also my mother, Steinunn Thorsteinson, has always been an astonishing source of strength and courage. I dedicate this book to my parents.

NOTE ON TRANSLITERATION AND TRANSLATION

I have followed the Library of Congress transliteration rules with a few exceptions for names that have a commonly accepted spelling in English (e.g., Mikoyan, Georgy Zhukov, Yevgeny Yevtushenko, Yuri Zhdanov). The same logic applies to Soviet organizations and institutions, where I refer to them either by their Russian acronym or name (such as Mezhkniga or Soiuzpechat'), or by the commonly used English term (e.g., Writers' Union).

INTRODUCTION

On April 25, 1945, on the banks of the river Elbe one hundred miles south of Berlin, Soviet soldiers advancing from Stalingrad in the east and American soldiers coming in from Normandy in the west met to cut the German army in half, signaling that the end of the Second World War was in sight. But the meeting on the Elbe did more than break up the German army. On that day, hundreds of Soviet and American soldiers experienced comradeship and solidarity they vowed never to forget. They exchanged handshakes, embraces, and gifts. Together, they played music, sang American songs, drank Russian vodka, and toasted to "the late President Roosevelt, President Truman, Prime Minister Churchill, Marshal Stalin, and 'everlasting friendship' between us all."[1] On this spring day in April, the prospects for peace and friendship seemed endless. Soviet and American soldiers had no inkling that the "spirit of the Elbe" would soon be sacrificed in a superpower struggle between the former allies.

A long time would pass before friendly interactions between the Soviet and American people were again possible. The onset of the Cold War brought with it an official anti-American campaign in the Soviet Union that reached all areas of political and cultural life and dramatically limited possibilities for contacts with the former allies. Furthermore, the official memory of the Great Patriotic War in the Soviet Union did not allow for any celebration of the cooperation with Americans, and all attempts by veterans of the Elbe meeting to gather and commemorate the event were hindered by the Stalinist regime.

It took ten years until Soviet and American veterans of the meeting on the Elbe were able to arrange for an official reunion, indicating dramatic changes in Soviet political and cultural policy. Starting in 1955, two years after the death of Joseph Stalin, Soviet and American officials slowly revived cultural relations between the countries and, consequently, ordinary Soviet people could better access American culture and personal interactions with Americans

2nd Lieutenant William Robertson of the US Army and Lt. Alexander Sylvashko of the Russian Army warmly greet each other at a historic meeting of East and West near Torgau, Germany, in April 1945. The end of the Second World War was in sight and many people hoped for better times after the devastating war experience. *National Archives*, 531276

became more frequent. At the same time, Nikita Khrushchev softened the anti-American rhetoric noticeably, by announcing a return to Leninism and making peaceful coexistence the dominant Soviet strategy in relation to the United States and the West. A few more years passed before the official narrative of the Great Patriotic War would include references to cooperation with the Americans, and only in 1959 was the wartime alliance openly celebrated and incorporated into the Soviet memory of the Second World War. In September 1959, Khrushchev became the first Soviet leader to visit the United States, and he used the occasion to emphasize the wartime alliance as proof of the two countries' capabilities to peacefully coexist.

The journey from the meeting on the Elbe to Khrushchev's visit to America epitomizes the way in which the Soviet authorities attempted to control, contain, and appropriate images of the United States. Under Stalin, the attempts to control and shape available images of America in the Soviet Union often led to a tension between the desired, state-controlled image of the United States on the one hand and the way America was perceived by those who claimed to know it through non-Soviet channels on the other hand. This applied both to Soviet cultural officials working on American matters and to Soviet people who were exposed to various images of America. In the early Khrushchev years, the Soviet approach moved from hostile confrontation of all things American to hesitant interaction with Americans and American culture. Rallying people around the task of competing with America was supposed to move the focus to the accomplishments of socialism, but simultaneously admitting that the Soviet Union had to catch up with the United States turned out to be more complicated than Khrushchev had bargained for. Increased interaction with America and Americans was a double-edged sword in that it made information gathering less difficult. And while it should have made competing with America easier as well, the nature of Soviet socialism prevented Soviet officials from taking full advantage of what they learned about how best to deal with images of the American enemy.[2]

Enemy Number One is about the many challenges and difficulties Soviet authorities faced in the cultural Cold War with the United States. It is an untold part of a story that we have heard many times before: American soft-power efforts during the early Cold War are well covered in the historiography.[3] But this is the first detailed account that analyzes the Soviet ideological campaigns that engineered the multilayered reactions to America and American propaganda in the early Cold War. The book focuses on the dominant ideological narratives about America in the Soviet Union in the postwar period, and whenever possible it looks at challenges to these narratives and the way the authorities dealt with them. The challenges came from within the propaganda system in the broadest possible sense. Agitprop's "ideological workers" were quite aware of the perceived reception of their work and tried to preempt positive appraisals of the United States. In relation to that, the judicial authorities reported on moods in the country and noted carefully how Soviet people approached the American enemy in various contexts, and, finally, well-meaning participants in cultural diplomacy activities sometimes challenged the ideological rigidity of the propaganda. All these actors were strongly influenced by the ruling elite at the time, first the notorious "Stalin team" and then, after Stalin's death in 1953, the Khrushchev "clan" that took over.[4] The identity of the leader in charge was critical to the differences in control and policies: Stalin's script for anti-Americanism was entirely different from Khrushchev's emphasis on peaceful coexistence with the West. Without de-Stalinization and without the Thaw, we would not have seen the shifts in the cultural administration in the Soviet Union and the international outlook toward the United States.

While political and cultural focus on the United States was not new in the Soviet Union, it reached its greatest ideological heights in these early years of the Cold War when both countries were adjusting to their superpower status and the adversarial roles they now found themselves in. With the bipolarity came competition and enmity on a larger scale than the two countries had ever seen in times of peace. The Cold War thus created a context where the Soviet Union's celebration of socialism as the superior ideology took place while it constantly compared itself to the United States, contributing to what Michael David-Fox has called "the Soviet superiority complex."[5] Earlier, in the 1920s and 1930s, while certainly anticapitalist, the young Soviet state had felt relatively secure in showcasing its alternative form of modernity,[6] but during late Stalinism, the Soviet cultural mission was reduced to "explaining" Soviet socialism to both domestic and international audiences. The preoccupation with the United States and the role it played in the anti-Western campaigns of the immediate postwar years emerged strongly in a fear of being misunderstood and misrepresented. Under Khrushchev, the focus was back on celebrating the accomplishments of the Soviet Union; although without most of the international admirers of the prewar years, it was an uphill battle.

Russian and Soviet Views of America before the Second World War

Far from being monolithic, Russian and Soviet images of America before the Second World War changed over time and took on many different forms. Praise and criticism of the United States have always coexisted in Russia and the Soviet Union, and only with the rise of the Cold War did Soviet authorities no longer allow for any admiration of the recent ally, as it became enemy number one. Reluctantly, however, postwar Soviet ideology and propaganda had to take into account several narratives of the United States. One narrative was dominated by earlier memories of Americans: from the late nineteenth century to the Second World War, the United States had occupied a place in Russian culture and consciousness, although it was secondary to European countries like France and Germany in influencing the Russian cultural and political outlook in tsarist times.[7] Many architects of the future socialist way of life and thinkers of the revolutionary guard had looked to the United States as a symbol of a new frontier and modernity and explored how the future socialist state should take after the United States.[8]

Personal encounters with Americans were infrequent, however, and impressions of America were more likely to come from Soviet fiction and the printed press. These accounts would often come from privileged individuals who visited the United States as they frequently wrote about their experiences and thus contributed to the way the Soviet reading public formed an image of the United States. This brings to the forefront a focus on America as a mythological place, a place to dream about and to believe in, without really knowing it, and in this way, literary works and travelogues about the United States played an important role in advancing an image of America in the Soviet mass consciousness.

Fictional realities fed off and contributed to the various images presented in the media and official communications, and it surely did not hurt that several of the most able authors of the Russian language gave America a prominent place in their writings.

From the 1890s on, the United States had a strong presence in Russian literary works. Such beloved authors as Vladimir Korolenko, Maxim Gorky, Aleksandr Blok, Osip Mandelstam, Vladimir Mayakovsky, Ilya Ilf, and Evgeny Petrov contributed greatly to the creation of a myth of America in the Soviet Union, showing progress and prosperity on the one side and discrimination and inequality on the other.[9] Their poems, short stories, plays, and travelogues about America gradually reached an increasingly literate Russian reading public, and together their works represent the ambivalence so evident in Russian views of the United States. Although the writers generally have in common a focus on perceived American greatness, upon closer inspection America fails to meet their expectations. In part, this narrative was regenerated over and over, because the writers were influenced by earlier readings about the United States and did not therefore see the "real" America. In this way, Milla Fedorova argues, the literary tradition "imposed" its framework on the travelers, who "read America rather than saw it" and adhered to and recreated the existing ideological narrative about the United States.[10]

In addition to the literary narratives, the United States became an important point of reference in the writings and speeches of Bolshevik leaders, from Vladimir Lenin and Leon Trotsky to Nikolai Bukharin and Joseph Stalin. Understandably, the respect the young Bolsheviks showed for the United States cooled considerably when American troops intervened on behalf of the Whites in the Russian Civil War (1918–1921), but nevertheless a period of peaceful co-existence followed the Civil War with increased economic relations. At the same time, however, newspaper articles about the United States started to present the country as a callous capitalistic country, "blind to the sufferings and exploitation of the poor and unemployed citizens."[11] This was telling of what was to come in the postwar period, when Soviet newspapers and journals mastered the idea of the two Americas.

In the 1920s, however, American technological superiority and prosperity were widely acknowledged in the young Soviet Union. The Bolsheviks themselves promoted the United States as an industrial model and sought to promote the production strategies of Henry Ford and the industrial vision of Frederick Winslow Taylor. The writings of Ford and Taylor were translated into Russian, and *Pravda* advocated their industrial visions and business strategies. American cars became symbols of modernity, and Soviet authorities considered American tractors as necessary tools for industrialization and building communism.[12] In the late Stalinist era, the quality of American cars and factories did not escape

Soviet audiences, and these were among the advantages commonly noted in pro-American narratives in the postwar period.

Purchase agreements for Fordson tractors, Ford motorcars, and Ford factory layouts brought American specialists from Detroit to Russia, and for a while, industrial progress and Soviet modernity seemed to depend on imported American ideas and products. Fordism and Taylorism became synonyms for positive aspects of the United States, which the Soviet elite built on in order to design the Soviet future.[13] In 1936, for example, Stalin sent Anastas Mikoyan, then People's Commissar for Food, to America in order to learn about the American food industry. He spent two months in the United States, traveled 12,000 miles, and came back with many ideas about, for example, mechanically producing rolls and buns and information on producing nonalcoholic beverages. Mikoyan claimed that the trip to the United States had turned out to be a good education for him, and that he had returned with concrete plans for how to transfer the experiences of a capitalistic country to the Soviet Union.[14]

However, the Soviet leadership certainly had no qualms about condemning the American way of life in the same breath it embraced American technology.[15] Increasingly, in the 1930s, images of American technological superiority, so prominent in the entertainment and media in the 1920s, took a secondary seat to an image that increasingly promoted the pressing social and racial problems in the United States. The social problems of the United States were widely publicized in Soviet visual media, perhaps most famously in the 1936 film *Circus* (*Tsirk*, directed by Grigorii Alexandrov) and also in the performance arts such as in real circus skits that played up the problematic "Negro Question" and the maintained suppression of American workers. The propaganda was everywhere; even children could not escape the bleak picture of American racial relations. The 1933 children's poem "Mister Twister" by Samuil Marshak, beloved to this day, thus depicts the travels of a smug, conceited, capitalist, and racist American family in the Soviet Union.[16]

As urbanization was becoming an important topic in the Soviet Union, major American cities often provided the surroundings for literary works. In Vladimir Korolenko's writing, the focus had been on Chicago, and throughout the 1920s and the 1930s, Chicago maintained an important status in Soviet literature. Indeed, the slang term for urbanization in Russia was *chikagoizm*.[17] Detroit was known as a city of productivity and industry in the Soviet Union, but New York became a symbol of all that the United States stood for, both good and bad. New York's skyscrapers, broad avenues, and the Hudson River were often praised in Soviet literature and travelogues, but also present was New York's decadence, the filth and dirt, its mobs, and visual social and racial inequalities.

Thus, the conflicting experiences Russian and Soviet writers encountered and mythologized in the writing about urban areas serve well as a script for the

Soviet image of the United States before the Second World War. The American people lacked sophistication, focused only on business, and their culture was unrefined, mindless, and extreme. American technology, however, and the possibilities to advance in the United States and work one's way up to the top, received due attention in the Soviet Union, especially among its peasants. The Soviet press, however, true to its educating role, repeatedly tried to reassure Soviet peasants and workers that the American idyll would have nothing to offer them, claiming that in America the rich got richer and the poor got left behind.[18] By the late 1930s, the rich American was exaggerated and mocked in Soviet coverage of America, and in general, the American contribution to technology in the fast-industrializing Soviet Union was now downplayed in the official media.

Soviet official language still emphasized the difference between the American people and American government, thereby indicating what was to come in the postwar period, when Soviet newspapers and journals promoted the official idea of two Americas. The major pipeline for official views, the Soviet media, dictated how the United States should be understood, especially during the Cold War when "[i]nterest in American actions bordered on obsession."[19] But long before the Cold War, the Soviet media were helping Soviet readers to reach correct conclusions about the "true" nature of the United States. America was to be admired for its industrial progress and ridiculed for its socioeconomic and racial conditions. From the beginning of Soviet journalism, the ambiguities about the United States, such as the "moral bankruptcy in the American social welfare system," were emphasized in the press while the increased international role of the United States in the post–First World War period was acknowledged along with American technology and efficiency.[20]

Therefore, in the time span of about fifty years, from 1890 until 1941, the United States was seen as a model in technological and agricultural progress, as well as an example of everything gone wrong in terms of racial, social, and economic equality. At varying times, the Soviets emphasized one extreme more than the other, but more often than not, these images of the United States coexisted in the Soviet consciousness. While parts of this narrative survived well into the postwar period, much changed during the Second World War. By the early years of the Cold War, a new challenge arose when Soviet authorities had to react to an unfiltered American narrative, namely American cultural and political propaganda, which was as equally ideological in tone as the Soviet official propaganda. But prior to the Cold War, the United States and the Soviet Union became allies in the Second World War and even if the alliance was relatively short-lived, it had a lasting impact on the way the United States was understood and portrayed, in both Soviet ideology and the popular consciousness.

The Fate of the Soviet-American War Alliance

In order to understand how Soviet authorities and the Soviet people approached the Cold War conflict with the United States, it is important to appreciate the importance of the Second World War in Soviet society. It has been argued that the Second World War became the foundational myth of Soviet society during the postwar era,[21] but the fate of the Soviet-American wartime alliance has not been covered in depth. Only by understanding the nature of wartime interactions do we fully comprehend the dilemma of Soviet anti-Americanism in the late Stalin era and the modest success of Khrushchev's peaceful coexistence. Because of the experience of the Second World War, the anti-American campaign was met with some ambivalence in the Stalin era, and likewise, Khrushchev's coexistence narrative depended on the fact that the two Cold War superpowers had been allies during the war.

The Second World War, or the Great Patriotic War as it came to be known in the Soviet Union, was a time of incredible hardships for the Soviet people. It is estimated that about 27 million Soviet citizens lost their lives during the war, leaving the population in a demographic crisis. On the geopolitical level, victory seemed to make the war effort worthwhile: the Soviet Union had established itself on the global stage and the socialist state had to be taken into account when debating a postwar international system. When the war ended, the superpower status of the Soviet Union on par with the United States was confirmed, but at home the effects of this newfound international status were not felt in the material, social, or political well-being of Soviet citizens, who continued to suffer shortages and harsh domestic laws in the late Stalinist era.

Russian historian Elena Zubkova has argued that the war did not change the relationship between the people and the regime. She maintains that supporters of the system backed it even more strongly after the war, while nonbelievers remained unconverted. Still, the social psychology of the conflict was potentially challenging to the government: "The war awoke in people the capacity to think in unaccustomed ways, to evaluate a situation critically, and never again to accept uncritically any exclusive version of the truth."[22] Zubkova especially attributes the change in disposition of the Soviet people to the final months of the war:

> A process of psychological reorientation was catalyzed by the last stage of the war when the Soviet soldier crossed the frontier and encountered another society, politically, culturally, and economically. As a result soldiers returned from the war in possession of a comparative experience and knowledge of considerable significance.[23]

The postwar Stalinist system did not look favorably upon the "comparative experiences" Soviet people made during the war, and this was reflected in the way Soviet authorities developed their anti-American strategy. Soviet ideology needed enemies, and with the rise of the Cold War, the United States took on that role. At the same time, the Kremlin also had to consider ordinary people's hopes for better times after the war, and thus one of the main goals of Stalin's postwar rule was to prevent dissent in the Soviet Union.[24] And certainly, with the Soviet authorities encouraging a rumor about a pending attack from the former allies, the United States became the most likely outside instigator of dissent in the postwar Soviet Union and thus became enemy number one.

To be sure, the Second World War had increased American influence in the Soviet Union. Aid in the form of Lend-Lease brought American tanks, jeeps, trucks, motorcycles, explosives, guns, and foodstuffs to the Soviet Union. Even though historian Robert Huhn Jones argued that Lend-Lease failed to give Americans an advantage in negotiations after the war,[25] its lasting image proved a plus for the American cultural offensive launched as the Cold War unfolded when people remained grateful for Lend-Lease products. In 2002, Eduard Ivanian, historian at the Institute for US and Canada Studies in Moscow, recalled how a family member held on to an empty American cigarette carton acquired during the Second World War. The cigarettes long since smoked, the carton remained on display in his living room, a symbol of another world, off limits and unattainable but nevertheless appealing.[26]

The Second World War also played an important role in increasing the chances for personal contact with the outside world. These personal experiences of Red Army units in the West with alternative realities had an enormous impact. In 1954, Oleg Anisimov, a Soviet émigré, claimed that the Soviet people were dis-illusioned with their realities now that they had firsthand knowledge that life was better elsewhere. Seeing the Baltic States, eastern Poland, Romania, Hungary, Czechoslovakia, and Germany during the Second World War had altered people's worldviews: "And they remember Lend-Lease. Personal observations naturally carry more weight for the Soviet man than the broadcasts of Radio Moscow. These observations have made him very critical of the Soviet economic system."[27]

Moreover, the American alliance had contributed to the success of big-band jazz during the Second World War, when American classics, such as "All of Me" and "Sunny Side of the Street" were in the repertoires of several American-style Soviet front bands. During the war, American music thrived on the Soviet frontline, and many remembered this cultural freedom fondly in the postwar years.[28] Jazz, how-ever, was also one of the first victims of the postwar anti-cosmopolitan campaign, with its focus on the "inferiority" of Western, especially American, art forms, witnessed most symbolically in the 1949 ban of the saxophone "as a symbol of American decadence."[29] Two years earlier, in 1947, the Voice of America started its broadcasts to the Soviet Union, and it is telling of the lasting popularity of jazz in the Soviet Union that the Voice of America's jazz programs remained the most popular programs broadcast across the Iron Curtain.[30]

More information about how people lived in the West, increased personal contacts with Americans, and the presence of American Lend-Lease products influenced many Soviet people. Despite the worsening of Soviet-American relations at the dawn of the Cold War, the Second World War both contributed to the comparative experiences of America and confirmed Soviet realities in ways that were difficult for the Soviet authorities to counter. A combination of all these narratives created a complicated image of the United States that the Soviet state and citizens alike tried very much to make sense of in the postwar period. As an example, Soviet authorities did not really know how to deal with remnants of American technology, still visible in their country since the 1930s industrial drive. In 1947, when the American writer John Steinbeck and photographer Robert Capa visited a "famous Stalingrad tractor factory," Steinbeck noted that "practically all the machinery was made in America, and we were told that the assembly line and the assembly method had been laid out by American engineers and technicians."[31] The Soviet guides forbade Capa to take pictures of the factory. The fact that the factory was basically American was too sensitive an issue in 1947, when postwar reconstruction was a major patriotic project and acknowledging openly that Americans had any part in it was out of the question.

Ideology and Propaganda in the Soviet Union

This book follows the development of Soviet cultural relations with the United States from a time of hostility to official formalization of cultural contacts, and by doing so it contributes to our knowledge of how Soviet ideology and propaganda developed in the late 1940s and continuing into the late 1950s. In the Soviet Union, the term "propaganda" remained in the good books of the party—perhaps most evident in the prominence of the Agitation and Propaganda Department of the Central Committee—but it was also consistently and benevolently used to describe the activity of shaping the "hearts and minds" of both Soviet and international audiences.[32] One of the central premises of this book, the importance of Soviet ideology, has recently been argued very convincingly by David Brandenberger, who claims "that ideology is best addressed from three different perspectives relating to its production, projection, and popular reception."[33] In his study of prewar Soviet ideology and propaganda, Brandenberger offers a broad account of how these three facets of ideological indoctrination were out of balance, as exemplified in the "failure of the party hierarchy to popularize its ideological worldview."[34] The Cold War focus on the American enemy follows the same trajectories, but nevertheless, the ideological narratives about the United States had selective success, especially when confrontation and animosity were taken (at least partly) out of the equation, as was the case with peaceful coexistence.

The focus on the United States as an enemy was ideologically driven and had strong roots in the various ambivalent Russian and Soviet narratives about America. It is worth emphasizing, however, that there was no shortage of enemies in Soviet history: internal and external, real and imagined.[35] The story of how first the Bolsheviks, then the Communist Party, created and persecuted enemies of the state is well documented, as is the amount of fear and tragedy this caused in Soviet society.[36] As David Caute so eloquently put it:

> Virtually everything in human life was defined in adversarial terms; in art as in life, the Soviet citizen was relentlessly judged in terms of his or her war, his or her allegiance—the civil war against the Whites, the economic war against the kulaks, the anti-fascist struggle and resistance to Nazi invasion, and finally the new cold war against America. Where did you stand, comrade, and how did you behave?[37]

Knowing who the current enemy in Soviet society was could be a matter of life and death for Soviet citizens, and it is therefore not surprising that people reacted to the ideological campaigns. This study goes as far as is deemed possible in trying to understand how Soviet people adapted their worldview to the postwar Soviet ideology, which almost overnight took a recent friend and ally, the United States, and turned it into enemy number one. Even with the long history of ambivalent attitudes toward the American other, this was a radical turn of events. Studying the Soviet cultural bureaucracy does not reveal what ordinary people actually thought about the Soviet Union and the United States, but relentless efforts in terms of controlling perceptions of America suggest that Soviet authorities feared that anything from favorable mention of the United States to consuming American culture would influence the Soviet outlook in unwanted ways. This fear is confirmed in the various sources, including judicial records, official strategies and reports on propaganda and cultural relations, travelogues, and personal letters that together cast new light on the Soviet side of the cultural Cold War.

The fall of the Soviet Union in 1991 caused many in the West to declare victory for the American way of life and to spell out the reasons for the failure of Soviet socialism. To date, however, we still have no in-depth study of the planned Soviet economy, let alone a definitive study of Soviet consumerism. Nevertheless, the view that the Soviet Union collapsed because it rejected American-style consumerism has entered into the popular imagination of how and why the Cold War ended.[38] While the fall of the Soviet Union seemed to confirm what American

Cold War propaganda had maintained, that Soviet people wanted freedom and democracy the American way, scholars have only very recently started to systematically compare the two systems and the "way of life" each country propagated.[39] This book aims to balance the history of Soviet-American cultural Cold War relations by providing a much-needed account of the inner workings of Soviet ideology and propaganda and its effect as it relates to its number one enemy.

The Soviet Union became known throughout the world for its propaganda techniques, and Soviet methods of mass mobilization have been studied in depth.[40] The Soviet authorities referred to the people involved in these activities as "ideological workers" and talked about them doing "ideological work." This study refers to the Soviet cultural bureaucracy when discussing the various units that dealt with anything from the creation of the ideological campaigns (Agitprop Commission of the Central Committee) to the organizations responsible for such matters as corresponding with foreigners, planning their visits, and monitoring their stays in the Soviet Union (such as VOKS, SSOD, Intourist, etc.).[41] With time, the early successes of Soviet cultural diplomacy were impeded, first by the Second World War and then by the Cold War conflict with the United States. A look at the inner workings of the cultural bureaucracy reveals a chaotic and ineffective propaganda mission in the postwar period.

Before the Second World War, the Soviet Union had been in the forefront of including culture in foreign relations, indeed mobilizing state, party, and Comintern resources to influencing—preferably converting—foreign public opinion.[42] But the onset of the Cold War ensured that the most successful methods of Soviet interwar cultural diplomacy, such as relying on front organizations and foreign intellectuals and sympathizers, no longer applied. As Michael David-Fox has argued, Soviet cultural diplomacy in the prewar period was highly original and visible also domestically, in that it relied in large part on "showcasing" the accomplishments of the Soviet Union. In practice, however, Soviet officials often talked about cultural relations (*kul'turnye sviazi*) with foreign countries and used that term to cover the interchangeable cultural diplomacy and propaganda activities of the prewar era.[43] To mark the importance of the official Soviet-American exchange agreement in 1958, this study refers to Soviet-American propaganda and cultural diplomacy activities that took place before its existence as "cultural relations" and makes it clear throughout what actors were involved: the focus on different actors is crucial as the form, content, and reception of Soviet-American cultural relations, ideology, and propaganda depended on who was involved at all three levels of "production, projection, and popular reception."[44]

In the postwar period, the fascination many foreign intellectuals had shown for the young Soviet Union and the impressive Soviet use of cultural diplomacy in the 1920s and the 1930s belonged to a distant past, and hesitant attempts to continue cultural diplomacy efforts were in vain. And later, when the intensity of the anti-Western, anti-American campaigns of the late Stalin era decreased, it was no longer possible to maintain the strict control over Soviet cultural diplomacy efforts.[45] Khrushchev's peaceful coexistence relied on an updated form of Soviet cultural relations, namely public diplomacy, which advocated for the use of individual contacts, sometimes in the form of "citizen diplomacy."[46] The focus on people and real exchanges changed Soviet cultural relations, so that even if they were controlled and influenced by ideological policies, these efforts paved the way for official exchange agreements with foreign countries and added an important dimension of interactions to Soviet-American relations.

The end of the Cold War improved access to formerly sealed Soviet archival sources at the same time that historians increasingly became interested in the role of culture in state relations.[47] In the historical field at large, a focus on images and perceptions gained momentum, and in Soviet history these larger trends are both visible in the focus on Soviet subjectivity and a renewed curiosity about what Soviet people actually thought about the Soviet system and the outside world.[48] This work combines all those threads and builds on recent works that acknowledge the important role of Soviet ideology.[49] The Soviet archival record unveils serious attempts to control and manipulate perceptions of the United States in the Soviet Union. Ideology, propaganda, and cultural relations played an important role as Soviet anti-Americanism depended in great part on cultural channels. Indeed, the policy of peaceful coexistence experienced its most lasting success in terms of institutionalizing broadly defined cultural relations, including official cultural and technological exchanges, between the two countries.

Khrushchev's visit to America in 1959 was the high point of an otherwise successful first full year of official Soviet-American cultural and academic exchanges. Peaceful coexistence had also put the focus back on the silenced Soviet-American wartime alliance, which was noticed in both official and nonofficial responses to Khrushchev's America trip. Just as the memorable Secret Speech had denounced the cult of Stalin and notably removed him from Thaw-era films about the Great Patriotic War, the wartime alliance, which had been silenced or ridiculed in earlier films about the war, was now openly celebrated and embraced by the Soviet people. This narrative of the wartime alliance, in the context of Soviet ideology and propaganda, gives meaning not only to the varied reactions to America in the Soviet cultural bureaucracy and among the population; it also explains why since the end of the Cold War, Russian and American leaders have recurrently used the wartime alliance as proof that the two entities can and should work together.

STALIN'S SCRIPT
FOR ANTI-AMERICANISM

THE ANTI-AMERICAN CAMPAIGN, 1945–1953

With the goal of confirming America's place in Soviet ideology as enemy number one, Soviet authorities designed and executed an official anti-American campaign in the early years of the Cold War. Its creators were Soviet party officials, and its main target was all of Soviet society (as well as potential sympathizers for the Soviet cause around the globe). Members of the Soviet creative intelligentsia also played a leading role as they were tasked with the project of writing, performing, and staging the anti-American campaign in Soviet society. The "workers of the ideological front" and Communist Party officials responsible for promoting patriotism and fighting the Cold War with the United States worked in close cooperation to dictate how Soviet ideology defined the American enemy in the early Cold War and to control how Soviet intellectuals executed the anti-American campaign as it was orchestrated top-down.

In the postwar years, Soviet propaganda pushed for a dual image of the United States, and the space inhabited by "progressive Americans against the warmongers" was called "the second America," or *vtoraia Amerika*.[1] Given that throughout the Cold War, the American enemy image often focused on "the Russians" as a monolithic group, it may come as a surprise that Soviet ideology was more nuanced in its approach to the American enemy. True to its Marxist roots, it dictated that the American enemy be analyzed in terms of class conflict and the struggle against imperialist powers. Official Soviet Cold War propaganda represented the United States as a place where ordinary Americans were victims of "evil" Americans. The "evil" Americans were depicted as greedy American capitalists who oppressed their socially progressive compatriots. On the contrary, the "good" Americans were usually favorably disposed toward the Soviet Union (such as fellow travelers or communist sympathizers) but also normal Americans who "were merely misled and manipulated by 'bad' Americans."[2]

Official Soviet agitators took on the role of frontline soldiers in the anti-American campaign of the late 1940s: the Central Committee's

Department of Agitation and Propaganda (Agitprop) bore responsibility for carrying out the anti-Western campaign.[3] Agitprop's weapons ranged from Soviet writers and artists to American progressive authors and fellow travelers. In 1948, "workers of the ideological front" were defined as "writers, performers, people of the press, and scientific and cultural researchers."[4] Old and new Soviet works of literature and art were put to use in the anti-American campaign, as were some favorite American authors in the Soviet Union. Agitprop's anti-American campaign seeped into all aspects of daily life through the print media, but in the creative arts especially, a diverse group of party members, agitators, critics, writers, playwrights, poets, and journalists contributed to the image of America as an enemy within the limits set by Agitprop.

The *Zhdanovshchina* and the Anti-American Campaign

The anti-American campaign can be seen as a part of the larger anti-cosmopolitan campaign that dominated the Soviet Union in the last years under Stalin's rule, and the anti-intellectual campaigns often referred to as the *Zhdanovshchina*. However, it has long been established that even if the fight against the Soviet intelligentsia is identified with the name of Stalin's close comrade and ideological chief, Andrei Aleksandrovich Zhdanov, it was Stalin himself who stood behind it.[5] Already in November 1945, Stalin wrote a note to the Politburo in which he denounced the decision to print a speech by Winston Churchill, claiming that "we need to be fierce in fighting servility before the West,"[6] thereby coining the expression that was to become the catchphrase for the anti-Western, anti-American campaign of the postwar era.

As one of Stalin's closest colleagues, Zhdanov was certainly a driving force behind the new Cold War mentality in the Soviet Union.[7] Zhdanov was in charge of two Central Committee departments: the Department of Agitation and Propaganda and the Foreign Policy Department. The Soviet Information Bureau (Sovinformbiuro), the Telegraph Agency of the Soviet Union (TASS), and the publishing house Mezhdunarodnaia kniga (Mezhkniga, International Book) were thus all under his control. So were "public organizations" such as the Jewish Anti-Fascist Committee, the All-Slavic Committee, and the All-Union Society for Cultural Ties Abroad (VOKS).[8] And even if it was Stalin who initiated the well-known purges of poet Anna Akhmatova and writer Mikhail Zoshchenko in 1946, they marked the beginning of the period that was to become known as the *Zhdanovshchina* and the attempt to "discipline the Soviet intelligentsia."[9] Fronting the attack on the Soviet intelligentsia in 1946, Zhdanov echoed the phrase coined by Stalin when he preached against "servility before the modern bourgeois culture of the West."[10] The focus on anti-Western elements was gaining momentum, and soon suspicion rose on all levels and all contact with foreigners became dangerous—including marriage, which was forbidden by law in 1947.[11] And out of this atmosphere of distrust and fear, came the anti-American campaign in the arts.

There was certainly a tradition of anti-Westernism in Russian history that preceded Stalin, but it took on a new form and intensity in the postwar period.[12] This can be explained by uncertainty and paranoia at the highest level—the way that Stalin ruled in the postwar years did not allow for criticism of his plans, and party ideologues maintained an atmosphere that cultivated fear among the creative intelligentsia. In the postwar years, Soviet patriotism could not coexist with any form of sympathy for the West, especially not for the United States, which had by now been assigned the role of enemy number one in Soviet ideology and propaganda. As of 1947, both domestic and international Soviet propaganda fought against the "reactionary ideology of American imperialism," which in the Soviet Union became a part of the broader anti-cosmopolitan campaign.[13] Spreading propaganda was so incorporated into everyday life and so intertwined with Soviet culture that these concepts need to be understood as part of one and the same goal: the mission of rallying the Soviet people around the cause of communism and promoting Soviet patriotism.[14] Furthermore, this goal was extended to proletarian internationalism, also central to the Soviet project, where anti-American themes came to dominate the larger propaganda project.

In the late 1940s, anti-cosmopolitanism was driven in large part by the continued emphasis on Soviet patriotism that started during the Great Patriotic War. A combination of 1930s Russian nationalism and Soviet socialism, postwar patriotism played a large role in the anti-Western atmosphere fostered by Stalin after the war.[15] As a nationalistic ideological doctrine, anti-cosmopolitanism entailed an attack on "anti-patriotism" in general, but more specifically it was aimed at anything non-Russian. Stalin's goal was to divide Soviet society into "patriots" and "antipatriots," and by doing that he managed to maintain a constant search for "enemies" among the Soviet population.[16]

It was inherent in Soviet ideology to look for enemies of the socialist project. Before the war, considerable energy had been devoted to othering the pre-revolutionary past of the Soviet state,[17] but the most successful effort at uniting the Soviet people against a common enemy had taken place during the Great Patriotic War, when the Soviet Union fought Nazi Germany.[18] The Soviet people had gotten used to thinking in terms of "us versus them" during the Great Patriotic War, and the government feared public confrontation in the absence of an outside enemy in the immediate aftermath of the war.[19] To that effect, the Cold War gave the Soviet authorities a much-needed focus on a new antagonist and they put considerable effort into securing the proper resources for spreading anti-American propaganda.

Stalin therefore saw the impending Cold War as an opportunity to unite the Soviet people, and communists everywhere, against a new enemy. The Cold War was in full force when, at the founding of Cominform (the Information Bureau of the Communist Parties) in Poland in September 1947, Zhdanov drew a picture of the world divided into two opposing camps. The "two camp" statement most likely originated with Stalin himself[20] and has been interpreted as a Soviet "declaration of Cold War against 'American imperialism.'"[21] Following Winston Churchill's Iron Curtain speech in 1946, and then the Truman Doctrine and the announcement of the Marshall Plan in early 1947, Zhdanov, most certainly in the name of Stalin, now confirmed that a fight for world hegemony would also become the guiding thesis of Soviet foreign propaganda.[22]

Anti-Americanism in Theater and Film

The ambivalence of the American enemy is perhaps most demonstrably found in Konstantin Simonov's anti-American play *The Russian Question* (*Russkii vopros*). Written in 1946, it was first performed on stage in 1947, and Mikhail Romm then directed the filmed version in 1948.[23] *The Russian Question* was without a doubt the most famous anti-American stage production in the postwar years. It highlighted in very simple terms the themes that were to become most prevalent in the anti-American campaign. The materialistic, imperialist, capitalist faction, often simply referred to as "Wall Street," was juxtaposed with the good, "second America."

Coinciding with the starting point of the postwar anti-American campaign in the arts, *The Russian Question* was set in President Harry S. Truman's postwar America and depicted greedy "Wall Street" players who repressed the honest, real Americans, embodied in the persona of the journalist Harry Smith.[24] In the last monologue, right before the curtain falls, the "good American" Harry Smith announces his epiphany: that there are two Americas. And he wants to find a place in the "America of Abraham Lincoln, in the America of Franklin Roosevelt."[25] Because of the wartime alliance, Roosevelt was generally looked upon favorably in the Soviet Union and he therefore represented the good American. Associated with the Truman Doctrine and the Marshall Plan, however, his successor President Harry S. Truman became an obvious target of anti-American sentiments in the postwar period. With the emerging Cold War, Truman came to embody the "imperialistic" aspirations of the United States in the Soviet Union, the aggressor against whom Stalin now positioned himself as a peacemaker.

The Russian Question set the tone for the ways the Soviet public was supposed to remember and treat the former ally, a topic that was repeated in the coming years.[26] Almost four years after the Elbe meeting, in March 1949, another anti-American film, *The Meeting on the Elbe*, premiered in Moscow.[27]

It was based on the play *Governor of the Provinces* by the Tur brothers, which had been staged to great acclaim in Moscow and around the provinces for two years.[28] Contrary to all reports of the actual meeting on the Elbe, the film is an unrefined account of American efforts to destroy any prospect of peace between the Soviet Union and the United States, and it is one of the most anti-American films of the late Stalinist period. In the film's opening scene, Soviet soldiers march proudly through the streets. One of them looks across the river, sees the Americans advancing, and says ironically: "Look, it is the last day of war—and finally we have a second front."[29]

This clearly shows how the anti-American narrative described the Soviet-American wartime alliance: it emphasized Soviet sacrifices against the Nazis and the late entry of Americans in the European theater after the Red Army had done most of the fighting. Instead of displaying the feelings of joy veterans on both sides claim to have experienced, the film shows playful—almost immature—Americans and disciplined Soviet soldiers, all speaking in Russian, except for the occasional "hello" and "thank you." Dark scenes from decadent American nightclubs and US officers' clubs in Germany, where most of the film takes place, depict promiscuous women and coarse American soldiers dancing to jazz music. Dmitrii Shostakovich wrote the score, famously using "Yankee Doodle Dandy," the theme song of Voice of America broadcasts to the Soviet Union.[30] Explicitly anti-American, the film narrates how despite Soviet attempts to sustain the newfound peace, Americans always opt for confrontation instead. It blames the United States for starting the Cold War and is an excellent example of how quickly friend turned to foe in the immediate aftermath of the Second World War. Both the play and the film adaptation were promoted in the Soviet Union as part of the broader anti-American campaign designed by Stalin and to show the way the former ally was supposed to be remembered. On its anniversary in April 1949, for example, the Elbe meeting was not mentioned in the Communist Party newspaper *Pravda*; indeed, not even the newly premiered film *The Meeting on the Elbe* was discussed on this occasion. Instead, the focus was on the newly established North Atlantic Treaty Organization (NATO) and the Soviet-sponsored World Peace Conference in Paris.[31]

By the end of the 1940s, favorable discussions of the wartime alliance had completely disappeared from official Soviet rhetoric. In theory, it was easy for Soviet agitators to manipulate the strongly rooted feelings of hatred toward Germans and subtly suggest that such sentiments be transferred to Americans. In practice, however, this proved difficult, as the memory of the war alliance and its economic benefits was too clear for Soviet people. With films such as *The Russian Question*, Soviet propaganda authorities worked hard at trying to convince Soviet audiences that the Americans had forgotten all about the common enemy and now focused their aggression on the Soviet Union.

Also, there is much evidence that supports the notion that the rumor of a new war terrified some Soviet citizens,[32] and *The Russian Question* manipulated this fear extraordinarily well. In the play, the "evil capitalists" want Harry Smith to write an account of a Russian war threat, but he resists, concluding that the Russians desire peace more than anything and the real warmongers in the story turn out to be the bad Americans.[33] It may have been hard for the Soviet people to imagine that the comradely feelings of the meeting on the Elbe—of the whole alliance for that matter—had been abandoned by the American side, but the memory of the war itself and the sufferings of the Soviet population probably made them more susceptible to rumors of a renewed war and thus troubled by the purported machinations of the former ally.[34]

The Russian Question was not the only anti-American work by writer and journalist Konstantin Simonov. A favorite of the Kremlin, Simonov had served as a war correspondent during the Second World War. His favored status allowed him to travel, and in 1946 he had gone on the first of three trips to the United States, where he reported back to *Krasnaia zvezda*.[35] His 1949 play *Alien Shadow* (*Chuzaia ten'*) continued the theme of the war scare in its focus on a Soviet scientist who discovers cure from a fatal disease, which the American enemy gets hold of and turns into a "weapon of extermination" in the coming war.[36] In 1949, Simonov also offered to write an anti-American play called *Gorky in America*, which would be based on Gorky's own "ruthless criticism of America."[37] Nothing seems to have come of this idea, but Simonov's proposal to do this shows that favored artists and intellectuals of the period were under severe pressure to respond to the demands of the state.

With the help of Simonov and others, the anti-American campaign was already off to a good start in 1947, especially in the theaters.[38] By 1948, anti-Americanism was a thorough part of every form of art in the Soviet Union, and the ideological witch-hunts were starting to spin out of control. By then, even a film with such a clear and strong anti-American message as *The Russian Question* could be "improved" to make the message even stronger. In a February 1948 report, Aleksander Egolin,[39] now a director and literary critic at the Academy of Sciences, maintained that the 1948 Mikhail Romm film adaptation of Simonov's play suffered "from essential shortcomings." He stated that, at the time of writing the play, Simonov had incorporated important international events into it, which the producers of the film had left out:

American imperialism is shown only in one way in the film, as the politics of a capitalist upper class, directed against the USSR and communism. It does not show the responsibility of capitalists for the approaching economic crisis in the USA—the terror, dictated by expansionist politics, aimed at weakening rivals, with the goal of capturing and enslaving free nations and instituting the global dominance of the dollar. The film does not expose the attempts of American imperialism to camouflage the aggressive tendencies of anticommunism and anti-Soviet politics.[40]

Egolin claimed the film did not have an "offensive but a defensive character" and the script should have taken better advantage of the possibilities to cast light on the varieties of American imperialism and evilness. He continued:

The film underlines only that the USSR does not want war. It insufficiently shows that American imperialism now has a stronghold on the global re-action, is preparing war, and that the USSR has an iron grip on peace, that communists of all countries expose and reject the criminal conspiracy of the imperialists against peace.[41]

According to Egolin, Harry Smith and his stenographer, Meg, who together personified the progressive America in *The Russian Question*, paled in compar-ison with the portrayals of the reactionary American embodied in the work by the publishers MacPherson and Gould. The reactionary Americans were, in his opinion, disproportionately strong and tough. He blamed this shortcoming of the film partly on the main actors, especially actor Vsevolod Aksenov's "uncon-vincing portrayal" of Harry Smith. Of course, Harry Smith's role was the most important one, as the character was sympathetic to the Soviet Union and had to be convincing. On behalf of the Council of Arts at the Academy of Sciences, Egolin recommended that the film be redone. The only positive thing he saw about the film was composer Aram Khachaturian's musical score, which Egolin thought fit well with the "gloomy, barbarous character of the capitalist American city."[42] It is likely that such a critical review coming from a leading literary critic at the Academy of the Sciences had more to do with Egolin wanting to show his dedication to the all-embracing anti-American campaign than anything else. The movie was not remade and has unanimously been considered a hit in the anti-American genre, securing Harry Smith's reputation as an "ideal American" in the Soviet Union for years to come.[43]

Mikhail Romm's *The Russian Question* was one of about a dozen films that explicitly attacked America and all that it stood for in the early Cold War. Other films of note are *The Meeting on the Elbe* (*Vstrecha na El'be*; Grigory Aleksandrov, 1949), *The Court of Honor* (*Sud chesti*; Abram Room, 1949), *The Conspiracy of the Doomed* (*Zagovor obrechennykh*; Mikhail Kalatozov, 1950), *The Secret Mission* (*Sekretnaia missiia*; Romm, 1950), *They Have a Motherland* (*U nikh est' rodina*; Aleksander Faintsimmer, 1959), *Dawn over the Neman* (*Nad Nemanom rassvet*; Faintsimmer, 1952), and *Silvery Dust* (*Serebristaia pyl'*; Room, 1953).[44]

Even if they were not very many in number, they were quite prominent, given that from 1946 to 1953 only 124 feature films were produced,[45] and from 1946 to 1959, 45.6 percent of villains and antiheroes in Soviet films were American or British.[46] World-famous Soviet composers wrote the music for these films, such as Dmitrii Shostakovich, who wrote the score for *The Meeting on the Elbe,* and Aram Khachaturian, who wrote for *The Russian Question.*[47] According to Agitprop's plan, more anti-American films were planned and discussed but not all of them went into production even though much preparation had gone into the film. Thus was the destiny of *The Dollar Exchange Rate* (*Kurs dollara*), which was abandoned in 1948 seemingly because of it no longer being relevant (the script had evolved around the Greek Civil War, which ended in 1948).[48]

Another planned film, *Farewell, America!* (*Proshchai, Amerika!*), based on the 1949 book *The Truth about American Diplomats* by American defector Annabelle Bucar, was abandoned after a third of the film had been shot. Bucar had worked in the American embassy in Moscow and when her book was published, it became a major success, with Stalin himself seeing its propaganda value and ordering the book to be translated into English, French, and Spanish.[49] In 1949, Dmitrii Shepilov, deputy chief of Agitprop, had recommended the filming of the book as a way to increase the production of anti-American films.[50] The well-known filmmaker Aleksandr Dovzhenko wrote the screenplay and originally received praise and support for the creation of the film, which had been ordered by Agitprop. Then, in 1951, Annabelle Bucar surprisingly switched sides again and Soviet authorities abandoned their plans to film *Farewell, America!* so that it would not cast bad light on Soviet propaganda.[51]

Agitprop authorities continued to strengthen and refine anti-Americanism's relationship with patriotism by disciplining artists and critics. In December 1948, Aleksandr Fadeev, the general secretary of the Soviet Writers' Union, gave a speech on the "antipatriotic drama critics"; in early 1949, the press publicly denounced artists that were accused of antipatriotic work in the theater,[52] and then, in the spring of 1949, the Department of Agitation and Propaganda of the Central Committee issued several measures for strengthening anti-American propaganda.[53] The measures called for more anti-American plays, books, variety shows, and circus skits. It also called for up to four hundred "new plays on anti-American topics" to be on stage all over the Soviet Union by the end of the year. The ideal topics were already laid out in the plan, sometimes even assigned to a certain writer. Thus, Nikolai Pogodin was called upon to write about "the activities of American warmongers," Nikolai Virta "about American intelligence activity," and Anatolii Surov "about the financial magnates of Wall Street." Konstantin Simonov, Boris Lavrenev, Lev Sheinin, and Arkadii Perventsev were supposed to write plays "exposing contemporary America."[54]

The plan stated that in addition to the anti-American plays already in the theaters, thirteen new ones were to be staged in big cities like Moscow, Leningrad, and Gorky, while others were to go into production in up to one hundred theaters in the provinces. These plays included *The Conspiracy of the Doomed* (*Zagovor obrechennykh*) by Nikolai Virta, which played in major theaters all over the country (later filmed), and a children's play by Sergei Mikhalkov, *I Want to Go Home* (*Ia khochu domoi*), which also played in twenty-five youth theaters in the provinces, in addition to showing at the Central Children's Theater in Moscow and the Leningrad Theater for Young Viewers.

Anti-Americanism was certainly not new to the Soviet arts, and one need only remember Marietta Shaginian's 1921 spy/science fiction novel *Mess Mend or Yankee in Petrograd* or the epic children's poem "Mister Twister" by Samuil Marshak from the 1930s[55] to recall how Soviet propaganda depicted the archetypical American capitalist and racist. What was new, however, was the level of initiative originating within the Communist Party on designing the subject matter and treatment of American topics. The Communist Party called on artists, playwrights, composers, and writers to "expose the reactionary politics and ideology of American imperialism and to dethrone bourgeois culture, customs, and way of life in contemporary America."[56] This they did not only by calling for general works; they also outlined the exact treatment a topic should get, such as in the mobilization of the playwrights.[57] But as with some of the planned Cold War films, many of the works ordered from above never came into being.

Responding quickly to the call from above, however, playwright Boris Lavrenev finished the play *The Voice of America* (*Golos Ameriki*) in the spring of 1949.[58] Utilizing the comradely feelings between the Soviet and American people during the wartime alliance, *The Voice of America* relates the story of American army captain Walter Kidd, who, during the war, had become a great admirer of the Russian people and had even been awarded a medal in the Soviet Union during the war. Upon returning to the United States, he became a suspect instead of a war hero and fell prey to the House Committee on Un-American Activities.[59] The play includes a host of American characters, stereotypical of the Soviet anti-American campaign. We have Senator Wiler who is an "American fascist"; Gangster O'Leary who "lacks every human quality"; Breasted who is a policeman and a drunk; and Skundrell as the agent of the Committee on Un-American Activities, personifying the "fascist stratum" of American society. Captain Kidd refuses to return the medal and barely escapes death at the hand of the "American fascists."[60]

The Voice of America was initially staged in two Moscow theaters, the Red Army Theater and the Maly Theater. At first, the play received much praise for its "truthful picture of contemporary America," but in 1950 the Maly Theater's staging of the play came under heavy criticism. Apparently, the stage designer,

Isaak Rabinovich, had included scenery based on American illustrated magazines. Critics were dismayed that he was not able to recognize that the prosperity exhibited in these magazines was not in line with official Soviet representation of American realities. As a Jew, Rabinovich became a victim of the broader anti-cosmopolitanism campaign, but by using American clippings as props, he was also guilty of "groveling before the West." The media portrayed this as a serious lack of judgment, and in May 1950, art critic Arkadii Anastas'ev wrote in *Pravda* that "the luxurious halls and exotic views of the sea presented on the stage clearly do not correspond to the life of an honest toiler such as Walter Kidd and give a false and distorted presentation of life led by ordinary people in America."[61]

Furthermore, some critics found flaw in the disposition and authenticity of the main hero[62] and faulted Lavrenev for not having chosen an American communist as the hero of the play. But Lavrenev defended himself, claiming that he had chosen to write about the tragic fate of a private, "prosperous" American. He wanted his hero to have "apolitical, undecided, and backward liberal views." Lavrenev's goal was to show how this person came face to face with the "barbarian degradation of the capitalist America" and how he aligned himself in the camp "against the America of Truman and Wall Street."[63] Anyone reading the play would be hard pressed not to come to the conclusion that Lavrenev had succeeded in his goals, but at the high point of the anti-American campaign, his colleagues at the Soviet Writers' Union had a different opinion.

At a September 1950 meeting of the Writers' Union, further reservations about the play were unveiled when playwright Anatolii Surov claimed that not just Lavrenev's main character but also the handling of the topic was faulty. He described the play as "an advertisement for the 'American way of life' and the American army."[64] And another critic, V. Zalesskii, did not find the character "cultured" enough for a socialist audience: "how were Soviet viewers expected to identify with 'the fate of an American everyman?'" he asked. Imagine Lavrenev's dismay. At his request, Aleksandr Fadeev, by all accounts a trusted Stalinist, had read the play and apparently made three valuable comments, which Lavrenev had taken to heart. With the approval of General-Secretary Fadeev, he was therefore understandably shocked at the kind of criticism he got from other members of the Soviet Writers' Union. Outraged that critics should find such basic flaws with his carefully written anti-American play, Lavrenev turned to Stalin to clear his name and emphasize his support of the Soviet cause.[65]

In a letter to Stalin, Lavrenev claimed that as a writer and commentator, he had always had a real interest in international politics. He felt strongly about the relevance of events in America for Soviet society, stating that "what is going on in America nowadays, the violent reactionary revelry, the impetuous fascism, the historical preparation of a new war against the Soviet Union" deeply concerned him. He was dismayed that Anatolii Surov had accused him of taking the easy way out by focusing on a non-Soviet theme: "I considered *The Voice of America* a timely, serious, and necessary political work. As a commentator devoted to international themes, I am used to thinking that the exposure of capitalism and the fight against it are significant and important, especially today, as objects of our literature."[66] Working on such a topic was not easy, he said; if it was to be done well, it was probably more difficult than writing about Soviet topics. Lavrenev also described how much work he had put into the play. He researched materials related to American "spirit, humor, and everyday life" and, as was usual, submitted the final product to the Agitprop Committee of the Central Committee, which had sanctioned it in April 1949. Finally, Lavrenev emphasized that of his six plays, "five cast light on Soviet life. Only *The Voice of America* brings forward themes of international politics, which nowadays are also Soviet and relevant themes."[67]

Lavrenev's letter to Stalin shows well the kind of atmosphere in which the intelligentsia was working at the time. Lavrenev struggled to make a point about his devotion to the campaign of anti-Americanism and the overall fight against cosmopolitanism. If for some reason writers or critics could not directly contribute to it, they found flaws with the works of those who did, showing how they themselves would have done things more patriotically, in a more anti-American way. *The Voice of America* has been described as "violently anti-American,"[68] and it was clear from Lavrenev's writing that it was intentionally so. He concluded his letter by appealing to Stalin to go see the play for himself and tell him "if he was right or wrong." Lavrenev wrote he would be eternally grateful, as Stalin's verdict would help him in his future career as a writer.[69]

Lavrenev's experience was far from unique. In 1949 and 1950, suspicion and backstabbing dominated the circles of the intelligentsia.[70] Those involved in writing about the United States struggled to convince Agitprop authorities that their efforts were worthwhile. The performance arts of the period celebrated the ideal socialist citizen and, correspondingly, looked upon foreigners with suspicion.[71] There was, however, a fine line between producing an anti-American play and an acceptable anti-American play. Asking Stalin to be the judge of one's performance was, of course, the ultimate test. Although there is no evidence that Stalin ever responded to the letter, Lavrenev continued writing to the leadership. A few weeks later, he wrote a letter to Central Committee Secretary Mikhail Suslov describing in great detail how he had not interfered in the staging of the play at the Maly Theater, although he had held reservations about the choice of Mikhail I. Zharov for the role of General Kidd, from the start. Zharov is "a great actor" he said, "but mostly experienced in playing simple Russian people" and therefore not qualified to grasp the "great complexity of the play." Lavrenev considered it vital to distance himself as a writer from the "deformity" that ended up taking place on the stage at the Maly Theater.[72]

After 1950, such polemics were not as prominent at the Central Committee level, but the paranoia and fear that dominated intellectual circles and contributed to the production of anti-American works decreased only after Stalin's death in 1953. By then, the theaters had plenty of anti-American plays to choose from, including the plays that had been written in the early 1950s to emphasize the beastly behavior of Americans in Korea, such as *People of Good Will* (*Liudi dobroi voli*) by Georgii Mdivani and *South of the Thirty-eighth Parallel* (*Iuzhnee 38-oi paralleli*) by Tkai Dian Chun.[73] Furthermore, the already classic works of the genre, such as *The Russian Question* and *Governor of the Provinces*, had both been filmed by the end of the 1940s, joining the ranks of the other anti-American films of the late Stalin era.[74] Indeed, theater, cinema, the circus, and the variety show came under strong attack in this atmosphere of anti-cosmopolitanism and left lasting anti-American images on the stage and the screen, but the preferred way to get anti-American views across to the population was still the printed word. In 1949, Agitprop had also called upon publishing houses and journals to issue articles and brochures on the "rotten musical culture of contemporary America" and the "rotten contemporary American arts—in paintings, theatre, and music."[75] Every side of American society was to be criticized and maligned, with an emphasis on its bourgeois elements and overall lack of culture, and the publishing world promptly answered the call from above.

Favorite Anti-American Authors

There was no apparent shortage of anti-American works, Soviet and foreign, old and new, in the field of literature. Plenty of Soviet works written before the war were perfectly good for use in the anti-American campaign of the late 1940s, so unlike in the film industry, it was not imperative to dictate topics and order new anti-American works of literature during the anti-American campaign. In 1949, Agitprop thus ordered variety shows and circus companies to include in their repertoires the "masters of dramatic readings," instructing amateur performance groups to focus on literature and musical productions with anti-American themes. For this purpose, the Central Committee suggested to the Committee of the Arts of the Council of Ministers that they should encourage performance groups to include in their repertoires the writings of Maxim Gorky and the poems of Vladimir Mayakovsky.[76] Both Gorky and Mayakovsky had written extensively on the darker sides of American life and propaganda in the 1920s and 1930s, and authorities correctly estimated that their work might also be useful in the postwar period.

Maxim Gorky, one of the most popular writers in the Soviet Union and a founder of socialist realism, was a staunch supporter of the regime.[77] In 1906, Gorky's six-month stay in the United States coincided with the rise of the revolutionary movement in Russia, and Gorky's accounts of his American experiences contributed to a growing skepticism about the United States. His negative perceptions were surely influenced by the way the American media and public treated him when they came to know the details of his relationship with Moscow actress Maria Fedorovna Andreeva, but the puritan American society was shocked to learn that the couple lived together in sin. It was common knowledge in Russia that Gorky had separated from his wife and lived with Andreeva, but upon finding this out, his American hosts, who had until then received them like royalty, turned very hostile to the couple; the media maligned them and puritan Americans turned their backs to them.[78]

Gorky's subsequent book *In America* (*V Amerike*) became an instant classic in the Soviet anti-American genre. Gorky's forceful account of an uncultured, superficial, and materialistic population was likely in part a reaction to the way ordinary Americans treated him, but it has also been argued that his portrayal of the United States fit his strong views of a cultured Europe versus an uncivilized America.[79] From the perspective of the Bolsheviks, his polemical attack of America fit with the revolutionary political agenda of the early 1900s, and it was later easily manipulated to fit the anti-American campaign of the postwar period.[80] References to staging and filming Gorky's work appeared repeatedly in Agitprop documents when the anti-American campaign was at its zenith in 1949. Dmitrii Shepilov, for example, wrote to Stalin about plans to make a movie based on a part of Gorky's essay "The City of the Yellow Devil" (*Gorod zheltogo d'iavola*).[81] There are references to these plans for filming "The City of the Yellow Devil" in several documents from 1949, but nothing came out of them.[82] "The City of the Yellow Devil" would certainly have made for a very anti-American movie, with New York as the setting for the American capitalistic city that is "ruled by a devil whose name is Dollar,"[83] and it provides endless images of poverty, violence, and inequality in the United States as such.[84]

In 1948, Agitprop made plans to republish Gorky's answers to an earlier questionnaire from American journalists.[85] The first question American correspondents had posed to Gorky was, "Does your country hate America and what do you think about American civilization?" Gorky prefaced his answer by ironically pointing out the absurdity of the question:

Yes, my country, my nation, hates America, all of its people, workers and millionaires, the colored and the white. We hate women and children, fields and rivers, beasts and birds, the past and the present of your country, its science and schools, its great technology, Luther Burbank, Edgar Allan Poe, Walt Whitman, Washington and Lincoln, Theodore Dreiser, E. O'Neill, and Sherwood Anderson. We hate all the talented artists and the beautiful romances of Bret Harte and Jack London. We hate Thoreau,

Emerson, and everything that is the USA, and everyone who lives in these states.[86]

It was clear to everyone familiar with Soviet anti-Americanism that this was irony intended to point out the divide between what was deemed acceptable about America and what was not: the Soviet people were cultured enough to admire the progressive aspects of the United States, the "second America" described in the quote. Like the Soviet Union, this "other" America was peaceful and its people lived in harmony. And to emphasize the unacceptable facets of America, Gorky was also explicit in describing his reservations about "American civilization":

> I think that your civilization is the most revolting civilization on our planet, because it so monstrously exaggerates all the different and shameful deformities of European civilization. Europe has enough trag- ically corrupted sons because of its own class structure, but all of Europe does not have the possibilities of such harmful and senseless actions, as your billionaires, millionaires, and such people, who give your country a degenerate name.[87]

Gorky's twenty-year-old text matched the ideological language of the anti- American campaign in the late 1940s perfectly. A Europhile, Gorky emphasized the peace-loving nature of the Soviet people while contrasting the acceptable, "second America" to the otherwise "degenerate" parts of the United States. He highlighted well the contrasts between the positive and the negative, and his im- agery was so vivid that no one could doubt the correct way of thinking about the United States. This ability to express oneself in the ideologically correct lan- guage of the time was a very important skill: anthropologist Alexei Yurchak has suggested that "ideological literacy," that is, "the technical skill of reproducing the precise passages and structures of that language in one's text and speeches," became the dominant form of expression in the party.[88]

Vladimir Mayakovsky, also well versed in "ideological literacy," had written a travelogue after his 1925 trip to the United States and secured his place as a favorite anti-American author. The book, *My Discovery of America* (*Moe otkrytie Ameriki*), was published in 1926 and became extremely popular. Moreover, Mayakovsky traveled widely in the Soviet Union to talk about his experiences in the United States in the 1920s, and even if the book received mixed reviews, Mayakovsky's impressions of America fit well with the regime's ideological posi- tion. In 1949, the Agitprop commission republished the book in a run of 250,000 copies, arguing that "it tears the mask off what has been called 'the American way of life'" and uncovers "the monstrous exploitation of workers and dreams about global dominance." Furthermore, the book offered a good account of the falsity of "bourgeois democracy," "bourgeois freedom," and "the corruption of bourgeois culture and morals."[89] Be that as it may, the authorities also worried that "Mayakovsky's text could at times be understood incorrectly," noting two or three places where the reader might have problems understanding Mayakovsky's relationship with America.[90] In spite of these problems, *My Discovery of America* was still considered one of the classics of anti-American literature, and it kept its status throughout the 1950s.[91]

Ilya Ehrenburg was another favorite among Soviet anti-American writers in the postwar period. After visiting the United States in 1946 as a part of a small delegation, Ehrenburg wrote several articles for the government newspaper *Izvestiia* about his travels in the deep American South. His first articles were unusual in the sense that they conveyed hope about the future of race relations in the United States and admiration for American technology.[92] In 1947, when he published a small book, *In America* (*V Amerike*), about his experiences in the United States, his descriptions were less positive.[93] But illustrating how quickly the tone of the ideological campaign was changing, by 1949 the book had fallen under attack at the Writers' Union when its own publishing house, Sovetskii pisatel' (Soviet Writer) announced it would not republish *In America* because it was "out of date" since it did "not sufficiently address the second America."[94]

In 1949, Ehrenburg had also written a little book on "the American Way of Life," including new essays as well as articles he had already published in *Pravda* and *Kul'tura i zhizn'*. The booklet, *Nights of America* (*Amerikanskie nochi*), started with Ehrenburg's claim that in his earlier writings, he had held himself back. Now, however, he would recount all the negative things he had learned in the United States.[95] In outlining some of the main problems of the book to the Central Committee, deputy chief at Agitprop Lazar' Slepov maintained that: "The limitations of the book lie in the absence of explicit borders between simple Americans and their oppressors." For example, Slepov complained that Ehrenburg did not include any discussion of lynching and his claims about ordinary Americans not wanting war at all were outrageous. He had also suggested that "hatred for Negroes" was not only a typically American problem but had a global character. Slepov suggested Ehrenburg should rework the manuscript and eliminate such passages.[96] The manuscript was never published. It is not clear if Ehrenburg withdrew it or if it was blocked, but later observers concluded that there was nothing in the book that went against Soviet propaganda and that it could easily have been printed as it was.[97]

Ehrenburg's biographers agree that he went to great lengths to compromise his views in order to please the state in Stalin's time,[98] and in many instances Ehrenburg was instrumental in executing the state's stance on anti-Americanism. In 1947, for example, his articles in *Kul'tura i zhizn'* marked the beginning of the Soviet response to the radio broadcasts of the Voice of America.[99] In 1949, however, even Ilya Ehrenburg's work was not up to the strictest anti-American standards. Upon finding out that his work was not "up to date," Ehrenburg appealed to the Central Committee, because he believed he had provided readers with enough information "to give them contempt and hatred for the 'American Way of Life' and its apologists."[100] But Slepov's rebuttal of his argument prevailed, and he concluded that the Central Committee's decision to not publish *Nights of America* had been the right one.[101]

The case of Ehrenburg, as well as that of Konstantin Simonov before him, illustrates well the pressure writers were under in the late Stalin era. If they wanted to keep writing, authors had to ascribe to the patriotic, anti-American themes required by the Soviet authorities and they also had to be able to stand the test of various party bureaucrats, agitators, and critics—who might have ulterior motives—in order to have their works approved. The creative industry is just one example of this; Nikolai Krementsov reached the same conclusions about one of the most highly publicized cases of antipatriotism during the late 1940s, when cancer researchers Nina Kliueva and Grigorii Roskin were put on trial after giving a talk on their research to American scientists. Also, Soviet researchers had to comply with the system's rules if they wanted to get by.[102]

While Agitprop's focus was on the arts and the "ideological workers," there were others who questioned their ability to do this properly and expressed the need for more accurate scientific knowledge about the United States. In a 1951 pronouncement "about the condition of scholarly work in American studies,"[103] several specialists on the United States complained that few Soviet students were interested in engaging in serious study of America. As a result, the Academy of Sciences suffered a shortage of highly qualified experts on the United States. The Institute of Economics had only nine specialists on America (both North and South), and there were only three each at the Institute of History, the Institute of Labor History, and the Institute of Law. Additionally, the pronouncement claimed that philosophers were poorly trained to study the ideology of American imperialism. Overall, there was a complete lack of training of new specialists on America at the various institutes of the Academy of Sciences in Moscow and insufficient numbers of people already working in this important area. The specialists claimed that a center dedicated to scientific and scholarly research on America was necessary in order to increase both the quality of training and the number of people involved in the area. For this purpose, they wanted to put the study of American history, economics, domestic and foreign policy, and American imperialism under one administration.[104]

The America experts also expressed much concern about the quality of published work on the United States. "The journals, as a rule, publish articles of low quality" and the authors of these articles seemed poorly qualified. They criticized the authors for "not knowing enough about the bigger picture, the local circumstances, and foreign policy of the United States through different times in its history." The scholars called for rigorous work, thoroughly based on the theoretical framework of Marxism-Leninism, as there were some examples of "bourgeois objectivity," or too much praise of the West in recent studies.[105] Furthermore, the authors of the report pointed out how many Soviet scholars relied too much on translated books on American studies. While such books "have an indisputable role" for the study of all things American, they should not be considered "a substitute for Soviet literature" on the subject: "It should be a priority of the Soviet state to publish books in which all questions related to the development of the countries in the Americas would receive true Marxist-Leninist treatment."[106]

It could certainly have benefited Agitprop had all study of the United States been moved to one center, but a separate Institute for US and Canada Studies was established only in 1967.[107] Not only that, the Academy of Sciences may have seen an opportunity in the anti-American campaign to advance the academy and secure a bigger budget for its research. Given the fact that the report was written around the time that the US government started to finance the establishment of Russian and Soviet area studies centers, it would not have been surprising had the Soviet authorities reacted favorably to the proposal.[108] The lack of responsiveness on the Soviet side, however, corresponded with the lack of organization in other areas of the Soviet cultural bureaucracy. Taking into account the extreme anti-American atmosphere and the difficulty in finding the correct anti-American tone, the authors of the report may even have put their careers at risk for suggesting this reorganization.

"Progressive" American Writers and "the Negro Question"

Under Stalin, access to American culture was limited, and knowledge about America was based mostly on Russian or Soviet works. A few American books, however, remained in circulation during the postwar period, mainly because their message was in line with the Soviet anti-American policy. Several American writers deemed acceptable by Russian and Soviet authorities had contributed to Soviet knowledge about American life and culture, although American writers and performers who maintained a good relationship with the Soviet Union during Stalin's last years were usually "friends of the Soviet Union" or "fellow travelers." In 1949, when the Central Committee encouraged performance groups to turn to earlier Russian classics in their emphasis on anti-American themes, it also recommended the works of some of those "progressive American writers."[109]

Several "progressive" American writers had long been popular in Russia and the Soviet Union.[110] Most anyone who enjoyed literature in the Soviet Union would have been familiar with Jack London's short stories or Upton Sinclair's novels.[111] From 1918 to 1959, Jack London's works were published in editions of more than twenty million copies in thirty-two languages of the USSR; Mark Twain in almost eleven million copies and twenty-five languages; and Upton Sinclair's work in more than four million copies in fifteen languages. The works of John Steinbeck were also very popular, as were those of O. Henry, Howard Fast, Theodore Dreiser, James Fenimore Cooper, Erskine Caldwell, Sinclair Lewis, Edgar Allan Poe, Walt Whitman, and Langston Hughes.[112]

Many of these authors were read in the years leading up to the Second World War and continued to be available in the postwar period in print runs that ranged from just over 100,000 copies for Langston Hughes to several million copies of works by Jack London and Mark Twain.[113] Standing before American audiences in 1949, Aleksandr Fadeev claimed that these numbers should be seen as proof that the Soviet people embraced American culture.[114] But most of the American authors whose works were printed in the Soviet Union were accepted only because they criticized American culture and politics in a way that was satisfactory to the Soviet authorities. In 1949, at the high point of the anti-American campaign, Agitprop issued that the "best books written by the progressive foreign writers" Mark Twain, Theodore Dreiser, Jack London, Sinclair Lewis, and Howard Fast were to be republished.[115]

These writers were seen as strong critics of American social, economic, and racial issues, both in the Soviet Union and back home. The acceptable American writers did not necessarily write within a Marxist-Leninist framework, but they wrote critically on subjects such as race relations or poverty in the United States. And not all, but many of the American writers accepted by the Soviet authorities, had at some point in their lives found the ideology of the Soviet Union appealing. Some of them, including Upton Sinclair and John Steinbeck, had a long-standing fascination with the Soviet Union and even visited the country.[116] Quite a few of these authors participated in the National Council for American-Soviet Friendship (NCASF), the most important Soviet front organization in the United States, cultivating a strong relationship with the Soviet Union and writing about the communist country and its policies for an American audience. The political beliefs of the American writers, however, are not the issue here, but rather how they or their works contributed to the Soviet image of America in the postwar period. These people were extremely valuable for Soviet authorities, not only to give their own anti-American propaganda a more legitimate voice but also because their major strategy in reaching foreign audiences was through these "friends of the Soviet Union."

While several of these authors are today part of the American literary canon and others are recognized for their contribution to American left-wing literature, not all American books published in the Soviet Union were deemed to be of very high quality. Melville J. Ruggles, then vice president of the Council of Library Resources in the United States, visited the Soviet Union in 1961 and researched the state of publishing and the contents of Soviet library stacks. In evaluating the quality of the American authors available to Soviet readers, Ruggles stated: "The appetite of Soviet publishers for literature critical of the American system is apparently not satisfied by left-wing American writers who can write. It leads them to scrape the bottom of the barrel."[117] He went on to say that

> The image of America projected by the American literature published in the USSR, however, seems to be fairly clear. . . . The America that the Russian knows from the American literature available to him is a land of Simon Legree, the coonskin cap, the heroic sled dog, the share cropper, the sweatshop, the dispirited, defeated, and depraved, the frivolous, the bloated billionaire, the regimented traveler in space. The American literature he is given opportunity to read conveys to him little notion of how we think, of how we live, of our true virtues or of our true faults.[118]

A study of American characters in Russian fiction reached a similar conclusion. The "Upper-Class Lady" was envied, hated, or despised, while the "Working-Class and the Middle-Class Woman" was admired and pitied. Similarly, American businessmen and millionaires, hated in pre-Napoleonic times and ignored in the early nineteenth century, ranged from being "hated" to "strongly hated" to "despised" as of the 1860s. Besides the "Worker," however, Russian fiction writers sympathized with no American character as much as "the American Negro."[119]

Not surprisingly, "the Negro Question" topped almost all other accounts about the United States in its perceived propaganda value: several American works were acceptable mainly for their value in showing the sufferings of African Americans in the United States. The most famous American novel dealing with racial issues--and one of the most widely distributed American books in the Soviet Union—was Harriet Beecher Stowe's *Uncle Tom's Cabin*. Stowe was the ninth most popular American author in the Soviet Union during its first forty years of existence, well into the 1960s.[120] Throughout Soviet times, *Uncle Tom's Cabin* was read in schools, was staged in theaters, and was widely available to the Soviet public. Serving as a testimony to the way American slave owners treated their slaves, it both reflected the Soviet stance on "the Negro Question" and became its constant point of reference. It was easy to make propagandistic use of a novel with recognizable characters, and references to the novel were often found in newspaper articles and cartoons of the period.

Supporting and advancing the cause of minorities was always a part of the Soviet position on colonialism and its global agenda. In the beginning, however, focus was mainly on African Americans and the "Negro Question" in the United States, only later expanding with the rise of black African liberation movements in the postwar period.[121] The Soviet side relied on the American Communist Party (CPUSA) to provide the theoretical framework for how to represent African Americans. Thus, when the American Communist Party started advocating for self-determination of African Americans in the American South, Soviet authorities also made self-determination of African Americans, and black people everywhere, their official policy.[122]

One of the most influential and popular African Americans in the Soviet Union was Paul Robeson, singer, actor, and activist. Emphasizing the similarity of Russian and Negro backgrounds—"they were both serfs"—Robeson remained a true friend of the Soviet Union throughout his lifetime. During the 1930s, he lived in London but traveled frequently to the Soviet Union, where his son went to public school. Because of the pending war, they moved back to the United States in 1938, but Robeson resumed his travels after the conflict. Following the 1949 Paris World Peace Conference, a propaganda initiative of the Soviet Communist Party where Robeson vocally expressed his views of the treatment of African Americans at home, he turned into somewhat of an outcast in the United States. He was not allowed to perform, and his passport was confiscated.[123] During this time, however, he worked diligently with the National Council for American-Soviet Friendship in the United States and mingled with Soviet delegations traveling there.[124]

During the late 1940s, when contact with foreigners was rare, Soviet propaganda authorities relied on their American friends to write about the Soviet Union for Americans and to relate stories of the wonderful things they saw in the country.[125] Propaganda authorities likewise counted on "correct" firsthand experiences of Soviet visitors to the United States, making plans to publish collections such as *Progressive Americans against the Wagers of War: The Second America* following the 1949 Congress of Science and Culture in the United States.[126] As with Soviet works, however, some American books were published in abridged form so that their text would fit Soviet purposes better. Such was the case with Lee Fryer's *The American Farmer*, a harsh critique of the working conditions American farmers faced in the postwar period. In 1948, the book was published but twenty-two pages were cut, because "a few parts contain praise for the evolution of American farming."[127] Very strategically, Soviet authorities offered books written by Americans as legitimate information about America. Stories of slavery, racial discrimination, beatings, lynching, suppression, and the like were used to represent the struggle of good Americans against the business tycoons and the aggressive American government. By showing parallels between

Russian serfdom and American slavery and by highlighting the oppression of African Americans in the postwar period, the Soviet Union aimed to present its own progressive ideas about socialist modernity while drawing out the worst aspects of the United States.

Conclusion

In Stalin's time, the creative intelligentsia was mobilized in the campaign to help people reach "correct" conclusions about the United States. The Communist Party controlled the production and publication of literary works, not only deciding which of the classic anti-American works were to be republished and in what form, but also instructing Soviet writers and playwrights to incorporate anti-American themes into their current projects.[128] Under the firm rule of Stalin, the anti-American campaign was the most spectacular effort the Communist Party carried out in terms of controlling the way America was perceived in the Soviet Union.

Although Soviet propaganda authorities often crudely represented the United States, they focused on real problems and issues in that country. Even if a majority subscribed to a capitalist ideology of abundance, differences and conflicts remained a sustenance of American society in the twentieth century. Often, the "oppositional elements" in America—especially issues of race and African-American struggles—held the highest appeal to observers in foreign countries.[129] In advocating anti-Americanism, the Soviet government certainly manipulated these "oppositional elements" to fit its story of a dual America, one where "progressive" Americans were fighting the "evil and rotten" businessmen of America.

While based on real conditions in America, Soviet anti-American propaganda was still grossly exaggerated and often represented the United States in a crude and misleading way. Despite the paradigm of dual America, it was therefore not always easy to promote anti-Americanism in the Soviet Union. The presence of American-made tractors and cars in the country suggested prosperity and possibilities that at times had been praised as exemplary but were now slandered. The Soviet authorities, however, did not rest in trying to control and monitor information in the Soviet Union. It was not enough to introduce anti-American topics into all Soviet media; it was also necessary to fight undesired information from America and to make sure that Soviet citizens understood how to "correctly" view the United States.

2 AMERICAN SOURCES OF INFORMATION AND SOVIET INTEREST IN THE ENEMY

Officials in Washington were perfectly aware of the forceful anti-American campaign in the Soviet Union, but deteriorating relations between the two superpowers in the postwar period made it difficult for Americans to counter it. During the late Stalin period, the State Department had only two official means to advocate for the superiority of the American way of life in the Soviet Union: the radio broadcasts of the Voice of America and the glossy magazine *Amerika*, published in the Soviet Union. Not surprisingly, Soviet authorities reacted strongly to this American propaganda effort and did everything in their power to control and counter these alternative sources of information.[1]

Emerging from the Second World War as one of two superpowers, American foreign policy took on an ideological dimension. The "American way of life" was to be protected and its version of democratic capitalism exported.[2] If there was some hesitation in Washington about the uses of psychological warfare against the Soviet Union in the postwar period, the dawning of the Cold War removed all doubt.[3] Around the time the Soviet state launched its anti-Western campaign, depicting the United States as "the leader of imperialistic expansion and aggression, the main stronghold of the global reactionary,"[4] the American government went ahead with its own anti-Soviet, anti-communist propaganda campaign.

In the fall of 1945, the assistant secretary of state for public and cultural relations, William B. Benton, was already facing a difficult task in terms of simultaneously clarifying American goals and justifying Stalin's expansion in Eastern Europe. In a draft analysis of how to deal with information policies toward the Soviet Union, Professor Harold Lasswell had warned Benton that the United States was facing a dilemma in that the Soviet Union was still admired for its role in the Second World War and it also had a reputation for being more tolerant than the United States with regard to race relations. Benton discarded

Lasswell's analysis in 1945,[5] but already in late 1946 the State Department made it clear that the Soviet Union was the most significant country to US foreign policy, and that as the Cold War intensified, "propaganda and information activities" were seen as "vital tools in combating communism."[6] In the beginning, those who were familiar with Soviet postwar realities, such as US ambassador W. Averell Harriman, warned against criticizing the Soviet system too much out of "fear of arousing Soviet patriotism," but fairly soon, the more aggressive "containment" strategy of George F. Kennan, however unintentional, prevailed.[7]

As the Cold War progressed, American propaganda toward the Soviet Union became more targeted and focused especially on the totalitarian aspects of Soviet society and countering Soviet propaganda about the United States.[8] In 1947, two Republicans, Senator H. Alexander Smith (New Jersey) and Representative Karl Mundt (North Dakota) advocated a strong information program to counter Soviet propaganda, and the Smith-Mundt Act took effect on January 27, 1948, calling for the promotion of a "better understanding of the United States among the peoples of the world."[9] To that effect, it anticipated mobilizing all modern media, exchange programs, and exhibitions in order to publicize the virtues of the United States.

Soviet propaganda authorities took strict measures to prevent American propaganda from reaching the Soviet population during the late Stalin period. American officials, however, believed that both the Voice of America and *Amerika* succeeded in lessening the impact of Soviet internal propaganda[10] and saw the strong reaction from Moscow as a sign of success.[11] As with much of our knowledge about the Soviet Union, however, this view was particularly stressed by Soviet dissidents and later supported by scholars who praised the efforts of American propaganda abroad as a form of Americanization or cultural globalization but based their conclusions on American evaluations of their own efforts.[12] Dissidents, scholars, and American cultural officials thus often made references to the Voice of America or *Amerika* in passing, mostly as proof of the perceived successes of American propaganda in the Soviet Union, but could not base their observations on studies of how Soviet authorities and Soviet people actually reacted to American propaganda during the early Cold War.[13]

The strong measures taken by the Soviet state to prevent access to American propaganda are indicative of how far Soviet authorities were willing to go in order to keep their ideological domination and control interest in the American enemy. Soviet authorities' intolerance for people's curiosity about the United States, let alone relations with Americans, was inherent in the anti-American campaign. Therefore, the Soviet state defined positive sentiments about America as counterrevolutionary behavior and repressed people who allegedly expressed interest in the United States of America, knew Americans personally, or listened to American radio broadcasts. Broadly speaking, the anti-American campaign of the early Cold War was not only about how to best represent "the second America" in Soviet cinema, theater, and literature or how to react to American propaganda about the superiority of the American way of life, but it was also about limiting access to all things Americans and extinguishing interest in the enemy.[14]

Official Soviet Reactions to *Amerika*

Amerika was first published in the Soviet Union in 1945 as a part of a bilateral agreement, with its circulation limited to 10,000 copies. In the beginning, the American embassy actually put out two different journals, *Amerika* and *Amerika Illustrirovannaia* (*Amerika Illustrated*), each published in a run of 5,000 copies. On April 24, 1946, however, the Soviet Ministry of Foreign Affairs announced that as of June 1, 1946, *Amerika* could be printed in runs of 50,000 copies. From then on, only the illustrated version of the journal was issued,[15] but soon thereafter, Soviet authorities regretted this decision and started to figure out strategies to limit access to the legal journal.

The Soviet side consistently denied that there was any demand for *Amerika* in the Soviet Union, but the Americans were certain that Soviet people would read the journal if it were easily available to them. In July 1946, the American embassy in Moscow complained that 22,500 copies of the fifth issue of *Amerika* (1945) were being detained in the warehouses of Mezhkniga, which was responsible for distributing the magazine. According to the Soviets, the Americans had jumped the gun; the increase in the press run was supposed to take effect only with issues no. 1 and 2 for 1946. Clearly concerned, the Soviet Ministry of Communications concluded that it was "necessary to decide what to do with the additional 40,000 copies of *Amerika*." Ministry officials claimed it would be "pointless" to allow the free sale of the journal, because it would not sell.[16] Thus, the relevant authorities tried to prevent *Amerika* from reaching readers outside of approved circles. It would still be possible for leading officials to receive the publication if they wanted to—but that would be done at the discretion of the party organs.[17]

In early 1947, Agitprop recommended to Zhdanov that the circulation of both the British journal *Britanskii Soiuznik* and *Amerika* be limited to 30,000 copies by subscription and 10,000 for retail sale. Clearly concerned about the readership, Agitprop proposed that subscriptions be allowed "only for patriotic workers of central party and Soviet organizations, the Central Committees of the Communist Party (Bolsheviks) in the Union republics as well as ministries of foreign affairs." Retail sales "should not exceed 4,000 copies."[18] This decision meant that audience was now very limited for both journals. From 1947, the foreign journals became privileged reading for the most loyal and trusted Soviet cultural

and political bureaucrats on the very doubtful presumption that they were im-
mune to ideological contamination from the West.[19]

With curbs on subscriptions and retail sales, whom did *Amerika* reach in the
Soviet Union? According to the Soviet overview for issue no. 7 in 1947 (when
it was still allowed to print 50,000 issues), 7,500 issues went to subscribers in
Moscow and another 8,300 issues went to Soviet institutions; 18,400 issues went
to subscribers outside of Moscow, and, overall, 14,000 issues went on sale (10,000
in Moscow). The final 1,800 copies were distributed to unspecified editors and
kept for inventory, according to the plan.[20] Soiuzpechat' (Union Print) kiosks
were supposed to sell *Amerika*, but they were located in only three Soviet
cities: Moscow, Leningrad, and Kiev; in other cities the leaders of the local party
organizations organized the sales.[21] Clearly, not anyone could just take out a subscription to *Amerika*, and in addition to limiting its distribution the party ideally
wanted only "patriotic" Soviet citizens to have access to the journal.

It is ironic then, in light of all the limitations put on the distribution and selling of the magazine, that two years later the Soviet side complained that "lack of
interest" in the magazine was causing financial losses for the Soviet organizations
involved. In November 1949, Nikolai Psurtsev, minister of communications,
complained to Agitprop and Comrade Vyacheslav Molotov, then first deputy
chairman of the Council of Ministers,[22] on behalf of the organizations responsible for printing and distributing the journal in the Soviet Union (Soiuzpechat'
and Mezhkniga) that the journal was not selling. Mezhkniga bought each press
run in full from the American embassy and was left with unsold issues and a loss
in revenue. Therefore, Mezhkniga suggested to Molotov that both the quantity
and the price of *Amerika* be reduced.[23]

Molotov reflected a bit on this question in his reply to Psurtsev's complaint.
He included a note to members of the inner circle Georgy Malenkov, Lavrenty
Beria, Lazar Kaganovich, and Nikolai Bulganin, who all had been getting copies
of the correspondence, claiming that Mikhail Menshikov, minister of foreign
trade, thought the suggestion on reducing the press run and decreasing the prices
of the British and American journals too strict.[24] Nikolai Psurtsev had stressed
that they could not really print fewer issues since they were already doing an absolute minimum to keep the terms of the contract with the Americans.[25] Still,
the Soviet side concluded that reducing the press run was the best option and
started outlining its conditions for continued publication of *Amerika*, stating
that since "demand from the population" was decreasing and the Soviet organizations Soiuzpechat' and Mezhkniga were suffering losses, they could not support
continued publication.[26] Stalin issued a decree stating that it was unacceptable
for Soviet organizations to suffer financial loss and dictated that the unsold issues
be sent back to the American embassy.[27]

Although American officials had been fully aware of the harassment Soviet readers of *Amerika* experienced as early as 1947,[28] the formalized complaints from Soviet authorities first reached American officials in December 1949 when Soiuzpechat' issued a statement about the unsatisfactory sales of *Amerika*.[29] Soiuzpechat' maintained that *Amerika* was on sale in more than seventy cities in the Soviet Union, in three to fifty Soiuzpechat' kiosks in each city, but up to half the run of every issue remained unsold in all these locations.[30] This was clearly not correct, as the internal reports on how to limit access to the journal show and the American embassy rightly said that this statement was "open to question."[31] The embassy correctly distrusted the figures about the availability of *Amerika* in the Soviet Union: American embassy staff had "failed to find *Amerika* on sale in twenty-four Soviet cities" and suspected that Soiuzpechat' had not distributed the magazine at all. They also found it strange that in the five years the magazine had been published, this was the first time the embassy had been notified of these unsatisfactory sales numbers. Finally, they estimated that Soviet readers had "great interest" in the journal and correctly concluded that Soviet authorities limited people's access to it.[32]

A November 1949 report from the Soviet Ministry of Communications actually predicted how a negotiation with the American embassy might go, with test questions and examples of good answers. An interesting feature of the report is that it stresses how it would be beneficial for the Soviet side to emphasize that Mezhkniga was a "commercial organization" following "normal practices" and thus appeal to the American way of doing business: "not one American firm would agree to work under such disadvantageous conditions."[33] Of course, neither Soiuzpechat' nor Mezhkniga were commercial organizations in the American understanding—they were state agencies subject to Soviet propaganda and censorship. Also, the conditions they were suggesting to the Americans, that is, reducing both the quantity and price of *Amerika*, were such that it was highly unlikely that the Americans would meet them. Eager to keep on publishing the journal, however, the Americans did not rule out meeting Soviet conditions. The American embassy was ready to explore a reduction in price, and embassy officials suggested that they could distribute the journal themselves and not rely on Soiuzpechat'.[34] This was unacceptable to the Soviet officials, confirming that they did not want to strengthen efforts to distribute the journal. After almost two frustrating years of Soviet and American debates about supply and demand, the Americans saw no other way than to cancel the publication in 1952, citing repeated efforts on the Soviet side to limit and inhibit the publication as the reason for doing so.[35]

In light of Soviet efforts to limit information about the United States, it is likely that the content of *Amerika*, and not the technicalities of distribution, was the real issue here. In a 1951 letter to Georgy Malenkov, then deputy prime minister as well as a secretary of the Central Committee, A. Khan'kovskii, member of the Communist Party and a self-appointed guardian of Soviet values, summarized the contents of the forty-sixth issue of *Amerika*, writing that:

> American propagandists try to present Soviet readers with utterly foolish fabrications about contemporary economic and social relations in the USA. Colorful diagrams, false numbers, dishonest facts, and other deceitful falsifications from the State Department try to impose on the Soviet readers an impression that America is a modern day El Dorado! *Amerika* maintains that, on average, American working families earn fifty-six dollars a week, they live in clover, and every week they can buy a men's suit, a lady's pair of shoes, stockings, and other clothing, eat lots of meat, eggs, butter and oranges, live in big three-room apartments, etc. This average worker even has a nice car, with a value of 1,700 dollars and a savings account.[36]

Dismayed, Khan'kovskii exclaimed, "Have you read this magazine?" He saw it as a challenge to the Soviet propaganda campaign, that the issues were produced on schedule, quickly distributed, and "always coincided with important events taking place in our country." He noted, for example, how the "famous decision by our party" to focus on forestation had pushed *Amerika* also to publish articles about forestation and the fight against erosion in the United States: "I am convinced that the dishonest propaganda of *Amerika* gives us plenty of wonderful material for counterpropaganda, to expose the American way of life, but we are not using these possibilities. It is unbelievable, but it is a fact!" Malenkov forwarded this letter to Mikhail Suslov, then editor of *Pravda* but formerly the chief director of the Agitprop Commission of the CPSU, asking him to familiarize himself with its contents.[37]

Khan'kovskii's concerns about the persuasiveness and accessibility of American propaganda in the Soviet Union reflect the overall fears of Soviet authorities. Continuing to worry about the ways American propaganda invaded Soviet society, Khan'kovskii sent another letter to Malenkov and Suslov in October 1951, expressing his disappointment with various publications in Soviet journals such as *Novoe vremia* and *Novyi mir*, which in his opinion "grossly distorted the facts of Soviet and American realities."[38] Khan'kovskii's letters show that Soviet authorities and audiences were aware of the danger of American propaganda emphasizing the superior quality of life in the United States. They also realized that the technique of indirectly attacking Soviet accomplishments by drawing out the successes of similar American projects had the potential to severely damage the Soviet cause.[39] It is therefore in no way surprising that the Soviet authorities were especially sensitive toward American propaganda that unfavorably compared the Soviet Union with the United States and that the Soviet responses remained harsh.

In the late 1940s, the American strategy was generally to avoid confronting hostile Soviet statements and propaganda while indirectly discrediting communism and the Soviet state. After the cancellation of *Amerika* in 1952, however, the US government was left with only one medium to propagandize in the Soviet Union: the Voice of America (VOA). Unlike *Amerika*, however, the radio broadcasts of the VOA were not bound into a bilateral agreement, making Soviet authorities fight even more fiercely against the broadcasts of the VOA than it had against the journal *Amerika*.

The Voice of America in Stalin's Soviet Union

The Voice of America (VOA) started its broadcasts to the Soviet Union on February 17, 1947.[40] The VOA was on the air every day for two hours: one and a half hours in the European part of the Soviet Union and half an hour in the Far East.[41] Over the following decades, it steadily increased its operation, broadcasting in nine languages to all parts of the Soviet Union by the mid-1980s.[42] American officials believed that the Soviet government would allow the broadcasts to go undisturbed, as any effort to limit them would signal their perceived appeal. The Americans were wrong. Not wanting to put a legal ban on listening to foreign radio broadcasts, the Soviet government opted instead for the costly and intensive jamming of VOA: jamming of the Russian-language broadcasts started on February 3, 1948.[43]

Maury Lisann, who worked as a consultant to the Voice of America during the Cold War, has claimed that the Soviet authorities had three ways of "coping with the problem" of foreign radio broadcasts: jamming, modifying the content of the broadcasts "at the source through diplomacy," or they could "remove the incentive for listening" by providing better information services at home and "discrediting foreign broadcasts through propaganda."[44] With diplomatic relations at an all-time low during the late 1940s and early 1950s, the jamming of foreign radio broadcasts in Soviet languages was the most systematic weapon the Soviet authorities used in the fight against this enemy propaganda, and domestic propaganda was also mobilized to counter the content of the radio broadcasts.[45]

The very first public response to the radio broadcasts was an article by Ilya Ehrenburg entitled "A False Voice," which appeared in *Kul'tura i zhizn'*, the Agitprop newspaper, on April 10, 1947.[46] Ehrenburg's article, in which he wrote that "the Voice of America has to market the most unmarketable goods— American reactionary politics," received much attention in the United States, where it was seen as a sign of interest on behalf of the Soviet people. The American ambassador, General Walter Bedell Smith, reported to Washington that the fact that Ilya Ehrenburg was chosen to launch the campaign against the Voice of America was "the most encouraging reaction we have seen,"[47] as it clearly showed that the Soviet side was concerned about the broadcasts.

When the jamming started in April 1948, the Russian-language service of the VOA had been extended into a twenty-four-hour operation.[48] The jamming, however, was neither exhaustive nor completely successful: in the late 1940s and the 1950s, American and Western broadcasters presenting an alternative image of both the outside world and inside realities succeeded in reaching an audience in the Soviet Union. To be fair, the estimated number of shortwave radio receivers needed to listen to foreign radio broadcasts was between three and four million in 1950 and about six million in 1955, but nevertheless, the Soviet domestic radio system was itself reliant on shortwave frequencies, and a ban on them would have severely limited the Soviet state's means for providing information to its citizens.[49] The irony here is that while the Soviet state was investing heavily in the jamming of the foreign radio programs, it was also producing and making available the technology needed for the enemy propaganda to be broadcast.[50]

So even if "few of those who did have receivers dared to listen to foreign radio broadcasts during the Stalin era," as one survey found out,[51] there is still evidence that the party-state considered the possibility for tuning in to the VOA as a problem to be solved. In 1950, the regional office of the Communist Party in the Karelo-Finskoi SSR reported that people were tuning in to foreign anti-Soviet radio broadcasts, and the local party apparatus seemed overwhelmed with how widespread the activity was in this region.[52] Similarly, the local party cell in the Chutkotskii region reported several incidents of people listening to the Voice of America, noting that they would undertake strict and intensive work against such radio broadcasts, without saying explicitly what those measures would entail.[53] Some of the measures for strengthening the fight against anti-Soviet broadcasts proposed by the first secretary of the Lithuanian Communist Party, Antanas Sniečkus, in April 1951, included the accelerated construction of transmitters designed for blocking the foreign radio broadcasts. This was presented as a matter of some urgency as parts of the city of Vilnius, and the towns of Klaipėda, Šiauliai, and Kaunas were not protected at all, and were "open to the penetration of hostile radio propaganda."[54]

Certainly, the content of the American broadcasts directly challenged the Soviet anti-American image of the United States. VOA radio hosts discussed, for example, how Western freedom fostered a thriving culture of artists and intellectuals, whereas the Soviet system stifled and often punished those with creative talent. VOA programs criticized totalitarian control over almost every aspect of private and public life, and they often put the spotlight on the right to travel abroad, collectivization, wages, long working hours, privileges granted to Communist Party members, limitations on creativity, and denial of freedom of religion, to name a few popular issues.[55] Furthermore, the VOA explained the US electoral process, emphasizing that the people selected their own leaders through free elections. The role of a free press was also discussed, but mostly VOA programming focused on the overall higher standard of living in the United States, better access to health care, abundance in consumer goods and leisure activities and the comfort of the American way of life.[56] By the end of the 1940s, Soviet propaganda against the VOA focused on countering "lies" about the United States.[57] Knowing that they could never completely prevent foreign radio broadcasts from reaching the Soviet people, the Soviet strategy was to counter information presented by the Voice of America with writings about the "second America."[58] This took precedence over trying to keep check on facts about the Soviet Union presented in American propaganda, which became more of a concern later. As of 1953, VOA changed its broadcasting strategy to focus more on Soviet domestic affairs and politics, much to the worry of Soviet authorities. But during the late Stalin era, the American broadcasts were mostly about life in the United States.[59]

While there was relatively limited access to the enemy radio broadcasts in the Soviet Union, the intense jamming suggests that the Kremlin perceived the American broadcasts as a threat to its ideological monopoly. And while it was not forbidden by law to listen to the Voice of America, discussing and disseminating information heard on enemy broadcasts could be interpreted as counterrevolutionary activity according to Article 58-10 of the Soviet criminal code, and people took a risk when they listened to the program, especially if they talked about it afterward. How the Soviet state dealt with the possibility of people's interest in the United States reveals much about the nature of social control in the Soviet Union at the time.

Soviet Interest in the United States of America

Soviet interest in the United States is well documented, even for this period of strong anti-Americanism. Several accounts have highlighted a not-so-hidden underground fascination with the United States and celebrated young people who imitated or adapted American culture during high Stalinism. Labeling themselves *shtatniki* or *stiliagi*, they embraced American popular culture, fashion, and music and, through their cultural consumption, believed that they had come closer to the quintessential American values of freedom.[60] Without concluding anything about the impact of American propaganda or culture in the Soviet Union, it seems clear that interest in American culture and values and the presumed effect of this curiosity about the evil other greatly worried Soviet authorities.

The campaigns against *Amerika* and the jamming of the Voice of America show that the Soviet authorities invested a considerable amount of energy in controlling the availability of information about the United States. As the Soviet government tried to channel the population's perceptions of the outside world with its anti-Western focus, Soviet authorities also collected reports from local authorities, who gauged "the mood of the population" in conversations and at party meetings, reporting back to the Central Committee on "unhealthy moods" in the Soviet Union. Local party organizations or surveillance establishments collected questions at various places, such as party or factory meetings around the country. Sometimes they were motivated by extraordinary events, such as strikes, but often they were a part of "the ongoing surveillance effort."[61] The collectors compiled the comments and sent them to the Central Committee in Moscow, where Soviet agitators were expected to take note of their existence.

Commonly known by their Russian name, *svodki*, these summaries of "moods of the population" were one way the Soviet state presumably kept in touch with "popular opinion" in the country, although the effect of such reports remain difficult to determine.[62] Soviet ideology was designed as a top-down process, a "tool for popular indoctrination and mobilization,"[63] and even if Soviet citizens wrote countless letters to various party organs, there is little evidence that either such letters or *svodki* had any effect on the strategy or execution of Soviet propaganda in general or the anti-American campaign in particular. Nevertheless, the existence of the *svodki* is here seen as suggestive of the regime's intent to mobilize the Soviet population and to streamline popular opinion. Read against the background of the anti-American campaign and the battle against American propaganda in the Soviet Union, some of the recurrent themes in the *svodki* are therefore interesting—not only because they mirror Soviet ideology and propaganda at the time, but also because they show a fear of the supposed impact of rumors and alternative sources of information in the Soviet Union.[64]

To be fair, the *svodki* did not focus only on American or foreign themes. This is particularly evident in cited remarks and questions about life in the Soviet Union soon after the war: "Why is there only one political party in the Soviet Union?" and "Why has our material position not improved, now that the war is over?"[65] Postwar reconstruction was obviously an important topic, and people wondered about everyday things such as when they would get an increased ration of bread; when clothes, shoes, and other industrial products would become more affordable; and whether they would be compensated for unused vacation time from the war.[66] Judging from such comments, as well as questions and concern about an impending apocalypse, Soviet authorities feared any skepticism regarding the official rhetoric about the pace of reconstruction, and any concerns about "outside danger" that would soon destroy the Soviet Union were duly noted. So even if the political indoctrination was a top-down process, Soviet people compared their realities to official representations and the authorities took note, if only to strengthen their own anti-American propaganda. Rumors of a pending doomsday were thus blamed on the new enemy.

In 1947, workers in Leningrad worried whether war between the United States and the Soviet Union was likely and posed challenging questions about the nature of the peace and the role that America would play on the postwar stage. "How much of a threat to world peace was the United States?" "Was America ready to go to war again?" "Would America use the atomic bomb again?" "In the case of an attack from the former allies, was Soviet strength sufficient?" "Would an American attack from Alaska pose a real danger to the Soviet Union?" [67] Tired of war, people asked who would benefit from the new superpower struggle: "Why is the Soviet Union competing with the United States and England? Would it not be better if our leadership surrendered to these countries?"[68] In addition to worries or speculation about a renewed war, the *svodki* also reported comments on the deteriorating relationship between the Soviet Union and the former allies, England and the United States. This is especially clear in questions on whether or not the American Lend-Lease aid would continue after the war.[69] Another similar question was, "[i]s it true that the United States would like to resume trade with the Soviet Union?"[70] And at one point, soon after the war, there was even a rumor about Stalin never returning from vacation and that the Soviet Union would be controlled by the United States.[71]

Party organizations from all over the country sent in similar reports, suggesting that these kinds of questions and comments were thought to be of interest to the central authorities.[72] As soon as the Cold War had started, Stalin's theory of the inevitability of wars between the capitalist powers took on a somewhat changed form in the Soviet Union.[73] Now, the government promoted the rumors about the possibility of a new war, this time against the United States. Having just gone through a horrible war, this fed a real fear among the population and created a variety of responses. While some people seem to have taken the rumor of war to heart, others questioned the integrity of this speculation and suggested that such a war would be senseless. Causing anything from fear and anger to disbelief and confusion, the Soviet regime used the rumor to agitate for continued patriotism and further sacrifices in terms of the seemingly difficult project of building socialism out of the ruins of the Great Patriotic War.[74]

Judging by the volume of comments and questions about the United States, Soviet authorities worried about Soviet citizens' presumed interest in the number one enemy. No other foreign country receives as much mention in the *svodki* of the postwar years, and the range and nature of questions about America is interesting in light of both the anti-American campaign, as well as American propaganda inside the Soviet Union. Following the themes of the anti-American campaign, questions on why the American working class was not actively fighting against their reactionary governments, "which carry on politics that are against the interests of their people," were noted in the *svodki*.[75] This last theme also suggests knowledge of Marxism and Soviet propaganda, which predicted that an uprising would of course be the logical goal of those inhabiting the "second America." Therefore, if the postwar *svodki*, like the *svodki* from the late 1920s, are mostly indicative of the state's interest about "where active unrest was likely to flare up,"[76] the numerous questions and comments about America that were noted in the *svodki* can be seen as symptomatic of the state's concern about American anti-Soviet propaganda and Soviet people's exposure to it. Similarly, questions on how to best represent the Soviet Union abroad[77] may suggest that knowledge of anti-Soviet propaganda, such as found in radio broadcasts and magazines, was not uncommon and that some people found this troubling.

Building on the analysis of the *svodki*, another way to approach the perceived impact of alternative sources of information and Soviet ideology on Soviet people is to browse through rehabilitation records for Soviet individuals who had been sentenced according to the infamous article 58-10 of the Soviet criminal code. Article 58 served as the foundation for the political terror that reigned in the Soviet Union; it defined anti-Soviet behavior and laid out the minimum punishment guidelines. The article consisted of fourteen clauses that dealt with people considered dangerous to society, namely, counterrevolutionary or anti-Soviet, but clause ten (58-10) specifically addressed the manifestation and the spread of anti-Soviet agitation: "Propaganda or agitation, containing a call for the overthrow, subversion, or weakening of Soviet authority or for the carrying out of other counterrevolutionary crimes, and likewise the distribution or preparation or keeping of literature of this nature shall be punishable by deprivation of liberty for a term not less than six months."[78]

These records, or review files (*nadzornye proizvodstva*) as they are called, are files that were put together when a victim of political repression had submitted a rehabilitation request in the 1950s to the Soviet Procuracy, the *Prokuratura*.[79] Like the *svodki*, these sources mirror the way Soviet ideology and the anti-American propaganda campaign of the postwar years reached far corners of the Soviet state; they too reflect the emphases and fears rampant in the Soviet bureaucracy in the postwar years. But additionally, the indictment and imprisonment of ordinary Soviet citizens who were repressed by the state for their supposed interest in the United States show the most extreme measure of the anti-American campaign in the postwar period.

This is not to say that these individuals were guilty of the anti-Soviet crimes they were accused of and often convicted for. Presumably, the victims may have been under surveillance already and the collected pro-American sentiments were used to compile a case against them. Also, the statements from the review files show neither support nor resistance to the Soviet regime, but rather that the developing superpower relationship and the pending Cold War caused concern in Soviet society, as well as in the administration: interest in the enemy did not equal lack of loyalty to the Soviet project. This is based on a reading of these files that is suspect of their origins, but finds the cited statements on the United States and the West to be of value in understanding how Soviet people may have reacted to both inside realities and the outside world. Just like the *svodki*, they are indicative of the international themes Soviet authorities worried about in the early Cold War.

There was certainly a variety of opinions about the United States. The chosen cases provide a cross section of Soviet society; these people had different levels of education; held different occupations ranging from peasant to worker to factory manager, accountant, and artist; and came from all over the Soviet Union. Furthermore, in some cases there are examples of some kind of contact with America or the West. The most common experience was fighting or living close to the front in the Second World War, but later the broadcasts of foreign radio stations, particularly the Voice of America and also the BBC, the Voice of Israel, and Radio Liberty, contributed to people's outlook on life.[80] Unlike the admiration certain groups, like the *shtatniki* and *stiliagi*, displayed for the West in the late Stalinist period, the review files show us a variety of opinions about the United States, ranging from positive to critical, from fascination and interest to doubt and disbelief in the alternative sources of information.

Analysis of more than two hundred review files of Soviet citizens who had fallen victim to the Stalinist persecution in the late 1940s and 1950s illuminates two themes related to the United States.[81] The first theme, also noted in the *svodki*, concerns the changing nature of the relationship between the Soviet Union and its wartime allies, the rising Cold War, and the comparative military strength and status of the two emerging superpowers. A second theme relates to discussions of American ways of life, democracy, the electoral process, freedom of speech, and individual choice, mirroring some of the most prominent themes in the radio broadcasts of the Voice of America.

The wartime alliance with the United States and the United Kingdom had clearly influenced the outlook of Soviet people, and the review files contain stories of former soldiers who regretted returning to the Soviet Union as they soon realized that the Soviet regime did not appreciate their newfound worldview. One war veteran, O., who suffered from tuberculosis during the war, was held in captivity from 1942 to 1945, and returned home an invalid, expressed ill will toward the authorities who confiscated his nice American suit upon re-entry into the Soviet Union. Instead of wearing it, he had to celebrate May Day in "a dirty sheepskin coat and torn boots." O.'s war experience changed his outlook on life: he regretted not staying behind with the Americans and moving to America, as there he would have "lived well and received the title of major in the American army." Yearning for the American way of life and the military power of America, he was cited for having claimed that the "Soviet people, who allegedly do not need anything, live much worse than Americans."[82]

The war made it possible for many people to see the West, for others to receive information about the West, and for rumors and hearsay about the West to travel much faster than before. Perhaps because of the traumatic effects of the world war on the Soviet people, new sources of information directed the betrayed hopes that some people felt toward the Soviet power into the creation of an American utopia: a Promised Land where people lived in excess and used white bread for fishing bait.[83] The case of a man who had spent the war in Germany illustrates this notion. Arrested on January 23, 1953, he was accused of having "actively worked against the Soviet Union by spreading slander about Soviet power and against one of the leaders of the CPSU and the Soviet state, and praised the way of life and culture in formerly fascist Germany." March 1945 found him in the American occupation zone in Germany, where he got to know an American soldier. According to the prosecutor, this man betrayed his motherland by promising the American officer that, upon return to the Soviet Union, he would fight against the hostile realities of the Soviet state. Repatriated in August 1945, he was accused of having spread anti-Soviet agitation from 1947 to 1953. He had reputedly maligned the Communist Party and the Soviet leadership, and criticized Soviet law, as well as Soviet print media and radio broadcasts, the living standards of workers in the Soviet Union, and Soviet realities in general. Furthermore, he was said to have expressed dissatisfaction with the kolkhoz system in the Soviet Union, while simultaneously praising the life, order, and culture in capitalist countries and in tsarist Russia.[84]

Although the Soviet regime had softened the official propaganda against the United States during the war, the state did not lessen its patriotic expectations of its citizens. Any criticism or doubt about the strength of the Red Army qualified as counterrevolutionary behavior, and, in the Soviet judiciary system, this was treated somewhat like treason. In 1943, a female medical doctor who had served in the White Army during the Civil War, a nun of gentry origins, was arrested for anti-Soviet behavior. Her class origins were only barely mentioned in the proceedings,[85]which emphasized her alleged gossiping about the poor performance of the Red Army during the Second World War. In fact, in 1941, this woman had ostensibly predicted a crushing defeat in the war, the end of Soviet power, and the subsequent escape of the Soviet leadership to America, which would "leave the nation at the mercy of fate."[86] One of the most serious anti-Soviet crimes committed during the war was talk of defeat such as that supposedly expressed by this woman.[87] Not surprisingly, the authorities often reported on such unpatriotic views in the borderlands or in formerly occupied areas. The *svodki*, for example, also reported on Polish nationalists, who sincerely hoped for the departure of Soviet troops after the war and for the help of England and the United States in attacking the Soviets in order to seize back Polish territories.[88]

Criticizing Soviet military strength after the war became another major offense. Some people, for example, were arrested for maintaining that, without the involvement of the United States, the Soviet Union would have lost the Great Patriotic War. Even worse was the assertion that the US military was superior to the Soviet: "Germany could not beat the USSR, but if America tried, it would take them one day."[89] These sorts of claims were probably a byproduct of the persistent rumor of a renewed war that circulated in the Soviet Union after the end of the hostilities—the *svodki* also reported on fears of a new war. Instead of adhering to the Stalinist paradigm of a military confrontation between Great Britain and the United States as they sought to establish themselves on the global stage, however, the "anti-Soviet citizen" feared war between England and America, on the one hand, and the Soviet Union on the other. Furthermore, almost all of these utterances entailed a Soviet defeat: "There will be war and then we will have an American spring."[90]

In the final stages of war, a Ukrainian Jew who was a professional musician was arrested for having supposedly maligned Soviet power and the nondemocratic nature of the Soviet state: "Everyone keeps screaming about democracy but every fool can see that we do not have authentic democracy, as they do in England and America. Nowhere else is there an NKVD that shuts up its citizens, nowhere else is there such terror—the prerevolutionary police was angelic in comparison with [the NKVD]."[91] The review file recounted this man's alleged anti-Soviet conversation as follows:

> I compared democracy in the Soviet Union with democracy in England and the USA. I said that, in some sense, the democracy that exists in England and USA does not exist in the Soviet Union. In England and the USA there is full freedom of speech; any person can say what he likes, when he likes, and where he likes. In the Soviet Union this is forbidden. That is why I said that we do not have democracy here. Genuine democracy exists in England and the United States.[92]

One man who testified against the Jewish musician claimed that he had not only heard anti-Soviet views from him within the privacy of the home but had also encountered them in talking to him on the street. He had apparently praised the life of workers abroad, expressing his wish of immigrating to the United States, where he would live well.[93] Two witnesses observed how, in judging the relationship between the USSR and its wartime allies, he had called the Soviet government subordinate to the governments of England and the United States, and said that Soviet authorities followed orders from the former allies.[94]

In line with the state's anti-American policies, newspapers gave much space to the "imperialistic aspirations" of the United States, such as the intervention in Greece, actions in Turkey, the Truman Doctrine in general, the nature of the Marshall Plan in Europe, and assistance to Latin America.[95] Especially the Korean War attracted much attention in the early 1950s, but often to discount Soviet accusations of American uses of bacteriological warfare. One man claimed that it was "rubbish" and continued to say that "America is a civilized country, if they would have liked to they could have crushed Korea a long time ago, they want to wage war [fairly]."[96] The authorities took special note of the issue of bacteriological warfare as more cases reported on skeptical views among the population—one man claimed that Soviet papers wrote about "infected flies" in a way that "does not resemble reality." This particular man claimed in March 1952 that "Soviet papers write lies about Americans dropping infected flies—Soviet propaganda does this in order to create hatred among the Soviet people toward Americans."[97]

In all official discussions of international affairs, propaganda aimed at showing the American predisposition toward domination and repression, in line with the core characteristics of the capitalist-imperialistic camp. This too is reflected in the review files, for example in a case reviewing a conversation at a synagogue about the Korean War in the winter of 1951, when V. allegedly responded to a claim about America being the most aggressive country in the world: "America is not an aggressive country, quite the opposite; it is the most democratic, strongest country in the world. As to invading smaller countries, that is only what strong and progressive countries do."[98] In his proceedings, V. admitted to having said that America was a strong country. But, he claimed, he had "never said that America was stronger than the Soviet Union."[99]

The VOA radio broadcasts of this period emphasized the American way of life, and spent a lot of on-air time discussing the working conditions of American workers, American technology, and democracy the American way. This theme of the well-off American worker, blessed with superior working conditions that enabled him to produce higher-quality products, was widely noted, and accusations of anti-Soviet behavior in the review files sometimes directly reference the enemy broadcasts. Take, for example, S., an engineer from Leningrad born in 1909, who accepted the criminal responsibility of having spread the contents of anti-Soviet broadcasts of the Voice of America, BBC, and Radio Free Europe among his friends. He was accused of maligning the Communist Party and its policies, as well as strongly criticizing Soviet democracy, press, and radio. He allegedly praised the living standards of working-class people in capitalist countries while disapproving of the conditions of workers in the Soviet Union.[100] In a later appeal, this man wrote that he did not deny having listened to and discussed foreign broadcasts, but he did not see this as anti-Soviet agitation.

He claimed, indeed, not to have commented in any way on the quality of the radio broadcasts, and his remarks should therefore not be seen as anti-Soviet.[101] Still, talking openly about what he had heard made him suspect of anti-Soviet behavior and a victim of the state's intolerance for alternative views on the status of the Soviet-American relationship.

In November 1951, M., a war veteran and former locksmith of middle peasant origins, was sentenced according to article 58-10 to five years of hard labor in the Gulag and disenfranchised for ten years. In 1950 and 1951, he had allegedly spread anti-Soviet agitation among kolkhoz workers in his home region of Karamzin. He supposedly "praised life in America, maligned Soviet realities, life on the kolkhoz, Soviet trade unions and praised American unions." In the summer of 1951 he had praised American and English production while degrading Soviet manufacturing: "everything is done by Stakhanovite methods—quantity matters more than quality."[102] Furthermore, he supposedly asked an acquaintance—who later testified against him—to find him a foreign bicycle, but "of good quality." M. told another that "it is all propaganda: goods may be cheaper, but wages are lower." He also claimed that the Kremlin exploited the peasants, especially those working on the collective farms, and that "the Americans tell the truth about us." Furthermore, he invited people to visit him in order to listen to "the true voice of America"[103] and spread the word of how "in America workers have more privileges. They may speak freely, they have a car, and we only have serfdom. People are not allowed to say anything, and if they do, they will find themselves in prison." This man's file was detailed and supposedly he did not tire of telling people in his kolkhoz about the "good life of peasants" in the United States, consistently complaining about his own life in the Soviet Union and doubting the Soviet system. Finally, he was accused of having insisted that "everything they write about England and America in the papers is a lie" and "radio 'Voice of America' broadcasts the truth about the Soviet Union."[104]

Similarly, in January 1952, a Russian woman born in 1896 was sentenced to ten years in the Gulag (with a possibility of a reduced sentence of five years) for repeatedly spreading "counterrevolutionary agitation." She had allegedly complained about the leaders of the CPSU, the Soviet government, the life of workers in the Soviet Union, and Soviet foreign policy. She had listened to foreign radio broadcasts and, based on what she heard, "told anti-Soviet anecdotes and praised life in prerevolutionary Russia and in imperialist countries." She denied the accusations, claiming that she had listened to the Voice of America once at her brother's house, then left for work where she told one colleague of her actions: "but it is impossible to call it anti-Soviet agitation . . . it is not true that I said America broadcasts the truth." However, the Soviet Procuracy chose to believe that what she had said was that "the American broadcasts say that our lives are bad, that workers get paid very little, and are forced to work. The Americans tell it as it really is."[105] Although the woman admitted to having listened to the Voice of America, she denied that the programs had made a positive impression on her. She had neither agreed with what she heard nor been inspired to malign Soviet realities. It was, however, enough of a crime to acknowledge the activity of listening to Voice of America broadcasts.

The final years of Stalin were tumultuous in all ways imaginable. In addition to the 1946–1947 famine, postwar reconstruction took its toll on the home front and the superpower conflict caused fear and uncertainty about the future. When Stalin died on March 5, 1953, many people felt grief and desperation, but mixed with those reactions was a feeling of insecurity among the population: who would protect them from the aggressive West now? Not only a leader but a father figure and a role model had left the scene. The Stalin cult of the 1930s had been a "means to mobilize the population's support and build a link between the people and the Party leadership."[106] Stalin had in many ways embodied the Soviet system, and it was to him that people declared their loyalty to the holy trinity: the leader, the party, and the state.[107] Fearing disturbances in the wake of Stalin's death, the secret police strengthened its campaign against anti-Soviet elements, which is also noted in the review files.

Following the death of Comrade Stalin, B., a railroad conductor, had listened to the Voice of America at her sister's house. She claimed that what she heard had deeply upset her. Completely indignant, she cried and railed against the Americans for broadcasting this slander.[108] All the witnesses provided the same testimony, that she had not agreed with what she had heard, and the court eventually ruled in favor of the defendant based on these testimonies.[109] In the end, she was only fined and not sentenced to prison, but one wonders whether the timing of her case—she was arrested on March 24—did not have more to do with the fearful atmosphere that prevailed in the Soviet Union immediately following Stalin's death earlier that month. Listening to the Voice of America made her guilty of anti-Soviet behavior, but denouncing what she heard certainly did not make her into a full-fledged "counterrevolutionary."

On March 6, 1953, after hearing on the radio that Comrade Stalin had died, a thirty-eight-year-old Moldavian male, married and of middle-peasant origins, made the following statement: "The leader of the Soviet government and the Communist Party was not a leader, but a dictator."[110] He continued by claiming that if the party would not change its policies after the death of its leader, "there will be a breakdown in the proletarian dictatorship."[111] Finally, he predicted a third world war, anticipating that the Soviet Union would be defeated and a new system would take over—"not American, but something completely new."[112]

Another man, accused of expressing happiness on March 6 when he heard about the death of the leader, claimed that now was the right time for America to start a war against the Soviet Union and to win an easy victory: "Then he would begin to live." This Azerbaijani (b. 1920), a veteran of the Great Patriotic War, was unemployed at the time of his arrest on March 16, 1953. Seven witnesses maintained he had demonstrated a hostile attitude toward Soviet power: he repeatedly made anti-Soviet utterances, and maligned the everyday material reality of workers in the USSR and the leadership of the Communist Party and the Soviet state. Simultaneously, he praised the life that workers led in capitalist countries, predicting a war between the USSR and the capitalist countries in which the Soviet Union would be defeated.[113] Two days later, in a conversation with one of the witnesses, he claimed that Stalin's followers would not be strong enough to govern the country and that this would, in the near future, contribute to the fall of the Soviet Union, when "the nation would be saved from torture."[114]

These allegations indicate how difficult it was to imagine a new leader replacing Stalin. Also, they confirm that the presence of the American Cold War enemy contributed to uncertainties about the future of the Soviet state. Especially the latter case reveals how Americans were simultaneously seen as potential attackers and rescuers. But the first case also illuminates the wish for neither the Soviet nor the American way of life, but a "new" world order. Together these cases indicate the exhaustion and disillusionment of the postwar period so well documented in the existing literature.[115] Not only had Soviet hopes for a better life after the Great Patriotic War been dashed by the harsh realities of reconstruction and late Stalinism, but the Cold War conflict had maintained an atmosphere of fear and uncertainties among the population. A new world order might help the Soviet people overcome the difficulties of the previous eight years.

While comments and questions from the *svodki* and review files were mainly as a "reflection of regime propaganda,"[116] especially the anti-American campaign, it seems unthinkable to not allow some kind of agency to people in Stalin's Soviet Union. The Soviet citizen harbored many—often conflicting—ideas of America and curiosity, and queries about both the Soviet Union and the outside world show several things. It is clear that anti-American propaganda in the Soviet media had not gone unnoticed; people thought about how the anti-American propaganda of the postwar period fit with earlier knowledge or what they learned through alternative sources of information. Along with reports on jamming of VOA and the controlled distribution of *Amerika*, this indicates that despite their earnest attempts, Soviet authorities did not succeed in fully limiting access to American propaganda. With a new world order on the horizon, people tried to understand the nuances of American foreign policy and how it would affect the Soviet Union and their own lives. Sometimes they did so by discrediting their own reality, but that was not always the case.

Conclusion

In Stalin's Soviet Union, people risked repression and prison sentences if they admitted to having listened to the Voice of America. Together, the campaigns against American sources of information and the accusations of anti-Soviet behavior represent the state's unrelenting but ultimately unsuccessful efforts at preventing Soviet citizens from making independent analyses of the outside world and domestic realities. Both the journal *Amerika* and Voice of America radio broadcasts were moderately successful in breaking the Soviet monopoly of information and knowledge:[117] their content was unacceptable to the Soviet authorities and their very existence embarrassed the state in its attempts to jam the broadcasts and limit access to *Amerika*.[118]

Without a full-scale content analysis of the American media, and without systematic sources on Soviet people's reception of them, it is impossible to assess the full impact of American propaganda. The official Soviet attitude toward it is indicative, however, of the anxiety American propaganda efforts caused in the Kremlin. Jamming of international broadcasts remained relatively stable during the late Stalin era, and ideological workers thought up strategies to obstruct the perceived effects of the radio broadcasts. The Soviet attitude toward the publication of *Amerika* is more complicated, since its publication was bound to a legal agreement between the Soviet Union and the United States concluded in 1944.[119] But the Soviet authorities actively limited people's access to the journal, and relentless negotiations between the two superpowers did not change that. Finally, the state's interest in people's utterances and questions about America and Soviet-American relations as it monitored the mood of the Soviet population and persecuted citizens for anti-Soviet behavior, including pro-American sentiments, is strongly suggestive of Soviet worries about the possible and much-feared impact of the American propaganda.

Soviet citizens were interested in the world around them as well as in their own survival and quality of life. With the dawning of the Cold War and the war of words it ignited, it was justifiable to link external circumstances to private interests. Interest in the outside world, however, does not necessarily indicate lack of loyalty or belief in the Soviet system. The people, whose alleged views are presented here, may have been targets of persecutions that labeled them anti-Soviet without them having doubted the idea of socialism and the Soviet Union. They may also have been victims of the Soviet state's notorious suspicion of all things foreign—including random observations about the nature of life in America. Interest in America did not necessarily mean that people had given up faith in the idea of the Soviet Union; it could, in some cases, mean that people disagreed with the road that the Soviet leadership had taken to reach socialism, or it could simply mean that they preferred to base their worldview on a variety of outlets, thus embracing alternative American sources in addition to Soviet information.

3 SOVIET-AMERICAN CULTURAL ENCOUNTERS IN LATE STALINISM

Constant efforts to control and monitor coverage of the American enemy were included in the Soviet foreign propaganda campaigns, and it is quite possible that the Soviet project won additional supporters the world over because of its anti-American position. Clearly, cultural relations between the two superpowers suffered as a result of this tone in the foreign propaganda, and Soviet officials involved in maintaining these relations often complained about both the unfavorable conditions in the United States and the lack of resources within Soviet institutions and organizations involved in Soviet-American relations. As early as 1946, officials working at the Soviet All-Union Society for Cultural Relations with Foreign Countries (VOKS) had concluded that because of anti-Soviet propaganda in the United States, it was necessary to "help American guests who visit the USSR reach correct conclusions about our country."[1] This concern applied not only to foreign visitors to the Soviet Union but also to international audiences outside of the country; indeed, helping people reach "correct conclusions" about the Soviet Union neatly captures the essence of the work Soviet ideological workers were tasked with.

After the war, the combination of the Cold War and the relative isolation of the postwar years changed the Soviet foreign propaganda mission permanently. Since the creation of the Communist International (Comintern) in 1919, Soviet foreign propaganda had sought to educate foreigners in how to perceive the economic, social, and cultural policies of socialism. This mission had been abandoned temporarily during the Second World War when Stalin, in order to please the Western allies, dissolved the Comintern in 1943. Other institutions and actors that were involved with the foreign information campaign were also inactive, as tourism and cultural relations were obviously a low priority during the horrible war. Foreign cultural relations were certainly not an immediate concern of the Soviet authorities after the war, but the rise of the Cold War and American anti-communist propaganda made it impossible for them to ignore this aspect of international politics completely. Cultural officials were quite capable of analyzing the problems potentially inherent in getting Soviet ideology across to Americans and suggesting improvements in strategy, but putting all the good advice into practice proved next to impossible as the Kremlin made it clear that any contact with foreign nationalities could be severely penalized.

At the same time, conditions for conducting cultural relations with the Soviet Union were deteriorating in the United States, where this period, commonly identified with Wisconsin senator Joseph McCarthy, was dominated by witch-hunts and political repression. Like Zhdanov in the Soviet Union, McCarthy came to symbolize an ideological campaign in the United States, but merely focusing on McCarthy tends to be too narrow. While McCarthyism focused on any critique of "white Protestant American norms," it is best known for creating and fostering a strong public fear of communism in the United States.[2] Ever since the war, the State Department had been suggesting an official cultural and scientific exchange program between the two countries, but with the lack of response from the Kremlin and then the increasingly difficult political context in the United States, these attempts were in vain. By the end of the 1940s, they had come to a full stop.[3]

During late Stalinism, Soviet authorities fought an uphill battle in countering American propaganda, not only in the Soviet Union but also in the United States. Looking at some of the very sporadic interactions on both American and Soviet soil in the late 1940s makes it clear that the weak attempts of Soviet officials to maintain a cultural relationship with the United States were controlled and monitored at the highest level—and in the end, they were almost completely in vain. Also, the Soviet anti-American propaganda was certainly not going to work in this context, although cultural officials always echoed the party line that if only Soviet accomplishments and the Soviet commitment to peace were adequately introduced, they would be embraced by the American public.

Soviet Cultural Institutions and Foreign Propaganda

The institutional organization of cultural relations reveals much about the ways that the Soviet Union sought to represent itself to foreigners. During their stay in the Soviet Union, all foreign visitors were under the auspices of a specific state- or party-controlled organization, travel agency, or the appropriate youth organization. The relevant ministries were involved with union delegations, and special agencies were in charge of diplomats and journalists.[4] All these types of organizational units often coordinated with both the Central Committee and the Soviet embassy in Washington.

During the early Cold War, the two Soviet front organizations most important for foreign propaganda were VOKS and Intourist (the State Joint-Stock
Company for Foreign Tourism), working under the labels of, respectively, cultural relations and tourism. Both these organizations were established in the interwar years and were given a seemingly benign role, but anyone paying attention
to the Soviet system knew that these organizations were not independent of the
Communist Party, thus the label "front organizations." Even if Cominform (established in 1947) was officially in charge of maintaining political relations with
like-minded parties, many of the people visiting the Soviet Union as part of a
delegation (and therefore under the purview of VOKS) or as tourists (the responsibility of Intourist) during the interwar years and onwards during the Cold War
were members of foreign communist parties or sympathizers of the Soviet Union.
Thus, most foreigners arriving to the Soviet Union were likely to be involved with
one or both of these organizations.

The Soviet Council of People's Commissars set up VOKS on April 5, 1925,
as a "public society,"[5] but it was clear to most foreigners that, even if it was
not officially a part of the Soviet state structure, so as to be perceived as independent of the government, VOKS reported to the Communist Party.[6] The
main goal of VOKS was to facilitate the establishment and development of
academic and cultural relations between Soviet and foreign institutions, public
organizations, and individuals and groups involved in academia and culture.
VOKS thus kept in touch with foreign friendship societies and independent
fellow travelers and sympathizers with the Soviet Union.[7] The corresponding
friendship societies in foreign countries had similar organizational charts,
depending on their size and importance, and were always in very close contact
with VOKS in Moscow.[8]

VOKS was also responsible for inviting cultural figures to the Soviet Union
who usually visited as a part of a delegation.[9] The structure of a delegation
was characteristic of the way Soviet authorities wanted to organize cultural
relations—a delegation was a carefully selected group that was easy to control.
The authorities designed a detailed itinerary for every delegation and shepherded
the delegates around the country. Soviet cultural officials invested much effort
in this technique, especially since they hoped the delegates would return home
and write positively about the Soviet Union for a wide audience.[10] Finally, there
is strong evidence that VOKS and other cultural organizations cooperated with
the secret police organs and supplied them with information on foreigners they
had hosted.[11]

The pressure to showcase socialism at its best was therefore not lessened
when Soviet organizations received fellow travelers whom they knew to be favorably disposed to the Soviet Union. On the contrary, they relied on their positive observations for an "authoritative" account of life in the Soviet Union, and

therefore VOKS officials worked very hard to impress fellow travelers. To this effect, VOKS officials were trained to promote Soviet socialism and both secure new friends and maintain relations with old friends of the Soviet Union.[12] Even if VOKS was to a large extent paralyzed in the late 1940s, the organization was revived along with the thaw in cultural relations after Stalin's death and remained, in somewhat changed form, an important player in Soviet cultural diplomacy throughout the Soviet period.[13]

Established on April 11, 1929, as the agency within the Ministry of Foreign Trade responsible for the management of foreign tourism in the USSR, Intourist was in charge of all technical and organizational details relating to foreign tourists in the Soviet Union.[14] Intourist issued visas and other necessary documents for foreigners, took care of transportation and baggage, published guidebooks and other information for foreign tourists, arranged for hotels and housing, and organized the sale of souvenirs. Early in 1939, the Soviet Council of People's Commissars also made the agency responsible for training a highly educated staff for working with foreign tourists. In this regard, Intourist played an important role in projecting Soviet ideology to foreigners, although mostly on Soviet territory,[15] but a key difference between VOKS and Intourist was the latter's focus on economic profit, as it was by definition a commercial institution.[16] Intourist took care of all foreign tourism in the Soviet Union until 1958, when a special agency, Sputnik (Biuro mezhdunarodnogo molodezhnogo turizma), was established to organize international youth tourism.[17]

In the postwar years, other front organizations dealt with international relations, such as the previously mentioned Cominform and the World Peace Council (established in 1949). These organizations were also firmly based on the anti-capitalist, anti-American rhetoric that dominated Soviet propaganda in the Cold War period, but most relevant for our purposes here was an organization established during the war, the National Council of American-Soviet Friendship (NCASF). According to the State Department, the NCASF was one of the most important Soviet front organizations in the United States. Formed in 1943 by the Communist Party of the United States of America (CPUSA), NCASF worked closely with VOKS[18] and had four main centers in the United States: Chicago, New York, San Francisco, and Los Angeles. The NCASF sponsored "goodwill tours" to the Soviet Union and enabled select Soviet citizens to travel to the United States. However, the State Department made the work of the NCASF very difficult by, for example, confiscating mail and passports of its members.[19] In the postwar Stalin era, NCASF was almost exclusively responsible for maintaining Soviet-American cultural relations on the American side. Until the slow revival of official cultural relations in the post-Stalin years, which saw the increased role of individual contacts and the eventual official participation of the American State Department in 1957, NCASF acted as an intermediary between Soviet authorities and American citizens interested in traveling to the Soviet Union or in corresponding with Soviet citizens.[20]

On paper, therefore, Soviet efforts in cultural relations with foreign countries or cultural diplomacy looked quite remarkable. Those involved were supposed to receive training in foreign languages and have access to otherwise restricted foreign culture and products in order to advance their work within diplomacy and cultural relations.[21] While this was perhaps the case in the prewar years, both VOKS and Intourist worked within the financial and political limits of the late Stalin period, and in practice, the staff was not well trained and did not have easy access to up-to-date information about social and political development in foreign countries. This made it difficult for them to control interactions between the few mutual visitors during the early Cold War and proved a challenge in the escalating cultural Cold War between the superpowers.

Soviet Propaganda in McCarthy's America

In 1945, VOKS, celebrating its twentieth anniversary, was prepared to take up renewed cultural relations with the United States. On June 23, only a few weeks after the end of the Second World War, Vladimir Kemenov, the chairman of VOKS, wrote to the National Council of Foreign Affairs and tried to draw Vyacheslav Molotov's and Georgy Malenkov's attention to the importance of conducting cultural relations with the allies by sending artists to America and England.[22] The Kremlin seems to have shown little interest in the initiative, even if VOKS maintained that it was especially urgent to crush rumors that exaggerated the role of England and the United States in winning the war while diminishing the accomplishment of the Soviet Union.[23]

Being on the winning side of the Second World War had filled the Soviet leadership with the hope that its country would be accepted as a leader on the world stage: Andrei Zhdanov stated in early 1946 that the victory would allow the Soviet Union to conduct its foreign policy "under much more favourable conditions than before," but this was a short-lived hope.[24] Also in 1946, VOKS concluded that the American government "put forth great activity in its goal of taking control of cultural relations between Soviet and American organizations and individual cultural agents,"[25] and this seemed worrying to Soviet authorities. The Soviet side obviously had no interest in establishing cultural relations on American terms, but it was also acutely aware of the growing hostility toward the Soviet Union and its front organizations in the United States and thus realized it needed to keep some channels open. VOKS officials closely monitored the development of the House Committee on Un-American Activities, which became a standing committee in 1945, and claimed that it "intervenes against alleged fellow travelers found in all American organizations friendly to the USSR."[26] This 1946 report of the American department of VOKS noted that the "outburst of reactionary and anti-Soviet propaganda, inspired by aggressive imperialistic cliques in the United States," was making their work more difficult, but also maintained that "interest in the Soviet Union [among the American people] has not decreased."[27] The question was just how to maintain that interest and best represent Soviet goals and ideas to an American public.

VOKS rightfully suspected the US State Department of wanting to limit the appeal of American organizations friendly to the Soviet Union, such as the American Russian Institute in New York,[28] but in the immediate aftermath of the Second World War the American authorities were more favorable to conducting cultural relations with the Soviet Union than vice versa. The American embassy in Moscow had been in touch with VOKS, suggesting that the Red Army Song and Dance Ensemble should tour the United States and the US Air Force Band should repay the visit. They also suggested that Jessica Smith, editor of *Soviet Russia Today* (later *New World Review*) and member of CPUSA, would visit the Soviet Union at the same time. Smith, however, had not raised the issue of reciprocity and did not seem to find it necessary for Americans to visit the Soviet Union. She was more focused on receiving the Soviet artists and imagined them contributing to a celebration of the twenty-eighth anniversary of the October Revolution.

VOKS suggested that "only if the Americans insist on it" should they invite Americans to tour the Soviet Union, and then preferably some important directors, who could benefit young Soviet artists. VOKS officials were clearly more interested in renewing cultural relations with Americans on American soil than in receiving them in the Soviet Union, and they noted that "conditions for conducting our work in the United States have deteriorated significantly." Since the war, informational reports from the Soviet Information Bureau (Sovinformbiuro) had stopped abruptly, and much less attention was devoted to the Soviet Union in the United States after the war reporting ended. They concluded by pointing out how the past months had seen an amplification of anti-Soviet speech in the United States and "in this regard, the Red Army Song and Dance Ensemble touring some major American cities would undoubtedly cause a strong wave of sympathy for the Soviet Union and bring us great benefits."[29] According to an American State Department report, this suggestion and other efforts to start the possibilities of cultural and scientific exchanges were met with absolutely no response from the Soviet side.[30] However, the story was more complicated than that: on behalf of VOKS, Kemenov had indeed pleaded with the Soviet leadership to take cultural relations with the United States seriously, but that initiative apparently died at the top level.

In both 1946 and 1947, VOKS officials in America continuously pleaded with Moscow to respond to the increasing anti-Soviet propaganda. They were full of ideas but lacking in materials and resources needed to execute a counter offense on American ground. In 1946, before the first Voice of America broadcasts to the Soviet Union, the Soviets concluded that American homes possessed more than sixty million radios, which were "an essential part of everyday American life." They claimed that the only way they would be able to get them to listen to Soviet broadcasts, however, was to "broadcast in American style to Americans." They noted that because Americans were so religious, Soviet broadcasts should emphasize that the Soviet Union allowed freedom of religion. Furthermore, they should appeal to American concern for rebuilding Soviet cities and industry, without leading Americans to believe that reconstruction also focused on strengthening the defense industry, since they could easily turn such information into complaints that the Soviet Union was preparing for war.[31]

Such VOKS reports, as well as numerous subsequent documents, assumed that if foreigners only learned about Soviet achievements and progress in social and economic spheres and the people's sincere dedication to peace, they would immediately warm up to the Soviet way of life. The functionality of this approach was proven, VOKS claimed, by the success of a 1946 delegation of Soviet writers to the United States who held "masses of Americans" captive during their meetings. They received so many "questions and friendly comments" about the Soviet Union that VOKS concluded: "the American people listen with attention and sympathy to the words of people who tell the truth about the Soviet Union."[32]

This high-profile delegation of Soviet writers representing Soviet newspapers visited the United States in February 1946 and, as they claimed afterward, "saw America."[33] Active participants in the Soviet anti-American campaign were writer Ilya Ehrenburg, representing *Izvestiia*; writer Konstantin Simonov, who wrote for *Krasnaia zvezda*; and Mikhail Galaktinov, the major general and military editor of *Pravda*. The three arrived as guests of the American Society of Newspaper Editors and were flown to the States via Paris in US ambassador Walter Bedell Smith's personal airplane.[34]

The American hosts proved a difficult crowd for the Soviet delegation, asking tough questions about working conditions in the Soviet Union, and the Soviet guests felt that they were not being treated with the respect and sympathy one would normally give visitors. The delegates were shocked and insulted at the directness with which the American hosts interrogated them about conditions in the Soviet Union, posing such questions as "what would happen to [them] in case [they] wrote an editorial advocating the removal of Marshal Stalin?"[35] Issues of censorship and correspondence were dominant during the visit. Famous American commentators on the Soviet Union, such as American journalist

Harrison E. Salisbury, who in 1949 became the first postwar Moscow bureau chief for the *New York Times*, angrily noted how the delegation avoided all uncomfortable questions, such as why it was so difficult for American correspondents to get admitted to Russia. Attempts by the delegates to represent the Soviet Union as a good place in which to live were overshadowed by the American focus on difficulties of traveling to and reporting about the USSR. Salisbury was later outraged to find out "that [Konstantin] Simonov came away and wrote a play [*The Russian Question*] about an American correspondent who was able to tour the USSR without the visa issue even being raised."[36] American journalists were well aware of the difficulties involved with getting a visa to travel to the Soviet Union and were not afraid to call the journalists on their statements about life in the Soviet Union.

On behalf of the American government, Assistant Secretary of State William Benton offered the Soviet journalists an invitation to travel the country as guests of the United States. They accepted the offer, but insisted on paying all costs. The American government then designed individual itineraries for each of the three guests according to their wishes: Simonov wished to see Hollywood; Galaktinov, Chicago; and Ilya Ehrenburg, the Deep South.[37] The journalists wrote about their respective experiences for Soviet publications, and even though Ehrenburg allowed himself some optimism in writing about the American South, claiming that "the South is on the threshold of decisive events,"[38] they adhered in most ways to the official Soviet anti-American standards in depicting the United States upon their return.[39]

Overall, Moscow considered the trip a success. VOKS claimed that the writers had been given much space to "tell the truth about the Soviet Union" in front of large crowds in the United States, where they "constantly provoked a variety of questions and friendly feedback."[40] Indeed, the trip had provided the Soviet authorities with plenty of information they could use to strengthen their propaganda about the horrors of American capitalism. The three journalists had witnessed both strikes and industrial unrest in major American cities, and they were extremely critical of the anti-Soviet rhetoric they witnessed in the media. To that effect, they repeatedly brought up the lack of ruins in America and contrasted it with the devastation and the human loss in Russia, making appeals to "American mothers" who they claimed were better equipped to understand the strong Russian desire for peace than "American correspondents."[41]

The "anti-Soviet" narrative the Soviet guests encountered in the American media was certainly a fact of the early Cold War, and a 1947 "explanatory note" from the American department of VOKS bears witness to the growing difficulties of carrying out an information campaign in the United States. In the note, VOKS voiced strong concern over "the diffusion of imperialistic, racist and militaristic ideas [in the United States], maligning the Soviet people and its culture."[42] In order to counter this, VOKS officials claimed that, in spite of the uphill battle, they urgently needed to familiarize American society with Soviet achievements in the social, economic, and cultural spheres. To this effect, they laid out seven recommendations about how best to "show the superiority of the Soviet socialist system over the capitalist system of the USA" by, for example, exposing American racism, "atomic politics," and the "dollar democracy" while all the time promoting the "preeminence of Soviet democracy as a higher form of democracy."[43] All the recommendations were focused on the written word, except the last one, which suggested the promotion of ideological Soviet art.[44]

In 1947, concern about anti-Soviet propaganda in the United States had increased in Moscow, and the American department of VOKS considered several ways to raise interest in the Soviet Union among the American people, especially intellectuals.[45] One of the ways with which VOKS attempted to counter anti-Soviet propaganda was by accepting an invitation to attend the American Cultural and Scientific Conference for World Peace in New York in March 1949.[46] Alexandr Fadeev, general secretary of the Writers' Union; Dmitri Shostakovich, composer; and Alexandr Oparin, head of the Biological Sciences Section of the Academy of Sciences in the Soviet Union, attended the conference on behalf of the Soviet Union. However, their attendance did not come about smoothly. In 1948, in the midst of an attack on "formalist composers" in the Soviet Union, the State Repertoire Commission (Glavrepertkom) had removed Shostakovich from his teaching posts at the Leningrad and Moscow conservatories and banned the performance of his works. When Stalin learned of Shostakovich's popularity abroad, he reversed the Glavrepertkom order four days before the delegation was to leave the Soviet Union and encouraged the composer to accept the offer to go to New York.[47] Mikhail Suslov, head of Agitprop, then gave Shostakovich permission to play for American audiences and address the Congress.

During their short stay, the Soviet representatives spoke only of Soviet achievements and dedication to peaceful relations between the two countries.[48] The main goals of the official Soviet mission of spreading the "truth" about the Soviet Union were clearly stated in Fadeev's speech:

> The peoples of the Soviet Union stand for peace. It is doubtful whether even one unprejudiced American or Western European could be found, who, coming to our country, would not feel the healthy, peaceful pulse of life in the entire atmosphere; in the plan for the reconstruction of Moscow projected for a period of 25 years; in the plans for the planting of forests encompassing the gigantic steppe regions of the European part of the USSR in order to insure a rich harvest; in the experiments of Academician Lysenko for distributing bush-like wheat; in the new productions of the Moscow Art Theater; in the life-loving, optimistic mood of our citizens;

Dmitri Shostakovich, composer, and Alexander A. Fadeev, general secretary of the Writers' Union, arrive at the American Cultural and Scientific Conference for World Peace in New York in March 1949. This was the last high-profile Soviet delegation to visit the United States until after Stalin's death in 1953. *Harry Harris/AP/REX/Shutterstock*

in the peaceful tone of the press; in the bright voices of the children—so many of whom are being born in our country, as a sign of the confirmation of life, its most beautiful and most hopeful symbol.[49]

When it became clear that part of the delegation's mission was to malign the US government, Americans turned increasingly hostile to it: Yale University declined to have Shostakovich perform on campus, and city councils and hotels refused to accommodate the delegation. Instead of allowing the members of the delegation to travel further in the United States, the State Department revoked their visas,[50] and this Soviet delegation was the last to visit the United States until after Stalin's death in 1953.[51]

Soviet diplomats in the United States certainly worked in unfavorable conditions, and in 1952 the Soviet embassy in Washington announced that, due to the communist witch-hunts of Senator Joseph McCarthy, VOKS was effectively paralyzed in the United States.[52] The repression of progressive individuals and organizations in the United States had blocked access to virtually everyone "loyally disposed to the Soviet Union." The embassy concluded that, without access to the progressive intelligentsia, possibilities for spreading the word about the Soviet Union were slim to none: "As is known, the work of VOKS can be successful only when there are possibilities for widespread and free relations with the progressive intelligentsia of a given country."[53] That possibility, however, had temporarily disappeared in the United States, and it was only after Stalin's death that cultural relations between the two countries would see a revival.

Rare Encounters: John Steinbeck Visits Late Stalinist Russia

From 1945 to 1951, VOKS documented only nineteen American groups with a total of fifty-seven visitors who had visited the Soviet Union under its purview. Most of the visitors were well-known American fellow travelers, such as Jessica Smith, who visited in 1945; Edwin Smith, director of the National Council of American-Soviet Friendship also in 1945; and Paul Robeson, singer, actor, and activist, who came on one of his many visits in 1949 and was one of only two Americans who participated in the Pushkin jubilee of that year.[54] Also, Elliott Roosevelt, son of Franklin and Eleanor Roosevelt, visited with his wife, the actress Faye Emerson, shortly after the publication of his controversial book, *As He Saw It*, which detailed his father's foreign policy and was labeled pro-Soviet.[55] Elliott Roosevelt met with Stalin in the Kremlin on December 21, 1946, and among the subjects they discussed was cultural and scientific exchange, with Stalin claiming that he favored a broad exchange between the two nations.[56] Stalin's position was met with optimism on the American side which, of course, was short-lived.

Apart from a very few delegations, Soviet travel abroad also came to a halt. In light of the anti-Western nature of the late Stalinist regime, it is not surprising that international tourism was almost nonexistent and Soviet authorities now encouraged domestic travel. Traveling in the Soviet motherland became a part of the postwar patriotic re-education of Soviet people, with its aim of creating a "correct understanding" of their own homeland, reassuring the population that conditions would improve and that the socialist future was filled with possibilities for leisure and comfort.[57]

In the immediate postwar period, very few foreigners visited the Soviet Union. The country was in ruins, and tourism or exchanges of delegations were not high on the list of government priorities. In spite of the few visitors, scant evidence suggests that, shortly after the war, Soviet authorities expressed interest in promoting tourism and cultural contacts but were overcome with the practical problems of reconstructing the tourism industry. Representatives of Intourist visiting a 1947 conference on international tourism in London speculated about the profits generated by the inflow of foreigners to Western European countries. They noted that Americans had started to travel abroad, but that the war-ravaged Soviet Union was not equipped to host foreign visitors: it lacked hotel space in Moscow as well as in popular tourist destinations in Crimea, Rostov-on-Don, and Sochi. Apart from inhabitable quarters, the Soviet Union also lacked air, land, and rail transportation, as well as qualified guides and translators.[58] The report also included information on how capitalist countries, "especially the USA and England," used tourism to their own economic and political advantage.[59]

The Soviet side responded harshly to the postwar aid Americans offered to European countries, especially the Marshall Plan, which encouraged postwar tourism as an effective way to re-establish European economies.[60] Moreover, tourism offered a means to change a country's public image, but Stalin's postwar Soviet Union was in no shape to invite foreign tourists to the Soviet Union. Therefore, very few Americans who did not openly sympathize with the Soviet system were invited to visit the Soviet Union during Stalin's last years. The great majority of Americans visiting were in some way connected to NCASF and thus to the Communist Party of the United States and, at least in theory, could be trusted to empathize with the state of the postwar Soviet Union and turn a blind eye to the visible challenges of everyday life.[61]

An exception to this rule was the 1947 visit of American writer John Steinbeck. Despite Steinbeck's open contempt for the communist agenda,[62] his 1930s novels, especially *The Grapes of Wrath* (1939), and his earlier visit to the Soviet Union in 1936 gave Soviet authorities reasons to believe that he would not malign the Soviet system or its people. In any case, Fadeev and Kemenov made several appeals to Zhdanov in early 1947 to invite Steinbeck to visit the country, which in the end were successful.[63] They were a bit concerned, however, because when Steinbeck and his traveling companion, the photographer Robert Capa, had been asked recently what they thought of the American Communist Party, they both called it "a sect that was leading stupid politics." Soviet authorities also strongly suspected Steinbeck of wanting to respond to Simonov's *The Russian Question* and worried what he might come up with.[64] When Soviet officials inquired about his plans, he claimed that "Americans usually expect the truth from me. I will also tell the truth this time."[65]

The case of John Steinbeck and his travels in the Soviet Union illustrates well all the concerns the Soviet government had with receiving and entertaining American visitors in the postwar Soviet Union. Steinbeck himself had spent the latter part of the Second World War as the *New York Herald Tribune*'s war correspondent in England, and he saw his trip to the still-devastated Soviet Union as "the final chapter of this war journalism."[66] The *Herald Tribune* published Steinbeck's articles from the trip in early 1948,[67] but the subsequent book, *A Russian Journal*, represents the larger genre of anthropological memoirs, travelogues, and journalistic accounts written by people who lived in or visited the Soviet Union. Such books were published in the United States throughout the Soviet period, and most of them aimed at getting to know "common people" or to present the "real Soviet Russia" to American readers.[68] Traveling to the Soviet Union mainly in order to report on the progress of reconstruction, Steinbeck's declared goal was also to write on the Soviet system and its people in such a way that mutual fears would be shattered and peaceful relations could be strengthened.[69]

In 1948, however, Soviet émigrés reprimanded Steinbeck for not trying to see what was behind the facade.[70] Steinbeck's refusal to look deeper was made all the worse by the fact that, in the fall of 1947, Ukraine was just beginning to recover from the famine that plagued the countryside in 1946 and 1947. Steinbeck, however, wrote about the show put on by the people working at Shevchenko I, a Ukrainian collective farm, seeing in it nothing more than hospitality: "The people in this village did put on a show for us. They put on the same kind of show a Kansas farmer would put on for a guest. They did the same thing that our people do, so that Europeans say 'The Americans live on chicken.' "[71]

Steinbeck's reports from the farm outraged émigrés who claimed to know the truth of the situation. The value of Steinbeck's observations, however, lies not only in his reporting of Soviet domestic circumstances but in his struggle to correct what he deemed inaccurate or false ideas about the United States. In that sense, Steinbeck was an important representative of the United States, causing people, such as little Grisha in Ukraine, to cry out in wonder, "But these Americans are people just like us!"[72] There are several instances in *A Russian Journal* where Steinbeck refers to popular interest in the United States, recounting how collective farmers, office bureaucrats, writers, and intellectuals expressed curiosity about the American people and their government. Steinbeck fielded typical questions about everything from America's agriculture to its structure of government: "they asked about wages, and standards of living, and the kind of life a workingman lives, and did the average man have an automobile, and what kind of house does he live in, and did his children go to school, and what kind of school."[73] People often expressed their fear of a new war and an American attack on the Soviet Union in conversations with Steinbeck and Capa:[74] "Will the United States attack us? Will we have to defend our country again in one lifetime?"[75] Memories of the American wartime alliance remained strong, and President Franklin D. Roosevelt remained a hero in the Soviet Union.[76] The anti-American campaign had already started, however, and people were wary of expressing fondness for American culture and values. Steinbeck concluded that the Soviet people in general had "a great deal of misinformation about America."[77] He observed that the general disposition toward the United States and particularly toward

Americans was friendly, but claimed that common knowledge about America was not deep. Slowly, he and Capa also "began to realize that America is a very difficult country to explain."[78]

Of course the Soviet authorities had a very different goal, namely to correctly "explain" their country to the foreign guests, and in an attempt to shape Steinbeck and Capa's work, the Soviet guides who shepherded them on their travels prepared personal profiles of their visitors, estimating what they would write about and photograph in the Soviet Union. Their guide in Ukraine, Aleksei Poltoratskii, writer and a former frontline reporter but now the deputy chairman of the Ukrainian Society for Cultural Relations with Foreign Countries (UOKS), concluded that their perceptions could harm the Soviet cause. Every effort had to be made to prevent them from "incorrectly explaining" the Soviet Union:

> Steinbeck is a man of conservative conviction and, in addition, he has recently become more right-wing oriented. That's why our approach to him should be especially cautious and we should avoid showing him something that can do us any harm.
>
> Capa, the photographer accompanying him, also needs to be watched to prevent him from taking pictures of what he shouldn't.
>
> The number of Steinbeck's questions should be limited and if need be, we must argue or even quarrel with him.[79]

Generally, Soviet officials hoped that Ivan Khmarskii, head of the American department of VOKS, who also accompanied Steinbeck and Capa on their travels, was right when he claimed that "Steinbeck will evaluate the Soviet people favorably and will emphasize its sympathy for the American people. He will describe to some extent the ruin and will positively evaluate the heroic work of the Soviet Ukrainian people."[80] They saw the closely monitored photographs captured by Capa as an indicator of the topics Steinbeck would write about. According to Kharmskii, Capa was sensitive when evaluating what to photograph:

> I was with Capa when he took all of his pictures. He had an opportunity to take pictures depicting beggars, queues, German prisoners of war, and secret sites (i.e., the construction of the gas pipe-line). He did not take photos of this kind and approached his photography without reporter imprudence. I can point to only two photos, which cannot be considered favorable. In the Museum of Ukrainian Art, he took a picture of an emaciated woman-visitor, and on our way to the kolkhoz, he took a picture of a kolkhoz family wearing shabby clothes; all of them including teenagers, were pumping water.[81]

The Soviet authorities concluded that Capa, whom they generally considered more open and talkative, was "more loyal and friendly disposed to us." They worried that Steinbeck, "in an underhanded way," encouraged Capa to photograph "vulnerable" aspects of Soviet life.[82]

Another worry was that even though the book would favorably depict everyday life in the Soviet Union, the authors would parrot American propaganda and unfavorably compare Soviet and American societies.[83] Everybody Steinbeck met with emphasized their favorable attitude toward the American people, and the Soviet guides correctly judged that Steinbeck was impressed with such interest in the American people. But his hosts in Kiev were not so certain whether Steinbeck believed that the Soviet people honestly wanted the Soviet and American governments to work together:

> As for the expressions made by our comrades about the unity of the people and government of the USSR, and that there are no sentiments in the USSR directed against the American people—these comments did not find any success since Steinbeck and Capa considered them "propaganda" and avoided discussions on this topic.[84]

After *A Russian Journal* came out, Soviet authorities finally decided that the Steinbeck-Capa visit had not been a success. Khmarskii, scrambling to redeem his formerly positive evaluation of Steinbeck's goals, now wrote a letter to the main editor of *Literaturnaia gazeta*, Vladimir Ermilov, claiming that most of Steinbeck's conversations with Soviet citizens were conducted while drinking: "his drinking seems to be a weakness."[85] John Steinbeck had failed to reach "correct conclusions" about the Soviet Union, and the only answer Soviet authorities had left was to discredit him, claiming he had been drunk the whole time and unable to "correctly" evaluate Soviet socialism. Steinbeck was unhappy with the Soviet reception of the book, especially a review published in *Izvestiia* that characterized him as having "sold out" to his bosses, as opposed to the "good American" Harry Smith from Simonov's *The Russian Question*.[86] After careful evaluation of the American media, however, Soviet analysts concluded that "Steinbeck—the author of *The Grapes of Wrath*—had long ago joined the ranks of writers who defend capitalism."[87]

The Steinbeck trip, in what was surely the most high-profile and prominent American visit to the Soviet Union in the immediate postwar period,[88] showed that Soviet officials went to great lengths in trying to control and monitor their guests' experiences. This ranged from staging prosperity and success in reconstruction in areas still devastated from the war, to choosing and preparing the people who talked to both Steinbeck and Capa. Soviet authorities realized quite well that a respected writer and war journalist such as Steinbeck had the potential to reach a large audience with his writings, and they hoped that he would report favorably on the Soviet Union. They took a chance on Steinbeck, and in spite of their efforts to show him only a staged socialist reality, his observations did the Soviet cause more harm than good.

Conclusion

During the late Stalin period, the two superpowers proved incapable of maintaining open cultural relations, and thus both sides resorted to an ideologically driven propaganda war. Soviet authorities found themselves under siege on all fronts: they were not reaching American audiences on American soil, they did not fully succeed in controlling the effects of American propaganda in the Soviet Union, and their most high-profile visit in the period, the Steinbeck-Capa trip, proved counterproductive in advancing the Soviet propaganda mission abroad. Stalin's Soviet Union was neither ready to be opened to the close scrutiny of international audiences in the postwar years nor was it able to convincingly counter American propaganda. In the aftermath of war, Soviet strategy was therefore to limit and control contact with foreigners and information about the outside world as much as possible. This was not just a reaction to the rising Cold War, but it also served the patriotic atmosphere of late Stalinist Russia.[89]

Despite all the challenges of the late Stalinist era, VOKS officials took their mission to conduct cultural relations with the outside world seriously. Even if the term "cultural relations" indicates mutual interactions, it should be remembered that VOKS and other Soviet front organizations were more interested in gaining followers for the socialist mission than in mutual exchanges of cultural events. In line with the anti-cosmopolitan campaign in the Soviet Union, where Soviet people were supposed to see both the West and Soviet realities a certain way,[90] it was also important to educate foreigners and helping them see the Soviet Union in the correct light. Although VOKS officials understood that earlier Soviet methods in international cultural diplomacy were not going to work in McCarthy's America, there was a lack of initiative in trying to renew and strengthen Soviet propaganda methods. The atmosphere within the Soviet bureaucracy was such that pointing this out to the Kremlin might have been an unnecessary risk for people working in the Soviet cultural bureaucracy.

Presenting their own version of a Soviet reality to both domestic and American audiences, the authorities were reluctant to admit that conditions beyond their control, such as McCarthyism, were not solely to blame for their struggles. The inherent failure in their mission lay increasingly in the fact that the Soviet definitions of peace and prosperity were flawed and the appeal of American propaganda was growing stronger internationally. Certainly, organizations on the Soviet side also lacked the official support to conduct cultural relations with the United States as was needed. But because of the anti-Soviet atmosphere in McCarthy's America, it remains doubtful whether resources and technology would have helped in the early years of the Cold War. More likely, the Soviet "truth" mission itself needed a complete overhaul, but the anti-American campaign and the larger anti-intellectual campaigns of late Stalinism made that impossible. To a certain extent, Soviet authorities used the political atmosphere in the United States as a cover: in reality, their own hostility to all things "capitalist" and "Western" made Soviet-American cultural relations impossible in the postwar Stalin period, and changing the Soviet approach and message did not become an option until after Stalin's death.

KHRUSHCHEV AND THE DISCOURSE OF PEACEFUL COEXISTENCE

FROM ANTI-AMERICANISM TO PEACEFUL COEXISTENCE

After the death of Stalin, a softer tone replaced the unrefined anti-Americanism in the Soviet Union, and the new official policy of peaceful coexistence came to define the cultural and political relationship with the United States. Internationally, peaceful coexistence was meant to bring respect, as Khrushchev wanted the Soviet Union to be taken seriously as a global superpower, and he wanted to be recognized as a leader of historical significance. For this purpose, Khrushchev played the role of peacemaker, wanting to take on the role of a pro-verbial middleman between the socialist and anti-Soviet blocs and be ready to reconcile with the number one enemy. Khrushchev also tried to win over former colonies in Asia, Africa, and Latin America to the socialist cause, and he attempted reconciliation with Tito's Yugoslavia. In this context, the slogan "For Peace and Friendship" became an integral part of Khrushchev's foreign policy campaign, where "peace and friendship between nations" remained a favorite toast and a symbol of Soviet nonaggression.

Already by the end of 1955, the Soviet All-Union Society for Cultural Relations with Foreign Countries (VOKS) concluded that the year had "marked the revival of Soviet-American cultural exchanges."[1] The year 1955 was indeed marked by several mutual visits of high-profile professional delegations and cultural events in both countries, a remarkable difference from the almost nonexistent Soviet-American cultural relations in the late-Stalinist period. Even if there had been scattered visits back and forth in the period from 1945 to 1955, the increase in overall cultural relations in 1955 was of note. As Eduard Ivanian, who started working at the Ministry of Culture in 1955 and later became senior researcher at the Institute for US and Canadian Studies (ISKRAN) in Moscow, claimed in an interview, the relationship with the United States started to mend in June 1955 and by the end of that year, the changes were felt in the ministry and among those interested in promoting cultural exchanges: "I wouldn't call them significant, but noticeable."[2]

The origins of the noticeable changes in the Soviet-American relationship are usually traced back to the summer of 1955, when American president Dwight D. Eisenhower, British prime minister Anthony Eden, French prime minister Guy Mollet, and Soviet premier Nikita Khrushchev met in Geneva to discuss the problematic German question.[3] In terms of hard agreements, the leaders did not accomplish much in Geneva, but the summit did open up a dialogue that helped to reduce tensions between East and West and the effects were noted immediately. The Soviet and the American sides made hesitant reconciliation efforts, and around that same time, Khrushchev's narrative of peaceful coexistence with the West really gained momentum. Even if peaceful coexistence ultimately failed as a foreign policy strategy, its most lasting legacy became the increased possibility for collaboration and interaction with the West, including the United States.[4]

The changes in official cultural relations between the superpowers were also due to the changed atmosphere in the United States. As of the mid-1950s, the power of Joseph McCarthy was diminishing, but VOKS perhaps overstressed the importance of conditions on the American side when the society claimed that the small success of 1955 was due to the fact that the "serious obstacles" to mutual cultural relations presented by the American government had somewhat been lifted.[5] Certainly, it was also clear that domestic conditions in the Soviet Union improved dramatically after the death of Joseph Stalin on March 5, 1953, and the immediate reforms played no small part in the way Soviet cultural organizations acted as of 1955.

Soviet cultural delegates and officials worked very hard to remove themselves from the ill-informed and distrustful Stalinist view of the American enemy, which resulted in a "noticeable revival" of Soviet-American cultural relations and the "rediscovery" of America in the post-Stalin Soviet cultural bureaucracy in 1955. However, the reports and discussions of some of the 1955 delegations show that while increased personal contacts continued to raise contentious issues for the Soviet bureaucracy, a real possibility for conducting cultural relations between the Cold War enemies had opened and the road was paved for what in 1958 was formalized in an official exchange agreement between the superpowers.

The Revival of Soviet-American Cultural Relations

After nearly a decade of almost nonexistent foreign exchanges, cultural organizations and institutions in Moscow were slowly coming to life again in the late 1950s. Institutions such as VOKS, Intourist, and the Ministry of Culture were finally able to work according to their assigned roles of maintaining foreign relation and exchanges in the cultural arena. Not just the relationship with the United States was on the mend; Khrushchev's dedication to improving relations with the West was evident, for example, by the signing of cultural exchange agreements, most notably with England and France. The immediate effect of Khrushchev's openness was increased exposure to British and French culture in the Soviet Union, and Khrushchev's visit to Great Britain in 1956 had also received much attention.[6] Finally, an agreement on cultural and educational exchanges with the United States was signed on January 27, 1958.[7]

In the three years leading up to the Soviet-American cultural exchange agreement, the Thaw therefore contributed to internal changes and increased openness in Soviet cultural organizations. Reports from organizations such as VOKS reveal much reflection, on both the prospects for increased cooperation in the cultural sphere and the outside context. Thus, by the end of 1955, Moscow VOKS agents reported that even with the progress in increasing relations, the possibilities of creating exchanges in the international climate had been "insufficiently taken advantage of"[8] and there was room for further improvement.

American friends of the Soviet Union were eager to help take advantage of the new opportunities; one of them was Elizabeth Moos at the National Council for American-Soviet Friendship. She urged VOKS officials to upgrade their propaganda with new films showing well-dressed people shopping in well-stocked stores: "Correct conclusions will be drawn from good pictures, showing works better than telling for our audiences."[9] She continued:

> Documentary films on the daily life of the Soviet people are urgently needed. They should not run more than a half hour each and have a minimum of commentary. In fact, the pictures with music and captions would be most useful, commentary could then be made by the person showing the film. Such pictures should show family life, an ordinary working day, industry, agriculture, recreation, trade union centers, an average holiday in the park, in the houses of culture; children in school, nursery and kindergarten.[10]

Moos observed that the documentaries the Soviets currently sent to the United States featured special celebrations and congresses of the Communist Party and thus did not create interest in the Soviet way of life.

> While these are beautiful, they are not as effective as educational material because they do not depict ordinary, everyday, life. In considering documentaries for the USA the producer *should* start from the assumption that the average person in our audience has utterly preconceived ideas that are false about life and work in the Soviet Union, particularly about

the family and trade unions. Pictures of the wonderful new projects and great buildings do not affect this false concept. Pictures of children and parents at home, people at the market, people enjoying themselves in the parks, libraries, etc., are helpful.[11]

The suggestion to focus on ordinary people and joyful everyday Soviet lives indicated that films showing Red Square marches and Communist Party congresses were not successful in convincing people of the superiority of the Soviet way of life. Showing images of family life and leisure would perhaps remove the idea many Americans had of Soviet people as submissive to the state and make them more familiar. According to Moos, Soviet propaganda needed to focus away from technological advancements and mass celebrations and show that Soviet people also bought groceries, played with their kids, and read books.

The well-meaning advice from Moos was a reaction to increased American curiosity about life in the Soviet Union after Stalin, and VOKS officials certainly felt this spike in interest as well. At the core of cultural exchanges was the focus on the personal, the idea being that "citizen diplomats" reach ordinary people better than political news about state leaders. VOKS was responsible for creating and maintaining these kinds of relations with foreign countries, but after the bleak years of war and late Stalinism when it was unable to fulfil this role, VOKS officials now rejoiced at being able to actually conduct cultural relations and in 1955 organized several exchanges of delegations and cultural visits with the United States. The mutual agricultural and journalistic delegations received much attention in both countries, as did the Soviet visit of the American veterans of the Elbe meeting. Additionally, American Olympic weightlifters, chess players, and a group of American senators and congressmen visited the Soviet Union; similarly, world-famous Soviet musicians, pianist Emil Gilels and violinist David Oistrakh, visited the United States for the first time.[12]

VOKS was also pleased to announce that upon return to their home country, many American visitors "were useful in spreading true information about our country in the United States."[13] Thus, Senator John Sparkman had given a speech at the National Press Club, expressing "satisfaction with the friendliness and the hospitality of the Russian people."[14] Furthermore, they reported that during the first ten months in 1955 they had received 350 letters from Americans looking to correspond with Soviet organizations and individuals, as opposed to 260 letters in 1954.[15] In general, VOKS reported the "steadily rising interest of American society in the life and culture of the Soviet people" and mainly credited this growing interest to the recent success of Soviet cultural organizations and their work with individual American citizens.[16]

Increased American interest in the Soviet project caused a sharper focus on how to present the Soviet Union to Americans. Elizabeth Moos had given some advice, but seemingly, VOKS did not act on it right away. In the beginning, VOKS treaded carefully and was more focused on celebrating the small successes that had been made than pushing for radical changes. Thus, a VOKS report applauded United Press Agency reporter Henry Shapiro's recent coverage of the situation in Moscow. He had just returned to Moscow after a two-year absence and found the Soviet Union completely changed. Before, he felt he had not been able to do much interesting journalism in the Soviet Union, as people there used to "run away from foreigners." Now, he claimed, the atmosphere was different. Shapiro reported on the "unusual politeness and friendliness" he was met with and how people actually sought conversations with him. He also observed that people were better dressed than before and that the stores had better products. This kind of reporting obviously pleased the Soviet authorities—this was precisely the kind of "propaganda" they themselves wanted to disseminate. It did not bother them that Shapiro's observations emphasized change, thus revealing that only two years earlier, the Soviet people did not feel free to talk to or display friendliness to American journalists. And Shapiro's discussion of the housing problem in Moscow did not seem to concern them either—for housing was one of the issues that the government planned on improving in the mid-1950s.[17]

Another observer of Russian cultural life, Isaiah Berlin, spent four weeks in the Soviet Union in 1956 and he noted the same kind of transition. He had spent four months in Moscow in 1945 and he observed how the death of Stalin had given people with official functions reason to be more optimistic: "the past had been terrible and the new freedom was full of promise: we were terrified, we are out of danger now."[18] Berlin was well connected in the academic world, and three different Soviet scholars told him that in November 1955, VOKS had given "the various academies of learning in Moscow" the message that cultural contacts with foreigners were now renewed and anyone with foreign language skills should "brush them up." VOKS officials also gave out instructions on how to treat and entertain "suitable" foreign visitors, with Berlin drawing the conclusion that people with a clearly defined status could expect closer contacts with Russians than before, while others would still encounter evasiveness and fear.[19]

Personal contact between Soviet and American people was therefore still a privilege very few people enjoyed. But with peaceful coexistence and Khrushchev's more relaxed attitude toward foreign culture, came also a comparatively large influx of American culture and literature in the Soviet Union.[20] A broad range of American cultural products now became available, such as translations of the works of Ernest Hemingway, John Steinbeck, and J. D. Salinger, who were published in hundreds of thousands of copies and easily available in public libraries all over the Soviet Union.[21] Another important source of information came from the well-known trophy films captured in Europe after the Second World War, such as the *Tarzan* series with Johnny Weissmuller and *His Butler's*

Sister with Deanna Durbin, which were popular and well known in the after-math of the Second World War.[22] Finally, the mid- to late 1950s also saw public performances by Americans such as the classical pianist Van Cliburn, stand-up comedian Bob Hope, the basketball team Harlem Globetrotters, and the staging of George Gershwin's folk opera *Porgy and Bess* in the Soviet Union, all of which had a profound effect on the Soviet people.[23]

Under Khrushchev, patriotic themes remained a priority in literature and the arts, but the anti-American tone was not as pronounced as it had been under Stalin. Certainly, anti-Americanism continued to play a role in the way American culture was presented in the Soviet Union, and in the 1950s, the increased press coverage of the American civil rights movement and its struggles made it excep-tionally easy for the Soviet press to manipulate stories of oppression as African Americans sought to participate in American society on an equal basis. The most dramatic moments of desegregation offered the Soviet side great propaganda opportunities, and it was only in the 1960s that Soviet writings about the "Negro Question" and American history were modified to include the achievements of the American civil rights movement and became more sophisticated.[24] In the 1950s, Soviet newspapers still took full advantage of stories such as the forced school desegregation in Little Rock, Arkansas, in 1957, and they repeatedly displayed cartoons featuring the Ku Klux Klan as a reminder of the repression African Americans had to tolerate.[25]

The Americans tried to address racial issues in ways that would not be harmful to US foreign policy, but Soviet anti-American propaganda was more interested in presenting the story from the African-American viewpoint. With that in mind, it is significant that in 1955 the African-American cast of *Porgy and Bess* was the first American theatrical group to travel to the Soviet Union.[26] That visit was a part of a four-year global tour, a part of a larger State Department propa-ganda campaign, which in part was aimed at raising awareness about progress in American race relations.[27] As early as 1949, the State Department had received a note from the American embassy in Moscow detailing the prominence of the "Negro Question" in Soviet anti-American propaganda.[28] Still, the state of bilat-eral relations with the Soviet Union was such that the State Department was not willing to provide financial support for the Soviet part of the *Porgy and Bess* tour in 1955, most likely because it was still not ready to reciprocate by giving Soviet performers visas to enter the United States.[29]

Somewhat cleverly, however, the Soviet authorities carried the cost of the Soviet visit themselves, and it has been claimed that by doing so, they "reaped a large part of the propaganda benefit inherent in the Porgy performances."[30] The staging of *Porgy and Bess* in the Soviet Union was an ambitious project, and the Soviet authorities invested in it in very real ways. For example, the Ministry of Culture, responsible for bringing the *Porgy and Bess* theater company, Everyman

Opera, to the Soviet Union, provided musicians and a grand piano and paid thousands of dollars to the company for the show.[31] Even if the State Department did not provide monetary support for the tour, it was very aware of the potential propaganda value of the show, which according to Ellen Noonan provided a threefold message. First, the play itself showed a past reality of African Americans in the United States but second, it was important that the behavior of the cast offstage should reflect how far African Americans had come compared to earlier periods. For that reason, the State Department was equally pleased with press coverage of the cast on and off the stage when they were traveling abroad.[32] This contributed to the third and most important message: to promote and raise understanding for the civil rights movement in America, and to counter the common view that racial discrimination and violence were rampant in the United States.[33]

It is not surprising, however, that the Soviet authorities emphasized the most basic message of the show, the reality of African Americans living in Charleston, South Carolina, in the early 1930s, and glossed over the accomplishments of the individual cast members or the advancements made in obtaining civil rights for African Americans in the 1950s.[34] It turned out, however, that the main problem Soviet authorities had with the very successful show was keeping track of the cast, who refused to spend their free time in structured group activities and wandered off on their own. An unidentified American Communist Party member ("Comrade from America") told VOKS in 1956 that, given the problems a large troupe such as that of *Porgy and Bess* posed, he would recommend inviting American soloists rather than such sizable ensembles to the Soviet Union.[35]

The show was an unequivocal success in the Soviet Union. Thousands of people saw it, and the Leningrad and Moscow audiences raved about the performance. Those not fortunate enough to get tickets congregated around the theaters, hoping to see cast members or be able to acquire a ticket.[36] A large cast such as that of *Porgy and Bess* was accustomed to garnering attention on their global tour; indeed, it was a part of their mandate to draw attention to their accomplished careers in the arts,[37] but it was not what the Soviet authorities wanted. Controlling the perceptions of foreigners and their own people abroad was much easier when cultural exchanges were focused on few individuals, such as the "Comrade from America" had proposed, or—even better—the preferred Soviet way of conducting cultural relations with foreigners, that is, by sending and receiving delegations, with controlled itineraries and approved agendas.

A Rediscovery of America

In addition to the success of *Porgy and Bess*, the 1955 revival of Soviet-American cultural relations was most noticeable in the exchanges of several high-profile delegations.[38] That year, a few Soviet official delegations visited the United States and vice versa, most notably from the fields of agriculture and journalism. A Soviet agricultural delegation visited the United States in midsummer, and in late fall a delegation of journalists traveled from coast to coast in the United States. The agricultural exchanges and the Soviet visit in particular indicated that the United States was once more a model for industrial and agricultural technologies, and the prominent Moscow-based journalists familiarized themselves with all aspects of print media, radio, and television in rural settings and urban areas. In addition to presenting developments in their respective professional fields, both delegations were charged with the task of spreading "true information about the Soviet Union" among Americans.[39]

The Soviet delegates received strict directives from the Communist Party on how to behave and how to present Soviet socialism to Americans. Overall, the Soviet authorities were "pleased with the positive treatment" and the media coverage the delegations received in the United States.[40] VOKS representatives attributed the positive treatment of the Soviet guests both to increased interaction with Americans and to better informational materials about the Soviet Union.[41] Upon return, the head of the Soviet agricultural delegation, Vladimir Matskevich, claimed that the American people had met the delegation with "warmth and hospitality," and the delegates "found great sympathy among 'ordinary Americans' toward the Soviet Union and the Soviet people."[42] American networks also aired footage about the Soviet journalists and they were recognized and greeted on the streets, where ordinary people "stopped the cars of the Soviet journalists in order to shake their hands and invite them to their homes."[43] Both the Soviet and American media provided much coverage of the visits, and the tangible optimism in the media bore witness to the rekindled energy of Soviet-American cultural relations.

Traveling across the United States and Canada from July 16 to August 25, 1955,[44] the Soviet agricultural delegation visited many American cities, familiarized themselves with dozens of farms, visited exhibits, machine manufacturers, colleges, and universities. Furthermore, the Soviets met with farmers, agronomists, and businesspeople. Everyone showed polite interest in Soviet agriculture, often expressing a desire to exchange experiences between the two countries in the agricultural sector.[45] The relentless talk about peace and friendship between the nations took on a new form when agricultural progress and sharing of information became a means to reach these goals. As Khrushchev later liked to repeat: "How much nicer it is to speak of corn than arms."[46]

Repeatedly, the delegates confirmed the success of "talking about corn" in the form of personal exchanges. As always, the Soviet cultural bureaucracy saw travel writing as a very useful way in getting a message across to the broader public, and in that spirit the agricultural delegation wrote lengthy accounts of its travels upon their return. In his book, Vladimir Matskevich claimed that the delegation had seen "many valuable things"[47] in North America. The book was overall very positively disposed toward American agriculture and the general hospitality with which the Americans greeted the delegation, but, predictably, descriptions of American hospitality and friendliness were countered with similar stories of the satisfaction of the American delegates who visited the Soviet Union. To be sure, the American agricultural delegation, which came to the Soviet Union in 1955, had also seen many "fruitful and interesting things in the Soviet Union."[48]

Matskevich claimed that they had traveled to places where "no Soviet person ever visited before,"[49] where Americans "tried to grab them" in excitement and claimed that American slander about the Soviet system only made them more interested in learning the truth about the Soviet people.[50] The Soviet delegates used every opportunity to remind Americans that the Soviet people did not want war and were "fighting for peace."[51] The antiwar narrative and the focus on peace was repeated in the coming years, showing a clear turn away from the Stalinist anti-Americanism, which had encouraged rumors about a pending war and forbidden all mention of the former alliance. The new focus on peace, corn, and coexistence was certainly welcomed, on both sides of the Iron Curtain.

All of this was in line with the general "spirit of Geneva," and more specifically with Soviet propaganda about how the Soviet Union and the United States, "the most developed agricultural industrial countries in the world," would be much better off if they cooperated.[52] Matskevich acknowledged that the United States was a step ahead in industrial production; "the USSR comes in second after the USA," but "with the speed of our growth, our country soon will leave the United States behind. Our planned national economy is, contrary to the U.S. economy, without crises and unemployment."[53] Certainly, Americans had also shown much interest in Soviet agriculture, but Matskevich made hardly any references to social conditions in the United States, focusing strictly on agricultural production and technology.[54] He did, however, hint that general topics had also been discussed when he claimed that the delegates had used every opportunity to "correct lies about the Soviet people, and to tell the truth about their goals, struggles, and expectations. We spoke of peace, about mutual understanding, about friendship, the foundation of mutual respect."[55]

Given Khrushchev's personal interest in agriculture and his commitment to increase corn production in the Soviet Union, it is no wonder that, in this case, he was interested in hearing what the delegation had learned about agricultural practices in the United States. On October 4, 1955, Khrushchev personally met with the Soviet delegation, asking several questions about what they had seen in America. He was interested in anything from detailed descriptions of American facilities and tractors to information about American strategies for growing corn, and the delegates answered all his questions in detail.[56] In the same month, Khrushchev himself hosted the American agricultural delegation in Crimea, taking a personal interest in the visit. This shows that even if the official Soviet mission was to promote friendlier relations with the United States, the Soviet side was also keen on learning from the American other. The growing of corn, however, was a topic that was more likely to reach Khrushchev's sympathetic ear than general suggestions about how best to conduct cultural relations and improve the Soviet image abroad.

Under Khrushchev, "corn diplomacy" thus became a way to take a non-threatening issue and use it as a way to cooperate and learn about the other. Khrushchev was sincere in his interest in corn and famously befriended Roswell Garst, a hybrid corn producer from Iowa, when he came to the Soviet Union as a part of the American agricultural delegation in October 1955. Khrushchev repaid the visit on his 1959 America tour, and their Iowa reunion became one of the media highlights of the trip.[57] The relationship between Garst and Khrushchev was widely noted in the late 1950s, such as in Adlai Stevenson's writings when he described the very "agreeable and profitable experience" Mr. Garst and Khrushchev had in Crimea, "talking about corn and drinking brandy."[58]

But even if the agricultural delegation reported unanimous success, at least in the official space, the exchanges could also raise questions and criticism. A report that the head of the 1955 Soviet journalistic delegation, Boris Polevoi, submitted to the Central Committee upon his return from the United States was surprisingly critical in its evaluations of the overall Soviet performance in presenting itself to the outside world. Just as Matskevich, Polevoi also published a book, *American Diaries (Amerikanskie dnevniki)*, about his travels in the United States.[59] Much more interesting, however, is his sixteen-page report about the delegation's experience in the United States. The document shows that the Soviet delegates had learned that it was not enough to talk only about corn if they were to reach the hearts and minds of Americans. They had come to realize that their knowledge about the United States was no longer up to date, concluding that if Soviet delegations were to represent their own country and its politics successfully, they would have to be better informed about the enemy's social and cultural issues.[60]

The members of Polevoi's delegation were privileged citizens of Soviet society so their ingenuousness and lack of knowledge about the United States was surprising. According to Frederick C. Barghoorn, the journalists were "suave, smooth, and thoroughly political,"[61] and in the Soviet Union, the journalists were both influential and well known. Polevoi himself was both a *Pravda* correspondent and a novelist on the governing board of the Soviet Writers' Union. Other members were also highly ranked in the Soviet bureaucracy. For example, Aleksei Adzhubei, then editor of *Komsomol'skaia pravda* and later editor of *Izvestiia*, as well as being Khrushchev's son-in-law, was present. Others were Vladimir Berezhkov of *Novoe vremia*, N. Gribachev of *Literaturnaia gazeta*, B. Izakov of *Mezhdunarodnaia zhizn'*, A. Sofronov of *Ogonek*, and V. Poltoratskii of *Izvestiia*.[62] All delegations were political—that was nothing new—but the journalistic delegation was indeed stacked with talented people who presented themselves in a cultured and correct Soviet manner. Their privileged position can also be noted in that at least two of the delegates went on repeated trips to the United States: Polevoi returned to America briefly in 1958 to attend a reunion of Soviet and American war veterans, and Adzhubei was a member of Khrushchev's entourage during his 1959 visit to America.

Despite the shock of learning that their information about the enemy was outdated, the overall experience was positive. During their busy schedule of getting to know the media business in the United States inside out, as well as visiting journalistic faculties at prestigious universities, the journalists received warm welcomes everywhere. Important people took the time to meet with them, such as owners and main editors of newspapers and television networks, departmental chairs and university professors. Everyone they met approved of the "renewal and strengthening of cultural relations, the exchange of know-how, mutual contacts and the growing exchange of delegations." The journalists also familiarized themselves with the "cultural treasures of America." They visited museums and galleries and went to concerts, but they also saw factories, mines, and farms and were happy to report that the print media had paid these visits much attention.[63]

Furthermore, Polevoi reported that "in line with the directive," the delegation had strived at all times to "explain the Soviet point of view" and clarify the Soviet way of life and the politics of coexistence and peace.[64] In order to do so, the journalists held press conferences and appeared on radio and television to reach a broad audience: "It was typical at these meetings for those present to almost always support the Soviet journalists, even showing sympathy to the Soviet speakers."[65] They had also been ordered to give interviews to "reactionary" media, so they spoke to *US News and World Report*, "which normally took an anti-Soviet stand on foreign issues" and seemed happy with the results, although Polevoi also noted that not all communications with the media had gone smoothly. *Time* magazine, for example, distorted the answers the delegates gave at a press conference and never published the letter the journalists sent to contradict the original article.[66] Polevoi likewise reported on the good behavior of his delegates: "in all conversations with Americans, during radio speeches, television broadcasts and during all interviews we gave to the press, in accordance with the directive, we constantly maintained a humble and friendly tone." Only once, wrote Polevoi, were they forced to change tone, and that happened in response to Senator Joseph C. O'Mahoney's (D-Wyoming) "abusive attack on the Soviet press." After listening to his criticism of the Soviet press and his "ignorant assessment of the Soviet constitution," the journalists gave him "an angry and sound rebuttal, which the next day, much to our surprise, was objectively noted in the Washington press."[67]

The US State Department planned the itinerary of the delegation, and it was closely followed, with the exception of leaving out Chicago and going instead to Salt Lake City. Foreseeing a big anti-Soviet demonstration in Chicago, the hosts wanted to spare the delegates the embarrassment. Although generally pleased with the schedule, the delegates complained to their escort from the State Department that no interaction with ordinary Americans was planned. This was clearly an important part of their mandate, because the delegates firmly pressed the issue and, as a result, they were allowed to meet with "ordinary American families" almost every night. They were divided into two, sometimes three, groups, and, according to Polevoi, this gave them "the most valuable material about the life and mood of real America."[68]

The delegates repeatedly emphasized how helpful it was to meet with Americans in their homes and how the personal gatherings were always pleasant and showed that Americans wanted to maintain friendly relations with the Soviet Union. Their hosts were from all walks of life: from simple tradesmen and office workers to millionaires. They met with many editors and publishers, but also insurance agents, milk farmers, and leaders of prosperous ranches. They met with business executives and representatives of commerce. In Hollywood, both "bigwigs and bosses" hosted them, as well as ordinary artists. Everyone was pleasant, and the Soviet journalists felt that they had learned much about Americans and their perception of the Soviet Union:[69]

> The most valuable impression from these dealings with Americans was that everyone who spoke to us sincerely welcomed "the Spirit of Geneva" even though many of them did not want the Cold War to end since they feared the cunning intentions of the Soviet Union (we were often told: "we are afraid of you"). Nonetheless, the people hate the Cold War, and all of them talked about the renewal and expansion of cultural relations, about the exchange of delegations, and how the doors for tourists should be more open in both countries.[70]

Even if Polevoi claimed that these meetings were valuable, he was also certain that the people they met with were instructed by State Department representatives to emphasize the need for greater cultural relations. It is not clear if that was the case, if the "ordinary American families" were prepped for their meetings with the Soviet delegates, but this was certainly how it would have been done in the Soviet Union. However, meeting real Americans was in line with American information strategy, which in the 1950s focused very much on American family values and an idealistic image of gender equality, contrasting them with the perceived image of hardship for especially Soviet women, who worked outside the home like men but bore the sole responsibility of the household.[71]

The American families and ordinary people the delegates spent their evenings with were apparently all friendly and open, but their political leanings remain uncertain. The journalists praised these encounters, saying they were much more impressive and informative than meetings with officials, but there was a catch. "We are certain," wrote Polevoi,

> that we were hurt by poor knowledge of American life, the superficial, vulgar illumination of processes going on in the country, and especially our superficial knowledge of the economy prevents the establishment of good relations. We are constantly harping on the dark side of American life, conducted in the same spirit of endlessly repeating one or the other outdated themes.[72]

This must have been a matter of some concern for the Soviet authorities, and it did not get any better when a friend of the Soviet Union, fellow traveler Paul Robeson, offered the delegation advice: "In the name of God, do not advocate for the Negroes with the methods of Beecher Stowe. . . . The Negro Question is more complicated than that."[73] Polevoi wrote that they had accepted Robeson's advice, and he strongly emphasized the need to update Soviet knowledge about the position of African Americans as well as black people all over the world. They should speak on behalf of "all cultured humankind," taking into account the substantial concessions Americans had made to African Americans, "of which they are very proud." Polevoi claimed that taking a position with "Negroes" as a whole against white people would only harm the Soviet cause, and would turn people off.[74]

Since Soviet-American cultural exchanges were still in the early stages, the exchanges of delegations in 1955 had much educational value. Polevoi not only pointed out lack of knowledge about American society, but also offered opinions on how to proceed with the exchanges without embarrassing Soviet officials and how to help them propagandize effectively about America:

> We think that we should completely rethink the system of propaganda about American topics. We should reject in every way possible provocative publications and concentrate in depth on the main points while clearly illuminating the problems of American life. To begin with, we could publish the materials written by the members of the delegation in their respective journals and magazines. Before that, it goes without saying; we need to have serious introductory conversations with the Central Committee.[75]

All the journalists published accounts of their trip in their respective publications, and, additionally, Polevoi and Gribachev wrote books that recounted their experiences. The delegates were under orders to adhere strictly to the "spirit of Geneva" in their writing and focus on what had already been achieved in Soviet-American relations, and it seems their efforts were met with approval. A 1958 Central Committee evaluation of "false portrayals of bourgeois realities in contemporary Soviet art and literature" complimented Polevoi and Gribachev on their publications.[76] This report praised their "especially successful" accounts of foreign travel as they "exposed the reactionary politics ruling in the bourgeois world, revealed the inhumanity of bourgeois society and the difficult position of workers."[77] In 1955, the journalists had argued that the publications could provide enlightening information about American life while "*not deviating from our principal ideological position*,"[78] and it looks as though they succeeded. They had wanted to "objectively shed light on the life and on the most interesting achievements of the American people,"[79] and certainly Polevoi's *American Diaries* presented its readers with a more attractive image of America than any other Soviet account of the postwar era had done.[80]

Publications about experiences abroad in newspapers, weeklies, and in travelogues were one way the authorities "helped" ordinary people to understand the West, and it has been claimed that the writings of this delegation marked a noteworthy change in the American image presented to the Soviet people. At the time, Frederick C. Barghoorn heard from "an American in Moscow" that Berezhkov of *Novoe vremia* claimed that the trip had marked a "rediscovery of America." Barghoorn also concluded that, in spite of the ideological language and the precautions about American life, the accounts conveyed "the teeming activity, material prosperity, and glittering gadgetry of America"[81] to the Soviet reader. Given the fine line Polevoi had to tread in showcasing an ideologically correct, yet alluring picture of America, the official verdict of his book is more than anything a witness to the literary skills of the writer Boris Polevoi.

Soviet authorities were torn between reconciling increased relations with the West and risking too much contamination by Western influences in general. Such concerns were even more pressing when attempting to control the experiences and reporting of people who traveled to the United States. Furthermore, the Soviet side also had an interest in learning from the Americans, especially on issues such as the growing of corn but also on how to successfully propagandize to Americans. In this last regard, they obviously still had a lot to learn. But unlike Stalin, Khrushchev realized that sending Soviet delegations abroad could prove helpful, and he relied on Soviet delegations to gather facts and—at least in the case of corn—he carefully studied the facts and information they brought back. Since delegation reports were sent to the Central Committee, there is a good chance that Khrushchev saw many of them. In any case, the advice of Soviet delegates—and sometimes of well-meaning Americans—reached high officials in the cultural bureaucracy and party hierarchy, and it may have contributed to the way that perceptions of cultural relations with the West rapidly changed in the coming few years.

Explaining the Soviet Way of Life to Americans

The delegation of journalists in 1955 had concluded that it was necessary for the Soviet Union to change its overall information strategy toward Americans, offering a long list of advice on how to go about accomplishing this goal. Getting Soviet propaganda across to Americans was the most important part of a delegation's mission, and the 1955 journalists were not altogether pleased with their preparation and subsequent lack of success. Polevoi claimed on behalf of the journalists "that we have finally learned how to actually propagandize the advancements of Soviet politics and the Soviet way of life in the United States." Most important, he claimed that "it is not achieving anything to rely only on our very limited and isolated group of friends of the Soviet Union." Those people are already convinced of the superiority of the Soviet way of life, he said.[82] In sum, they had been preaching to the converted.

Polevoi pointed out how Western ambassadors, embassy workers, and journalists used every opportunity to give public talks anywhere they could get an audience: at prominent universities, on the radio, and on television. Soviet diplomats and journalists in New York and Washington had not once taken advantage of this opportunity and had a reputation for being "hermits" among foreign journalists in these cities. Curious, the delegates inquired about the roots of this inactivity of their compatriots abroad and were told that they were not supposed to deviate from the prepared text "from above" anyway. It was a problem, the journalists concluded, that these people seemed to have lost the ability to trust their own judgment. Had everyone forgotten, for example, the work of Soviet diplomats and journalists in the 1930s and during the Second World War? They had been good representatives of the Soviet way of life and had advocated for the establishment of mutual understanding between nations. The delegates were also in shock to find out that the staff of the New York TASS agency had poor knowledge of English and little understanding of American life.[83] The problem was serious: "We really need to do something and we need to do it now, because we have this problem not only in the United States, but also in other capitalist countries, and we have much to lose and [our behavior] indulges anti-Soviet legends."[84]

In his suggestions on behalf of the journalists, Polevoi recounted several things that might be nourishing stereotypes of the Soviet Union and its people as uncivilized and uncultured. Soviet cultural organizations, for example, were notorious for letting requests from abroad go completely unanswered.[85] No Soviet city, not even Moscow, had tourist information readily available, but in the United States even the smallest city had "colorful brochures" loaded with photographs that contained information about the city, about its sights, and a map of the city with an index of hotels, theaters, museums, and restaurants. With growing numbers of tourists to the Soviet Union, this needed to be quickly improved; the expenses could be justified because they were in line with the government's aim to introduce Soviet achievements to foreigners.[86]

The journalists were also impressed with the welcome Americans gave them. All the cities they visited had put together a welcoming committee, staffed with local intellectuals or eminent citizens. Members of these committees invited the Soviet guests to their homes, and escorted them to the theater or cultural events. "Such a committee would help create warmer contacts with the guests and would remove the outward appearance of state organizations involved in control that always have a bad effect upon representatives of foreign countries."[87] This was remarkably reflective, and whether or not the idea came from Polevoi, the Soviet organizers of the 1957 World Youth Festival put much emphasis on local receiving committees in all small cities and towns en route to Moscow, and local welcoming committees became a constant factor in all cultural activities that involved foreigners in the Soviet Union.

A welcoming committee, however important, would still not be the "gate to the country." That honor went to Aeroflot, the first Soviet experience a foreigner traveling to the Soviet Union would have. An American farmer, John Jacobs, "a man favorable to the Soviet Union,"[88] gave them the following advice about Aeroflot: "as a 'gateway to the country,' it served no purpose. If the gateway is bad, nothing good can be expected to follow." To be sure, Jacobs said, he himself did not assign great importance to the Soviet gate; he was very satisfied with the Soviet achievements in science and technology. It was only for the sake of other people flying to the Soviet Union that he wanted to convey this information, namely that a foreigner stepping on an Aeroflot carrier in Prague or Helsinki immediately noticed a very strong difference in service. It was long known, Polevoi wrote, that "our IL's [Iliushin aircraft] lag behind the airplanes of the capitalist countries, but what we are talking about here is service, which normally is understood as 'servis.' "[89] The Russian word for service (*usluzhenie*) clearly did not begin to grasp what the American term entailed.

Polevoi complained that the delays in flights were outrageous, and the crew completely incompetent: "They do not know languages, do not offer newspapers or magazines, and do not pay any attention to the passengers."[90] Furthermore, "breakfast was served without napkins, straight from a box. The food was cold, two days old, had been prepared and brought in from Moscow and was dried up." It got worse; the "misses" [*devushki*] told them that the base gave them only "*two pieces of sugar per passenger.*"[91] If a passenger wanted an extra cup of tea, the "misses" had to pay for the extra sugar and tea themselves. "This is odd, but it is a fact," Polevoi wrote and apparently, this was not an unknown problem. What Polevoi warned against though, was that with the increasing numbers of tourists to the Soviet Union, the lack of service could potentially cause the Soviet image "serious, even political damage."[92]

As the Soviet visitors realized that their knowledge of the United States, both the country and its people, was superficial and outdated, they tried to convince the authorities that better preparation was in order. Participants in cultural relations—officials, delegates, and well-meaning friends of the Soviet Union—argued that the Soviet image needed to be modernized, the travel and tourist industry had to be more service-oriented, and the image of state-controlled activities had to be removed. Furthermore, the lack of "correct" materials about the Soviet Union for Americans, both in the United States and in the Soviet Union, hurt the mission of "telling the truth" about the Soviet Union, especially as they had lost access to "friendly circles."

People involved in cultural relations with the United States had to find the right balance between getting to have hands-on experiences with American society and searching for negative aspects at the same time. Though their accounts of America were heavily influenced by the expectations of the Soviet government, these encounters left an impression on the Soviet participants that often went beyond their mandate. This is very clear in the published journalistic accounts of 1955. In fact, the books written by Polevoi and Gribachev seem exceptional, both in their popularity and in how much they pleased the authorities. In 1958, the Cultural Department of the Central Committee of the Communist Party conveyed its disappointment with recent publications in the travel genre (with the exception of Polevoi's and Gribachev's work). The report explicitly expressed a longing for writings in the style of Gorky and Mayakovsky, "who exposed social conflicts of the bourgeois world while praising the arrangement of Soviet, socialist ideology."[93] This "fighting tradition" seemed to be lost: the officials felt that the new travelogues were written more generally and did not focus enough on "Soviet ideology and morals, the Soviet way of life and Soviet art."[94] They attributed this partly to the fact that, during a short visit, perceptions of a country could not go much beyond "exhibited sides of life." These would be put on show to advertise "bourgeois propaganda," and therefore the perceptions did not cover "the inconspicuous contradictory realities in the bourgeois world."[95] The report was focused on representations of "bourgeois" realities in literature, popular magazines and art and the authors argued for the importance of taking a firm stand on this issue, as this perceived misrepresentation was "causing much damage," especially among the young people.[96] Apparently, the changes in the way foreigners and foreign experiences were dealt with were a step too far for some members of the cultural bureaucracy.

As time went by and Soviet ideology moved from the strict anti-American dogma, one can speculate that some Soviet delegations were less aware of the necessary nuances in presenting America to Soviet readers. However, the struggle to control the experience and perceptions deriving from increased travel, openness, and flow of information so that they would not have people recount their experiences in a "spirit of servility"[97] always went hand in hand with the mission of telling the "truth" about the Soviet Union and its accomplishments. Lacking in resources, tools, and qualified people, the Soviet side found itself on the defensive in this battle. Interestingly, however, it often thought that the "superficial" nature of these trips was a major cause of their problems—people needed better training in how to look behind the facade of what they were being shown in America.[98]

During these first years of renewed cultural exchanges and foreign tourism, this posed a problem for Soviet officials. How were they to properly prepare their own people for trips to the West? How were they to prevent them from returning and recounting enthusiastically what they had been told and shown? Tourists and delegates alike were, according to Soviet authorities, not sufficiently prepared to take on the task of viewing American accomplishments through a socialist lens while simultaneously representing the socialist way of life. This was an ongoing struggle within all organizations and government departments involved in cultural and personal exchange with the United States. While explaining Soviet socialism to Americans was a main priority, it was difficult to maintain that goal when the outcome of the trip was negative comparison for the Soviet way of life.

From the Elbe to the Potomac (via Moscow)

On one front, there was no negative comparison for the Soviet Union: Polevoi reported that Americans showed great respect for the sufferings and achievements of the Soviet nation during the Second World War. This feeling of empathy, he stated, could be utilized better in the Soviet propaganda, which emphasized the "reconstruction of mutual understanding and trust between our two nations."[99] Reminding Americans of the wartime alliance would surely be effective in terms of rekindling friendly relations—after all, the end of the Second World War was only ten years earlier. This was close to Polevoi's heart, for he himself was a veteran of the 1945 meeting of Soviet and American soldiers on the Elbe in Germany.[100] In fact, the meeting on the Elbe had been Polevoi's first personal meeting with Americans:[101] as for so many Soviet people, his most impressionable encounter with America was related to the Second World War. In his *American Diaries*, Polevoi wrote about how his 1955 American trip was spent searching for John

Smith, whom he met at the Elbe in 1945. Ten years later, he lamented in the book, he was unable to find "a 'real American'" such as Smith.[102] Throughout the book and especially in the conclusion, Polevoi appealed to "John Smith" to not be afraid of communism and for the Soviet and American people to "not interfere in each other's lives." Instead, he proposed for an increased understanding of the differences between the two countries and "let us each live as we want." This strong focus on peaceful coexistence would be best served, according to Polevoi, by remembering the "joint fight against Hitlerism, sealed there on the clear, spring day at the Elbe."[103] Incidentally, Polevoi's next trip to the United States was in 1958, when he attended a reunion of Soviet-American veterans: the first reunion celebrated in the United States.

The very first joint reunion of Soviet and American veterans of the Elbe linkup, however, had taken place in Moscow three years earlier, in May 1955, only two years after Stalin's death. Even if the Cold War had made it impossible for the veterans to travel across the Iron Curtain, most Soviet and American veterans of the Elbe meeting had not forgotten the "spirit of the Elbe" or the oath they took in April 1945 "to do everything possible to strengthen the friendship between the peoples of the USSR and USA, not to allow another war ever to occur."[104] Veterans of the meeting on the Elbe remained sympathetic to each other for life, believing that someday "the spirit of brotherhood will truly prevail along the banks of the Elbe, Volga, Mississippi, and every other river on this our earth."[105] It took ten years, but as with cultural relations in general, 1955 was also the year Soviet-American veterans of the meeting on the Elbe saw progress in their efforts to reunite and celebrate their accomplishment and their everlasting friendship.

The Soviet government was especially skeptical of veterans' efforts to hold reunions and jointly celebrate the linkup. Thus, when in 1955, the American Veterans of the Elbe Linkup invited Soviet comrades to celebrate April 25 with them in Washington, DC, the Soviet side backed out at the last minute. Joseph Polowsky, the secretary of the American Veterans of the Elbe River Linkup organization, claimed that in 1955 the Soviet veterans of the Elbe meeting had "made inquiries concerning the issuance of American visas at the United States Embassy" but had found out that "they would have to be subjected to fingerprinting in order to visit the United States."[106] This was a deal-breaker for the Soviet government, which expressed frustration with the American insistence on fingerprinting all entering aliens, a practice it labeled "degrading to the dignity of the Soviet people."[107] The Soviets dramatically accused the American government of having raised an Iron Curtain around the United States.[108] So even if within the Soviet bureaucracy, the year 1955 marked a turn of events in terms of a revival of cultural contacts between the Soviet Union and the United States, Khrushchev was still not ready to send Soviet veterans to the United States.

With the Soviet withdrawal, however, came an invitation to celebrate in Moscow on May 9, the official Victory Day in the Soviet Union, and nine American veterans accepted the offer. It is tempting to attribute the choice of the May date over the April anniversary date solely to propaganda purposes, but practicality also mattered. The Soviet decision not to accept the American invite came so late that an earlier visit would have been difficult to pull off.[109] The Soviet side seized the opportunity to lavishly display Soviet hospitality. Before the trip, two Soviet newspapers, *Krasnaia zvezda* and *Trud*, formed a committee of six people, which identified up to two hundred Soviet participants of the meeting of Soviet and American troops on the Elbe. They recruited forty people to participate in the activities related to the stay of the American veterans in Moscow. During the four days in Moscow, the Elbe veterans met with more than 750 veterans of the Second World War, attended a reception held by Soviet marshal Vasily Sokolovsky, and visited the Lenin-Stalin Mausoleum. They were also shepherded to a collective farm in the Krasnogorsky district, taken to museums and theaters, and shown around the capital.[110]

American veterans of the 1945 Elbe linkup visit the Soviet embassy in Washington, DC, on the ten-year anniversary of the meeting, April 25, 1955. A portrait of Stalin looks on as the Soviet ambassador, Georgy Zarubin (left), shakes hands with veteran Murray Schulman (right). *John Rous/AP/REX/Shutterstock*

According to a report to the Central Committee, "the majority" of the American veterans were reserved and wary of making any statements that "in their words, 'could be used for propaganda purposes.'"[111] Apparently, they often avoided photo-ops and in the report, Marshal Georgy Zhukov, now newly appointed Minister of Defense, and Aleksei Zheltov, head of *Glavpur*, the Main Political Administration of the Ministry of Defense,[112] wrote that this behavior became much more pronounced after the delegation had visited the American embassy on the evening of May 10. In addition to this, the Americans were very hesitant and uncommitted to the Soviet proposal of making a joint appeal to veterans of the Second World War, with Polowsky apparently expressing concerns that such an appeal might cause diplomatic complications.

Overall, the Soviets concluded that the Americans were satisfied with their stay in the Soviet Union. They quoted Polowsky in claiming that the American veterans had expected more mistrust and tension but "the endless warmth and hospitality" had dispelled all such fears. The veterans did agree on a final joint appeal, which declared a determination to campaign for friendship between the Soviet and American people and for peace throughout the world, and the final evaluation on the Soviet side was that the meeting had been successful.[113]

Although pleased with the outcome of the reunion, the Soviet organizers suspected that three of the nine Americans were not really veterans of the Elbe linkup but had come to the Soviet Union "with ulterior motives." They maintained that the three had showed a marked interest in atypical circumstances in the life of Soviet people. According to the Soviet hosts, the three suspects had vigilantly monitored the behavior of their own comrades and avoided all political statements as well as topics that revealed any unpleasant realities of American life. The Soviets claimed that the behavior of the other six, as witnessed in photos and conversations, showed that they were real veterans of the April 25 meeting on the Elbe—two had even received the Soviet order of the Red Star. But the other three gave the impression of individuals sent to the Soviet Union "with ulterior motives."[114]

Whether or not the American authorities had infiltrated the delegation with CIA agents is up for debate. Both the American authorities and society at large had strongly supported the visit, starting with the "authorization" of President Dwight D. Eisenhower, who had an open dialogue with Marshal Zhukov.[115] According to Joe Polowsky, the State Department had also "facilitated the success of the good will mission at every stage" and "the women of America" funded the trip after an appeal on a CBS television network program, sponsored by the Colgate-Palmolive company.[116] Furthermore, New York governor W. Averell Harriman, and high-ranking politicians such as Senators Ralph A. Flanders of Vermont and Richard B. Russell of Georgia (who was chairman of the Senate Armed Forces Committee), supported the reunion and the sentiments of the veterans. Senator Russell expressed hope that the Americans would succeed in getting the Soviet veterans to visit the United States, "to see how a democracy functions."[117] The American veterans worked hard to fulfill this mission and during the 1955 meeting, the Americans expressed their wish that the next reunion could take place in Washington, DC.[118]

Three years later, in 1958, five Soviet veterans, led by writer and journalist Boris Polevoi, celebrated the thirteenth anniversary of the meeting on the Elbe with American veterans on the Potomac in Washington, DC.[119] The first official visit of Soviet war veterans to the United States would not have been possible without the changes in the Soviet Union in the aftermath of Stalin's death and the cultural and political Thaw that followed Khrushchev's 1956 Secret Speech, in which he denounced the crimes of Stalin.[120] But more important here, Khrushchev's shift to peaceful coexistence and Soviet-American negotiations on cultural and scientific exchanges that started in the summer of 1957 were showing results. For example, Polowsky claimed that—"to the overbrimming joy of all the Elbe veterans"—the return visit of the Soviet veterans was only possible after the Department of State announced the elimination of fingerprinting, which had been in effect since the 1952 Immigration and Nationality Act, on October 10, 1957.[121]

Conclusion

With increased interactions came the slow realization that Soviet knowledge of the United States, the country, and its people was superficial and outdated. The atmosphere of late Stalinism had not allowed for real knowledge or information about the United States, neither in the form of scientific study nor in cultural relations. However, peaceful coexistence allowed for a reopening of travel and personal contacts, but the Soviet authorities still discouraged any infatuation with the West on behalf of Soviet citizens, as they feared that familiarity with American popular culture and values would easily convert them. They realized, however, that it was difficult for delegates to balance their information gathering about US industrial supremacy while simultaneously expecting them to criticize the American social system and praise all things Soviet.

The problem of reconciling the various goals of the Soviet cultural mission was an ever-present one. Polevoi's conclusion, that the Soviet strategy of relying on friendly circles abroad, that is, front organizations, was bankrupt, started to hit home in the mid-to-late 1950s. By 1955, it was slowly becoming clear that lagging behind in "service" and the general availability of consumer goods harmed the image of the Soviet Union in the United States and at home. Following the moderate successes of 1955, Soviet delegates and at least some members of the cultural bureaucracy reached the conclusion that their strategies and institutions needed to be updated and modernized.[122] But, coexisting with the doubts and recommendations that circulated among those who experienced the alternative reality firsthand were the real changes and the hope that cultural and ideological workers experienced in terms of their work in 1955. Perhaps the biggest change, though, was that Polevoi dared criticize and suggest improvements to the Soviet cultural bureaucracy based on his experiences. This would have been unimaginable during the late Stalin era, where Soviet intellectuals dealing with foreign topics and foreigners were submissive and lived in fear.

The paradox of advocating for peaceful coexistence in the form of travel and interactions while simultaneously fearing the conversion of those involved ended up becoming a real problem for the Soviet leadership. Scholars have even claimed that cultural exchanges and personal contacts worked so much in the United States' favor that they helped the country win the Cold War.[123] And judging from the experiences of Soviet delegates and cultural workers, the Soviet authorities certainly were on the defensive in almost all aspects of the cultural Cold War. But at the time, the Soviet Union seemed very robust, and there was no reason for the number one enemy not to take the other superpower seriously. Full of confidence, Premier Khrushchev continued down the road of wanting to increase cultural relations with foreign countries and pushing for an official cultural exchange agreement with the United States. Khrushchev's optimism and the delicate opening to the West is the subject of the next chapter.

5 THE PARADOXES OF PEACEFUL COEXISTENCE, 1956–1957

The mid-1950s revival of Soviet-American cultural relations coincided with the slow beginning of the Thaw period in the Soviet Union. On February 25, 1956, Khrushchev delivered his fiery denunciation of the Stalin cult at the Twentieth Party Congress and started the official process of de-Stalinization in the Soviet Union. In that legendary Secret Speech,[1] Khrushchev declared that the Central Committee now "resolutely condemned the cult of the individual as alien to the spirit of Marxism-Leninism."[2] By aligning himself with Lenin, Khrushchev's policy of peaceful coexistence became an integral part of his de-Stalinization campaign, in which he advocated strongly for a return to Leninism and a peaceful relationship with the United States and the West.

Though this was undoubtedly an important change, there was also a very noticeable continuity in the way Soviet ideology chiefs thought about and reacted to challenges from abroad. During the mid- to late 1950s, "reformist intellectuals" debated the extent of the Thaw in culture and society, but they soon learned that Soviet ideology as such proved very resistant to change.[3] Furthermore, while this period saw a popular reaction to the perceived changes in the Soviet Union, it also witnessed increased political persecution.[4] These conflicting social processes would end up creating a paradox in international and cultural relations, since the decision to open up the Soviet Union inevitably caused much more influx of people, cultural artifacts, and ideas. Internal discussions in the cultural administration show how difficult it was to accommodate the ideological rigor that still dominated Soviet life with the renewed openness and the increased exposure to the outside world that followed. However, the creative intelligentsia was now less fearful in its dealings with the cultural bureaucracy, daring to make suggestions for improvements and contributing to a dialogue about the limits of peaceful coexistence. This was of course clearly noticeable in the domestic Thaw, which entailed "drastic reduction of political violence in Soviet society,"[5] but in this new era, the ideological apparatus had to take into account Khrushchev's new vision of the Soviet Union's relationship with the outside world.

The paradox of opening up the Soviet Union while simultaneously continuing to want to control people's access to and perception of the outside world is seen in both the cultural bureaucracy and the legal system, which once again reacted strongly to people's perceived interest in the United States. Among other things, the "spirit of Geneva" had paved the way for increased visits by delegations and a 1956 official agreement on the renewed circulation of *Amerika* in the Soviet Union and of *USSR* in the United States.[6] Voice of America broadcasts, however, continued to be jammed for the most part, but under strong pressure from the State Department, Soviet authorities also showed some lenience in their attitude to the broadcasts in the late 1950s. The cases of *Amerika* and the Voice of America illustrate the paradox of peaceful coexistence in direct relations to the Soviet view of American propaganda and people's access to it: American official propaganda was tolerated within the limits of official agreements, but at the same time, it was important to control popular reactions to it.

If the Soviet Union was so keen on controlling images of the West, then why did it slowly open up its borders in the mid-1950s? After the isolation of the late Stalinist years, Nikita Khrushchev's decision to open up the Soviet Union came with the conviction that the Soviet system ultimately would compare favorably to the capitalist West, especially the United States. To that extent, Khrushchev decided to show off Soviet accomplishments. In addition to opening the country to foreign delegations and tourists, Soviet authorities were to hold the Sixth World Festival of Youth and Students in Moscow in the summer of 1957 in the certainty that the accomplishments of Soviet socialism would impress the foreign guests. The festival was certainly a successful mass event, but its legacy quickly became tainted by the fact that it also confirmed to Soviet people that capitalism—and by way of association, the United States—was not as bad as Soviet propaganda had claimed.[7] When Khrushchev's international ambitions as well as his confidence in Soviet socialism were put on display at the 1957 World Youth Festival in Moscow, the paradoxes of peaceful coexistence became remarkably clear. In the period from 1956 to 1958, the simultaneous goals of coexisting with the West, celebrating socialism, and controlling people's reactions to both, posed challenges to the Soviet system that only increased with time.

The Domestic Life of Peaceful Coexistence

Peaceful coexistence also had a domestic purpose. In order to implement the social projects he had planned, Khrushchev needed to divert resources from the Soviet war machine and thus advance the socialist economy and lifestyle at home.[8] In the post–Secret Speech era, Soviet citizens hoped for better times, and there were lively debates about social and cultural matters in intellectual circles, but the invasion of Hungary in late 1956 and the consequent hardening of policies in the Soviet Union and its satellite countries stalled prospects for fundamental changes, if only temporarily. Soviet authorities now dissuaded freedom of speech: the Secret Speech had been interpreted "too loosely," and Khrushchev started talking about Stalin's "appropriate place in Soviet history" in spite of his "great shortcomings."[9]

The Thaw, however, was already underway, and Soviet society saw slow but important changes in the coming years. Despite the damage done to Khrushchev's image abroad, he kept highlighting his wish for peaceful coexistence with the West and adamantly upheld the slogan of peace and friendship with other nations. In the aftermath of the Soviet invasion of Hungary, he magnified this image of himself as a crusader for peaceful coexistence. Under Khrushchev, the Soviet Union campaigned to establish itself as the leader of the "non-aggressive world"—and attempted to actualize this role by inviting, for example, world youth to Moscow in 1957 and pushing for meetings with American and Western leaders.

The Cold War historiography of the Khrushchev period has emphasized the initial willingness of the regime to reform itself and overcome the crimes of the Stalin era. What has become increasingly clear with the partial opening of Russian archives, however, is that the beginning of the cultural Thaw in the Soviet Union barely influenced the regime's tolerance of alternative political opinion. In fact, postwar political repression did not end with Stalin. A wave of political persecution in the wake of Khrushchev's Secret Speech, which peaked in 1957 and 1958, temporarily impeded the effects of the cultural Thaw. In this period alone, 3,764 Soviet citizens were convicted of anti-Soviet activity, a testimony to Khrushchev's attempt to reform the system of social control, without the terror of the Stalin era.[10]

Little research has been done on this phenomenon, and the historical memory has tended to brush over the political repression of the late 1950s. Remembered as a period of "liberal reform" in the Soviet Union, the late 1950s has only recently come in for revision[11] but a December 1956 decree of the Central Committee called for the intensification of political work and the elimination of anti-Soviet and harmful elements all over the Soviet Union.[12] This campaign followed a more relaxed period from 1953 to 1956, when the authorities sought to minimize repression and released large numbers of prisoners from the Gulag, and is yet another testimony to the exceptionality of the year 1955.[13] Interestingly, Papovian shows how the intensification of the anti-Soviet campaign in the late 1950s also marked the beginning of the transferring of the education role of the state to the population—in 1959, the state dramatically reduced political persecutions, but instead called upon the Soviet people to take responsibility for themselves—and others.[14]

This period, from after the Secret Speech until 1958, also saw the emergence of the term "public opinion" in Soviet parlance. In 1956, in the ten months from February until December, members of the literary (often reformist) intelligentsia had delved deeply into a critical discussion about Soviet society, encouraged by the Secret Speech. In December, Khrushchev put an end to further evolvement of this discussion by issuing a closed letter, entitled "Strengthening work of party organization in cutting off the attacks of anti-Soviet, enemy elements," and what followed was an intensified repression campaign.[15] This was in part a reaction to an emerging public opinion in the Soviet Union, and it is clear that Soviet authorities wanted to avoid this kind of challenge and did not want reformist discussions about Soviet society to get out of hand. According to the party, this type of discussion was considered non-socialist and an example of negative foreign influences.[16]

Therefore, the attention on anti-Soviet activity in 1957 and 1958 once again put focus on popular interest in the Cold War enemy. It is important to reiterate, however, that interest in the United States did not equal a rejection of the Soviet system, but rather that it was sometimes used as a point of reference when criticizing or doubting Soviet actions.[17] For example, the 1956 Soviet invasion of Hungary sparked strong reactions and even, in some cases, dreams of overthrowing the regime. A group of eighteen-year-old students in Kyrgyzstan tried to mobilize their fellow students:

> Comrade Students! Do not be frustrated. Let us organize an insurrection like the one in Hungary. We will win the big kids over to our side; students of various cities in the USA, England, and France will help us. Our stipend was illegally taken away. Anyone who wants to participate come to the square tomorrow at 12 noon. Do not think that this will be risky. No! It is the honest truth. Do not tell any of the teachers.[18]

The focus on renewed repression also brings out a well-known struggle for the Soviet authorities, namely how to deal with alternative sources of information. The Procuracy review files reveal that also in this period, foreign radio broadcasts were a popular source of information. A young student in Byelorussia allegedly listened to "anti-Soviet radio broadcasts from London at the time of the events in Hungary"[19] and also called out: "Comrades, slaughter as many communists as you can, so that soon there will be none. There will be America, and we will be with her."[20] During this time, pleas to America and to President Eisenhower were commonly cited in the review files, as the outcries from a forty-two-year-old Russian peasant who "threatened" the leaders of the party and government show.

He offered to "personally kill them all and leave for America." He had apparently come to Moscow in order to fulfill these actions and had "fifteen thousand people behind him" who would fulfill his mission if he failed. He ended by stating that "soon Eisenhower will come and put things in order."[21]

A Gulag inmate also held Eisenhower in high esteem, claiming that "soon the Americans will take our side and destroy the communists. Soon Eisenhower will be our father. We will be surrounded on all sides, and then all communists will be kaput. I will personally hang all the communists, and the people will destroy them."[22] In complaining about his felt boots, he said, "if these felt boots were on display in America, people would run a kilometer to get away from them. In America they also have felt boots, but only sixteen people in the Soviet Union have felt boots like the Americans do: the people in the Kremlin."[23]

According to the Procuracy review files, many people expressed contempt for the Soviet leadership and often used the propaganda slogans of the regime in expressing themselves. Surely, most Soviet people were well versed in propaganda slogans, as parades and official celebrations were embedded in the socialist value system. But imagine the dismay when a Soviet citizen cried out that "Truman is the only one capable of providing us with freedom!"[24] The cult of the leader was thus often turned inside out, as, for example, when a group of drunks allegedly shouted so that many people heard them:

> Long live Capitalism!
> Down with Communism!
> Down with Soviet power and down with Communism!
> Long live Eisenhower![25]

Many of the voices in the Procuracy review files echo statements about the United States from the late Stalin period. In the early Khrushchev period, an era that saw comparatively more optimism in Soviet society but has recently come under scrutiny for its repressive policies, the relationship with the American enemy was also central in terms of what kinds of activities and utterances were considered anti-Soviet.

The dilemma Khrushchev faced in terms of simultaneously coexisting with and controlling images of the West, was also clear in the way his regime dealt with dissent; increased student activism; ethnic, military, or religious social conflict; and the rise of public opinion, to name a few domestic issues.[26] In short, Khrushchev's will to reform the system was sincere, but so was the regime's repressive effort. In a way, then, the authorities overinterpreted the uprisings and riots of the period for a direct attack on the Soviet system.[27] In this regard, the Kremlin worried about "bourgeois" influence on the Soviet consciousness and acted out of fear.[28] In the midst of the Cold War conflict, therefore, the Soviet regime was not able to remove the American enemy from discussions of domestic reform, and for some people the Soviet tradition of thinking in opposites only accentuated the focus on the United States in this period. This was due in no small part to the renewed influx of American official propaganda, which shamelessly pushed for comparing and contrasting the communist and the capitalist systems. But alas, the renewed focus on America also contributed to the continued repression of anti-Soviet behavior.

Amerika and the Voice of America in Khrushchev's Soviet Union

One of the signs that the easing of official tensions in Soviet-American relations was real was improved and increased access to official American voices. The Central Committee announced that, as of October 22, 1956, *Amerika* would again be distributed in the Soviet Union, now in eighty-four cities. Simultaneously, *USSR* would go on newsstands across the United States. Fifty thousand copies of *Amerika* went on sale,[29] and the American embassy in Moscow had the right to freely distribute two thousand copies of the journal as it saw fit.[30] However, seemingly more tolerant than they had been only five years earlier, Soviet authorities still saw the legal publication as a threat to socialist values, using possession of *Amerika* against some of its citizens.

Such was the case of Viktor Mikhailovich Lukhin, born in 1930 near the city of Tver. He joined the army young and served in Moscow, but after Stalin died he moved to Barnaul, where he started studying at the Agricultural Institute. He got married to a fellow student. They shared the same values, read a lot, went to the movies, and actively participated in student life.[31] In his autobiography, he wrote how "everything was coming together nicer than it ever had," but "then came 1956, the year of the 'historic' Twentieth Congress of the CPSU." Lukhin described how in 1956, students began exchanging their opinions about domestic and international events. He himself was often vocal at student gatherings, advocating for a better dormitory and a student cafeteria, and criticizing the authorities for inertia and deception. Lukhin and his friends were clearly influenced by the events of 1956 and openly started expressing themselves more critically. In general, universities and academic institutions provided fertile grounds for such discussions and the Agricultural Institution in the Siberian town of Barnaul was no exception.

On March 9, 1957, however, Viktor Lukhin was arrested for anti-Soviet behavior on the grounds that for two years, from 1955 to 1957, he had actively spread anti-Soviet propaganda. His review file says that he was accused of having both verbally slandered the Soviet leadership and spread anti-Soviet brochures maligning the Soviet leadership and the Communist Party's international and domestic politics. Allegedly, he had also praised the quality of life and the "political order" in capitalist countries.[32] During a search, the police found two issues of the journal *Amerika,* and on one of them he had apparently written: "I bought this with the last money I had but I feel happy."[33] The police purported that, in conversations with students, he had praised American freedom of the press while pointing out that the Soviet media never published critical articles, and "if such an article appeared, its author would end up in prison and maybe even dead."[34]

In the 1990s, Lukhin became an intrepid advocate for repressed Soviet citizens, fighting for the stories of repression not to be forgotten. In his unpublished autobiography, he recounts how he had indeed bought the magazines, emphasizing how they were legally sold in kiosks. According to his account, the police were concerned that he had taken *Amerika* to his institute, showing it to students and "maligning Soviet realities while praising the economic and political quality of life of the American people." His interrogators were also interested in his "anti-Soviet views" on the events in Hungary.

In the wake of the 1956 Twentieth Party Congress, Viktor Lukhin had become something of a student activist, and this could have been enough to put him on the radar screen of Soviet security organs. But it is fascinating how prominent a role the journal *Amerika* played in both his own writings and in the files of the Soviet Procuracy. By reading the journal, showing it to students, and, allegedly, complaining about student life in the Soviet Union while praising the life of students in England and America, he only added to the police's suspicion of him as an anti-Soviet citizen. He repeatedly claimed that it was legal to buy the journal; he did not own up to having committed any anti-Soviet crime.[35] Viktor Lukhin's story shows that despite Soviet willingness to open up to the outside world, the authorities were not going to tolerate complete freedom of information inside the Soviet Union. That is crystallized in the paradox of simultaneously advocating for peaceful coexistence and arresting citizens for anti-Soviet behavior when they took advantage of available, legal information about the outside world.[36]

By all accounts, *Amerika* continued to be a rarity in the Soviet Union, so notwithstanding the renewed circulation of the journal, radio remained the main tool Americans had to spread propaganda in the Soviet Union. It is telling that while the Soviet government allowed *Amerika* back in circulation, American officials tried to no avail to get the Kremlin to cease jamming VOA broadcasts in 1956.[37] Voice of America music programs, however, were usually not jammed, which is why American jazz and later rock and roll were not unknown in the Soviet Union, but all programs that entailed "information" were jammed.[38] American voices describing the American way of life were considered dangerous and therefore silenced. It was much easier to limit the sales of *Amerika* than it was to control the reception of the broadcasts, and at least on the surface, jamming was a very effective type of control mechanism.

In line with the increased cultural contacts, A. N. Kuznetsov, a director at the State Committee for Cultural Relations with Foreign Countries, accepted an invitation in late December 1957 to visit the Voice of America offices in Washington and learn about its operation. Kuznetsov met with George Allen, the director of the United States Information Agency (USIA), at the Soviet embassy in Washington, who confirmed that Americans were deeply concerned about the one-sided and biased information the Soviet people received about the United States. He emphasized the importance of allowing the Voice of America to get through to its audiences and stressed that the USIA was willing to "change the tone of the American propaganda" if that would help. Kuznetsov was skeptical, however, as he felt Allen had not specified "how, on whose initiative, and under what circumstances this could be done."[39] During the meeting, the American side emphasized that Radio Moscow was easily heard in Washington, clearly appealing to the reciprocal tendency of Soviet diplomacy and expressing hope that the jamming of VOA would cease in the Soviet Union.[40]

In the coming years, the Soviet cultural administration slowly admitted that, in reality, jamming was not very effective in stopping foreign radio broadcasts from reaching the Soviet public. The radio broadcasting system in the Soviet Union, with both wired and wireless receivers, dictated that those with a wired set could listen only to domestic radio, but wireless sets, including short-wave radios, received foreign radio broadcasts as well. In the 1950s, Soviet production and ownership of short-wave radios increased multifold and almost reached the ownership of wired radios.[41] In 1958, the Central Committee estimated that more than twenty million short-wave radios were in circulation in the Soviet Union (as opposed to up to 200,000 before the war and 500,000 in 1949),[42] which in theory could give many more listeners to foreign radio broadcasts.

With the signing of the Soviet-American cultural agreement in January 1958, the Soviet side was forced to show some tolerance for the availability of American propaganda in the Soviet Union, as is evident in their discussions of a VOA Saturday evening program, "Life in America." The discussion concluded that the show's stories about quotidian American life were harmless.[43] In cooperation with the State Committee for Cultural Relations, the KGB declared that "Life in America" did not contain direct anti-Soviet propaganda and could thus be broadcast unjammed, even though it sometimes "takes on a provocative character."[44]

However, the Soviet authorities also discussed how they would "silence" the program if it took on an anti-Soviet character.[45] And A. Romanov, deputy head of the Department of Propaganda and Agitation in the Soviet Republics, recommended that the Soviet Union reciprocate with a similar show.[46] The State

Committee on Cultural Relations decided to launch a Soviet counterpart, "Life in the USSR," and broadcast it to America. It was sixty minutes long and also planned for prime-time Saturday broadcasts; the State Committee's chairman, Iurii (Georgii) A. Zhukov, said that it would be done "the way the USA does this in their special broadcast 'Life in America.' "[47]

The Central Committee continued to view foreign broadcasts, especially the VOA, as "hostile ideology," especially as it estimated that 85 percent of all short-wave radios were in the European part of the Soviet Union, where "our own broadcasts cannot be heard on short-wave and people can only listen to enemy radio."[48] Jamming, they said was not very effective: "Hostile radio can be heard all over the country, with the exception of the centers of Moscow, Leningrad, Kiev, Riga," and "even in separate areas of Moscow, Leningrad, Kiev and in their suburbs, the broadcasts of BBC, the Voice of America, and others are audible."[49] Apparently, enemy radio broadcasts were received all over the Soviet Union in spite of the costly jamming. Therefore, in addition to damaging the Soviet image abroad, as it so strongly suggested that it feared the "hostile" broadcasts, jamming also seemed to be ineffective in reaching its ultimate goal of preventing Soviet audiences from listening to and receiving information from foreign radio propaganda.[50]

Soviet authorities were still trying to control and limit the effects of American propaganda in the Soviet Union, but compared to the Stalin era, much more information about the outside world was now available. Not only was jamming not fully succeeding in preventing foreign radio broadcasts from reaching Soviet audiences, but the legal publication of the journal *Amerika* continued to worry Soviet authorities, especially as their own journal *USSR*, distributed in the United States, did not live up to their expectations. Interestingly, they turned to their (admittedly few) American friends for advice.

American fellow travelers had on occasion offered advice on how the Soviet Union should present itself to Americans, none more bluntly than Paul Robeson in his 1955 discussion of the "Negro Question." But the archives reveal several instances in which Soviet cultural officials asked their American friends for advice on how to best appeal to American audiences. Both in 1944 and later in 1956, the agreements on exchanging journals had included a Soviet counterpart to *Amerika*. Earlier named *Information Bulletin*, the Soviet journal was renamed *USSR* when publication started again in 1956. The Soviet side struggled with what to publish in *USSR* but decided that general stories about the life of Soviet people as well as pieces about famous Soviet writers, art, and music would interest American readers. They also decided to dedicate an issue to Marshal Georgy Zhukov, "whose name is popular in the USA," and focus on photographic material. [51] But once again, the Soviet cultural administration proved to be behind the times in its approach, and the content of *USSR* did not appeal to Americans.

To address this particular issue, the Soviet ambassador in Washington, DC, helped assemble a group of twenty Americans identified as "American readers of *USSR*." They met with the editor of *USSR*, Comrade Mamedov, on April 12, 1957, and shared their take on the journal, criticized it, and offered their opinions on how to develop future issues.[52] One of the Americans, Marcus Goldman, a Ph.D. in geology, had visited the Soviet Union in the 1930s and was considered to have "a progressive disposition." He advised the editor not to write so much about machines and technical issues: a recent article on a mechanic had been both shallow and uninteresting to Americans. Goldman suggested they publish more stories and poems and go more deeply and more professionally into cultural and scientific issues. He specifically criticized an article about popular Soviet scientific films, which he thought both superficial and poorly illustrated. An African-American mechanic, Clarence Martins, especially interested in articles about science and technology, also said that the articles were superficial and did not explain issues in detail. He admitted that his perception might differ from that of other readers who had less knowledge of technological issues, but he claimed that "more depth" would increase interest in the journal because "middle Americans have an adequate grasp of technology."[53]

Several of the reviewers also commented on how difficult it was to find the journal in the United States and noted the poor quality of the English translations.[54] The fact that Soviet authorities needed Americans to tell them to publish more articles on contemporary literature, art, films, and exotic places of interest in the Soviet Union—Moscow, Ukraine, and Georgia were regularly on the itineraries of foreign tourists and deemed adequately covered—and decorate it with color pictures is astonishing. The report concluded that all those present at the meeting had expressed the wish for a continued dialogue, and the editorial group was urged to think about planning similar meetings outside of Washington, DC.[55] Repeatedly, Soviet agitators reveal their amateurish methods and lack of understanding of their target audience, in this case American readers of *USSR*. On the one hand, it was smart of them to reach out, but on the other hand the results were just yet another indication of how inadequate Soviet cultural authorities felt in the propaganda war against the United States.

By 1958, the Soviet cultural administration had plenty of evidence to conclude that the Soviet strategy of promoting the country and socialist values to foreign audiences was not working. It had been clear for a long time that the front organizations were preaching to the converted, and while the Soviet Communist Party wanted to modernize the mission of promoting the image of the Soviet Union, it was simultaneously burdened with its need to "help" foreigners reach "correct" conclusions about socialism while controlling their own people's perceptions of the West. In addition to the numerous reports and memorandums that circulated in the cultural bureaucracy in the mid-to-late 1950s, no event of the 1950s illustrates the complexity of these paradoxical goals better than the Sixth World Festival of Youth and Students, held in Moscow in 1957.

A Celebration of the Socialist Way of Life

After Soviet tanks stormed Budapest in November 1956, the Soviet state had to work hard to convince both some of its own people and the outside world that the socialist reality was a worthwhile democratic and peaceful alternative. For this purpose, Soviet authorities embraced the 1957 World Youth Festival as an opportunity to show the rest of the world the bright future of socialism. What could possibly go wrong with displaying the happy faces of Soviet and international youth on the broad avenues of Moscow? Both the Soviet cultural bureaucracy and leadership were perfectly aware of the challenges this type of event created and thus they installed a strict system for maintaining public order during the festival. This was a balancing act for the Soviet authorities. On the one hand, they wanted to maintain exemplary public order throughout the event, but, on the other hand, a peaceful, socialist democracy could not appear too controlling. And certainly, Soviet efforts to monitor and control their guests' experiences were highlighted in the Western media as proof of a flawed system, but in spite of Soviet attempts to keep order, the festival had some unforeseen consequences for the socialist state.

Contrary to the Kremlin's expectations, the World Youth Festival in 1957, which was meant to show off the accomplishments of the socialist state, saw only partial success in that regard. Khrushchev's personal goal was to establish that the Soviet Union was an equal of the United States. The country might be lacking in the availability of consumer goods but was ahead in technology and education and should thus be taken seriously. Khrushchev knew very well that inviting foreigners en masse to the Soviet Union would entail opening up the country further to anti-Soviet elements, namely, "bourgeois ideology,"[56] but Khrushchev also realized that "Western perceptions of Soviet life were dominated by the image of downtrodden women engaged in manual labor and that visitors took home the impression of a backward and uncivilized country,"[57] and he wanted to correct that image.

The decision to host the World Youth Festival in Moscow was reached before the return to repressive measures in late 1956. Even though the organizers realized the risks it would entail to invite thousands of foreigners to Moscow, it was too late to back out.[58] The World Youth Festival was instead celebrated as an opportunity to showcase both the advancements of Soviet socialism and Khrushchev's commitment to peaceful coexistence with the West. Indeed, the festival provided the Soviet authorities with an excellent opportunity to display socialist values and is now a great case study for examining how the meaning of socialism was created, shared, shaped, and controlled in the Soviet Union.

With respect to the relationship with the United States, the Soviets' main Cold War rival decided to not officially acknowledge the World Youth Festivals. As soon as it was clear that the United States did not want to use this venue to compete for the attention of global youth, the World Youth Festivals did not have an impact on the superpower conflict per se. Rather, the context of the Cold War was important in that the Soviet Union knew that when hosting the festival in Moscow, it had to show the rest of the world that it was worthy of its status as one of two superpowers in the world, and thus enemy number one was omnipresent in the Soviet showcasing of socialist culture and progress as an alternative to Americanized Western modernity. Even if the United States did not acknowledge it, the World Youth Festival was also useful for American propaganda and the American press used it vehemently to advocate for their own anti-Soviet agenda, making it possible to see the festivals as a microcosm for the cultural Cold War between the superpowers.[59]

Western countries tried to send mixed delegations to the World Youth Festival in Moscow—mainly because of right-wing criticisms at home, which denounced the festival as an international propaganda scheme.[60] And surely they were right, for the Komsomol organizers wanted every guest to receive "propagandistic literature" about the successes of the Soviet Union and the life and work of Soviet youth. Emphasis was placed on the remarkable recovery of Soviet society from the horrors of the Second World War,[61] not for the sake of just the international guests, but also for domestic audiences, as Moscow was expecting more than 60,000 Soviet youth from all over the country in addition to about 34,000 foreign visitors.[62]

In 1956, the Committee of Youth Organizations of the USSR had issued an appeal to the youth of the Soviet Union calling for help,[63] and Soviet youth built stadiums and rail lines, painted and cleaned, planted millions of flowers, prepared concerts and phrase books, and made thousands of souvenirs to exchange with the foreign visitors upon arrival.[64] Pre-festivals took place all over the country, with the smallest festivals taking place in factories, on collective and state farms, and in schools, offices, and colleges. In May 1957, regional, territorial, and republican festivals began, with finals held in Moscow; the winners at the national festival finals represented the Soviet Union at the festival main contests.[65] Besides exceptional sportsmen and artists, those who had delivered "outstanding" work to advance society were also invited to participate in the festival. The official Soviet delegation comprised 3,719 participants, but an additional 60,000 Soviet youths came to the capital as "festival tourists."[66] Travel to the World Youth Festivals, at home or abroad, was always a reward for good service to the socialist state, and the prospect of travel provided encouragement for Soviet youth to work hard in all their voluntary activities.

In some ways, the World Youth Festival resembled earlier festivals and celebrations in the Soviet Union. Their objectives were multifold and often contradictory: the Soviet state wanted to strengthen relations between the people and the state but simultaneously sought to control and guide the population on how to behave. The masses were to march and display the power of Soviet socialism through physical manifestations and acclamations.[67] The World Youth Festival in Moscow, while similar in setup, presented several additional challenges to the organizers:[68] most important, the festival was meant to celebrate socialist accomplishments and not to institute a new Soviet culture or celebrate victory— the Soviet public had to appear convinced of Soviet socialism and its superiority as a governing system.

Sixth in a series of World Youth Festivals, the 1957 Moscow festival saw first-time participants from seventeen African, Asian, and Latin American countries, and it was the first time since 1947 that Yugoslavia participated in a World Youth Festival. Even though the organizers aimed at attracting non-European youth, Western youth eagerly took advantage of the opportunity to look behind the Iron Curtain and, for the first time since the Second World War, to interact with Soviet people on their own soil. Therefore, the Moscow Youth Festival had to appeal to foreigners, who had to be guided in how to experience and perceive the socialist way of life. For the first time, Soviet authorities were faced with the task of impressing a foreign audience on a mass scale on their home territory, and they invested much energy and organization in the event.

The task of presenting the Soviet Union as a progressive, nonaggressive, and democratic state was intertwined with an elaborate system of surveillance. The Soviet state and the Communist Party, clearly the leading actors in creating meaning in the Soviet Union, were also in charge of social control. Although the 1950s witnessed changes in many aspects, the systems of surveillance and social control did not see major modifications until 1959, when the Twenty-first Party Congress called for the creation of comrades' courts and people's volunteer squads (*druzhiny*), which were to "substitute organised social control for the courts and the regular police."[69] Until then, the Communist Party played a leading role in issues of social control in the Soviet Union and was thus the main actor in organizing, overseeing, and maintaining public order during the 1957 event.[70]

The Soviet Ministry of Internal Affairs (MVD) aimed at creating an ideal facade wherever foreign delegates passed through.[71] Toward this goal, homeless people, waifs, hooligans, and prostitutes were removed from Moscow, and prisons and temporary orphans' homes in Moscow were emptied so as to have plenty of space to put delinquents during the festival.[72] Not just Moscow, but towns along the railroads leading to Moscow, as well as cities delegates planned to visit, such as Leningrad, Minsk, Kiev, Odessa, Stalingrad, Sverdlovsk, and Tashkent, were to see strengthened security and makeshift restoration. The trains themselves, traditionally a relatively free space in the Soviet Union, also saw strict control—foreign delegates should not witness any deviation from socialist behavior and standards. Furthermore, all trains were to be equipped with radios that would broadcast the festival program and practical information about life during the event.[73] This was without doubt also a measure to show off not only technological progress but also the modern and democratic nature of the Soviet Union.

Soviet authorities realized from the beginning that it would take more than slogans about peace and friendship to show the superiority of the Soviet way of life. They needed tangible displays, and to that effect both the Lenin Stadium and the area around the All-Union Agricultural Exhibition (VSKhV) in the Ostankino district of Moscow were built to show off the cultural and technological advancements of the Soviet state.[74] More sport stadiums and swimming pools were built on the occasion, and the Komsomol undertook a monumental effort to create infrastructure for tourists in Moscow.[75] Foreigners were also to see a selection of factories, institutions, schools, and kindergartens in Moscow and Moscow Oblast. The places chosen as showcases were decorated especially well, and some of them produced informational brochures or films about their activities.[76] Sport was likewise a real instrument with which to show the strength of communism and the Soviet way of life; the Third International Youth Sports Games that coincided with the Moscow Youth Festival were an excellent tool to spotlight the aptitude of socialist athletes.

The focus on real accomplishments did not mean that slogans were not important during the festival. Indeed, the official slogan "for peace and friendship" was very successful if judged by memoirs and historical narratives of the event.[77] Early in 1957, the Soviet Ministry of Culture sent its recommendations for slogans to the Council of Ministers and a few suggestions for the themes and ways the slogans should be constructed. The slogans should, for example, neither be "one-sided" nor hard to understand.[78] Out of a list of forty-eight slogans that were suggested, eleven were marked as worthy of attention. Needless to say, all the suggested slogans dealt with peace, friendship, and youth's role in reaching the goal of a decolonized, peaceful world.[79]

As much as they could, the police monitored spontaneous interaction between Soviet citizens and foreigners. Early on, five foreigners exiting the Canadian Embassy approached an elderly Soviet woman (born in 1873) and offered her a ruble for bread. She answered that she did not need money and "lived better than they did."[80] Parroting the official propaganda was of course favorably looked upon; it was the impossible act of monitoring what went on behind the doors of private homes and hotel rooms that left the police perplexed, but not powerless.

In the course of several days, the police registered thirty instances of foreigners visiting Soviet homes and Muscovites entering hotel rooms of foreigners. Each case was reported to the KGB.

Out of fear of looking totalitarian, the police did not forbid foreigners to enter Soviet people's homes, but the police reported the incidents to the KGB, thereby making sure that there could potentially be consequences for the Soviet citizens involved.[81] Most often, it seems that Soviet citizens were driven by their curiosity about foreigners and wanted to mingle with them on normal terms. What went on behind closed doors was often unknown. A man in Kiev invited a couple of Norwegians into his home and spent "two hours hitting the bottle" with them.[82] A Soviet tenth grade student invited an Englishman to his apartment, "located in a basement room," where, accompanied by two other comrades, they "spent a long time talking."[83] The fact that it was a basement room was seemingly disconcerting—maybe because it was not what the authorities wanted to present as an ideal living space for a socialist way of life.[84]

Many Soviet people were concerned about presenting both the Soviet Union and socialism in the most positive light possible. On a bus tour to Tushino, delegates from Iceland and the Netherlands protested the planned tour to look at dams on the Moscow River, asking instead to see the construction activities in the town and to observe how the workers of Tushino lived.[85] Their guides declined the request and the tour proceeded as planned. Similarly, the police frowned upon (but were helpless against) uncensored photography and were dismayed when a French tourist staying at the Hotel Tsentralnaia repeatedly took photographs out of the shower room window of an unsightly courtyard filled with construction garbage.[86] Muscovites were especially protective of their city, and one city dweller expressed disappointment when an Austrian delegate photographed three houses with grass roofs, pointing out that it was "shameful to photograph only bad things."[87] In their final report about the festival, the police acknowledged the role of those Soviet citizens who had "actively helped the police in maintaining public order."[88] Surely, there were instances of Soviet citizens taking it upon themselves to correct or even punish detrimental behavior during the festival, but no issue got as much attention as the question of socialist morality and the decadent behavior of young Soviet people.

One of the most durable public memories of the festival is the recollection of female promiscuity.[89] Overall, 107 women were arrested for "promiscuous behavior" (*legkoe povedenie*) during the festival and, judging by the lasting impact of stories about promiscuous Soviet girls, this was an issue that touched a raw nerve among Soviet citizens, some of whom took it upon themselves to punish girls who had "associations" with foreigners. Take, for example, the story of a twenty-two-year-old Soviet woman who took several walks with a West German man she got to know at the festival. One time a girlfriend and her Italian male friend joined them on a walk, and that evening young Soviet men took the law in their own hands: "A number of Soviet youth told [the girls] what they thought about their conduct with the foreigners. Then they put them in a car, drove to the town of Babushkin, left the car, and sheared them (*postrigli ikh*)."[90]

Branding girls as promiscuous was not the mass phenomenon that the public remembered, and these rumors were "intimately related to broader social anxieties about female sexuality and the end to Soviet cultural isolation."[91] Societal fears of this sort are well documented in other cultures—foreign sailors in exotic ports have long been perceived as a threat to prudence and local masculinity, and local reactions often take on a heavily nationalistic character.[92] According to Soviet Cold War ideology, just as the national culture needed to be shielded from foreign infiltration, women need to be "protected" from seductive foreigners.[93] Whether the arrest of 107 women indicates that female promiscuity really was a mass phenomenon remains irrelevant. Rather, these rumors were symptomatic of a greater problem—namely that the free intermingling of Soviet and foreign youth was worrisome and the effects of the dancing in the street caused concern among those charged with maintaining social—and socialist—order in Moscow and the Soviet Union.

In 1956, Soviet authorities had already expressed their worries about the weak ideological-political training of Soviet youth—suggesting that youth was rarely exposed to

> lectures, reports, and conversations about the successes and accomplishments of the Soviet people in building communism, about the advantages of the socialist system over the capitalist system, about patriotism, proletarian internationalism, about the advantages of vigilance and the rearing of a great social discipline.[94]

According to the report, party organizations were not giving the students enough guidance—leaving the education role to organizations such as houses of culture and youth clubs, where the youth preferred spending their evenings "dancing to jazz." As an example, they cited how a group of engineering students had organized a get-together and the youth spent the night (11 P.M.–6 A.M.) drinking and dancing to jazz with "solely Western dances."[95] The Komsomol worked hard against Western influences in the early Khrushchev era, launching an anti-*stiliagi* campaign in August 1955 with the aim of exposing and alienating youth they deemed too "westernized."[96] It should thus not have come as a surprise that some Soviet youth jumped at the opportunity to establish contacts with foreigners. While interest in the West had thrived among the *stiliagi* since the end of the Second World War, the post–Secret Speech atmosphere paved the way for the emergence of an "independent youth culture."[97] By the late 1950s, it was difficult to distinguish Soviet *stiliagi* from foreigners, and this suggests that the subculture had become relatively mainstream—youth as such was now an easily identified group with relatively universal ideas about fashion and popular music.[98]

The youth did not gather in the streets and parks of Moscow only to dance, sing, perform, and hold hands;[99] they were also interested in discussions about political and social topics. Predictably, the Soviet organizers planned anti-Western discussions on NATO and colonialism, but they were not always successful in shaping the conversation according to their wishes. The main topic the Soviet authorities were sensitive about was, of course, the turmoil in Eastern Europe, particularly in Hungary, and much effort was made to show that the Eastern European delegations were all favorably disposed toward the Soviet state. There was considerable anxiety that the Hungarian delegation might include some disloyal youth; several Hungarians without invitations to the festival were sent back at the border.[100] Any sort of behavior from the Hungarian youth that could possibly be interpreted as anti-Soviet was also reported, such as when a group of delegates on their way to Moscow dubbed Soviet girls in a dance ensemble "cows" in Hungarian.[101]

Later during the festival, when delegates from England and Hungary took a boat tour together, the English youth openly expressed their opinions about Eastern Europe: "They said that in the socialist bloc, there is allegedly no authentic, real freedom, and workers live at a low level." Apparently, the Hungarians tried to correct "the falsehood of their views," and the English had then "recognized the accomplishments of the socialist countries and their peaceful nature." The Soviets were dismayed that the English would "provoke" the Hungarians, who expressed "only friendly feelings" in relation to the Soviet Union, but they were relieved when everyone walked away talking about peace and friendship—the main goals of the festival itself.[102]

Most of the meetings between delegations were peaceful and friendly. The police reported on a few anti-Soviet incidents but, judging from the reports, they seem not to have done much more than to note incidents of anti-socialist behavior. Soviet authorities realized that the festival would increase the risk of unmonitored interaction between Soviet citizens and foreigners and that, no matter how extensive the measures taken, an assembly of one hundred thousand youth was bound to produce unforeseeable results. As the poet Yevgeni Yevtushenko remembered: "For the first time in my life, my socialist lips touched so-called 'capitalist lip[s]' because I kissed one American girl, breaking any Cold War rules. Not only me, many of my friends, . . . [were] doing the same . . . on the streets of Moscow, in all the parks."[103] The youth celebrated their relative freedom during the festival and not just "Cold War rules" but also the rules of socialist public order were broken in many regards, but even this is not that surprising—the astonishing thing is that the police let most of these interactions go on undisturbed.

The police watched and reported on deviant behavior all they could, but in the majority of cases they refrained from interfering.[104]

The police were, however, much more worried about "speculation," and, even before the event, they had arrested several people they suspected of planning to buy foreign products at the World Youth Festival.[105] During the festival, the police tried to control the trading of foreign goods by setting up controlled trading points (*skupochnye punkty*) outside of the main hotels where foreigners were staying. The guests quickly got down to business and, during the last two days before the festival began, on July 26 and 27, they had already sold various products, ranging from suits, underwear, pieces of cloth, and wristwatches, valued at 240,000 rubles. The majority of these products belonged to the Finnish and Polish delegations—a Finnish delegate sold 817 Pallas wristwatches at 270 rubles each and many Omega wristwatches.[106]

Most of the action was reported to have happened in the neighborhood of Vladykino, where many foreign delegates were staying. According to police documents, delegates from Poland, Finland, and Norway dominated these trading points. The dealers seemingly got good prices for their items (and sometimes their personal belongings):[107] 305 woolen sweaters went for 150 rubles each, 200 plastic raincoats for 65 rubles. A Swedish delegate sold 180 pairs of nylons for 25 rubles, while an Italian got 35 rubles for each of his 35 pairs of nylons.[108] Overall, 2,302,259 rubles changed hands at these legal trading points at the festival (July 24–August 11), and hundreds of pairs of jeans, nylons, and various toiletries were now in the hands of Soviet citizens.[109]

Black-marketeering also flourished during the festival. The police reported several instances of Soviet citizens obtaining things from foreigners—and sometimes trying to resell them. Upon return to her hometown of Ruza, a Russian girl who had been courted by a Hungarian during the festival sold gifts he had given her and was reported to the KGB.[110] The police cited students of higher-education institutions as the most active in illegally obtaining things from foreigners—on August 6 alone, fifteen students (at least two of whom were Komsomol members) were detained for buying items from foreigners.[111] In most cases, the students were reprimanded and reported to their Komsomol chapter—correspondingly, factory workers were reported to their party cell.

Another thirty-nine people were detained on August 8 and 9 for buying goods from foreigners, among them students, workers, and Komsomol and Communist Party members. In these cases their permits to visit Moscow were confiscated and "administrative actions" were taken.[112] As the festival went on, more and more foreigners seemed to have caught on to the great demand for goods, and the police repeatedly intervened when foreigners set up shop on the streets close to the legal trade points. They noted how they "touted buyers" and "outbid each other" in selling watches, toiletries, glasses, combs, towels, and other things.[113]

"I wonder if Khrushchev realizes what he is risking," a member of the Polish delegation in Moscow told American *Life* correspondent Flora Lewis in 1957.[114] If, as Lewis speculated, the 1956 "unrest" in Eastern Europe was mostly due to the Warsaw Festival of 1955, the Soviet authorities should have been more worried about the consequences of the youth celebrating in Moscow. The Soviet organizers were clearly concerned: pondering whether to organize regional meetings during the festival, they stated that while they might be of use, "they should certainly not be organized the way they were in Warsaw. No *mass* meeting, but a smaller *Forum* for *debate. No resolutions!*"[115] Not surprisingly, many Soviet participants later assessed the Moscow festival as a kind of turning point in the development of their own view of the world.[116] The contact with another culture, the very idea of having consumer choices, which was reflected in a wide variety of styles, contrasted sharply with the monotony of official Soviet consumer products.

Interestingly, the Komsomol worried about the potential isolation of Soviet youth, stating that "politically" it would not be advisable to keep them apart from the foreign guests. It tried to make sure that the communist youth intermingled "normally" with other delegations. At the same time, the Komsomol hoped to be able to control these interactions—they arranged for special meetings with "certain people" who would provide "concrete information" about specific, predetermined questions.[117] The Komsomol also concluded that it would be "erroneous and politically incorrect" if the communist youth were not more visible among the participants,[118] for the Kremlin was slowly realizing the power of personal contact. It turned out that members of the Soviet delegation did not socialize enough with foreigners during the festival—at least they did not carry their Komsomol pins and were thus not recognizable as official delegates. The authorities had no choice but to trust the youth's commitment to the Soviet state and encourage them to mingle normally at the festival, but as always, they were apprehensive about unwanted influences.

It is hard to judge the impact of the festival, but in psychological warfare interaction with people is always the most useful weapon. The evidence suggests that, at least partly, the outcome of the festival was not the outcome Soviet authorities anticipated. As Flora Lewis reported: "The easy camaraderie permitted for the festival surprised visitors but left Russians breathless with a taste of forgotten freedom." It seemed that "the sheer presence of foreigners made more impression than their words. Wherever delegates appeared, the Russians thronged—to see how they dressed, how they chattered and laughed, how they sang, how they danced, how they flirted."[119] The Soviet authorities were obviously concerned about the presence of foreigners in their country, but they had to accept the fact that foreigners talked to Soviet citizens. It was in their interest to appear open to a dialogue about Soviet accomplishments and therefore they encouraged personal contacts, in the hope that Soviet youth would proudly defend the socialist motherland.

After the festival, the organizers presented city authorities with a list of questions that were frequently asked during the festival. The questions all had to do with the way of life in Moscow: How had the construction of housing changed after the Twentieth Party Congress? How much did people pay for an apartment? Why were there residential buildings in industrial neighborhoods? How much did a car cost in Moscow? Why did underwear and ready-made dresses cost so much in the Soviet Union? How much did a television set cost and how many TVs were there in Moscow? Why were there so few cafes in Moscow? Why did women do hard labor in the Soviet Union? Does Moscow offer "'variety shows' . . . with girls?"[120] Much to the Kremlin's dismay, many foreigners were thus more interested in understanding the living standards of Soviet people than in viewing displays of technological advancements.

As early as 1957, however, it became clear that Soviet leaders had underestimated the power of the cultural Cold War and the role living standards, convenience, leisure, and fashion were to play in it. While Khrushchev himself would have preferred to make outer space the playing field of the Cold War, as there the Soviet Union was a player of superpower status, the Cold War of the late 1950s boiled down to issues of consumerism and living standards.[121] By promising improvements in housing and lifestyles to the Soviet people, Khrushchev himself was partly to blame for the attention these issues got at the Youth Festival. The authorities realized that, in the end, the sound of rock and roll, the look of abstract canvases, and the softness of "capitalist lips" would tempt Soviet youth more than they themselves could impress the rest of the world with slogans declaring peace and friendship. For the sake of keeping up appearances, they— for the most part—tolerated the dancing in the streets of Moscow. As a majority of the participants were already leaning to the left politically, the planners could be happy just to have the guests confirm their interest and belief in the system, because the World Youth Festivals failed in its main goal of attracting global mass support for the Soviet project. Quite the opposite, hosting world youth in Moscow had increased interest in foreign cultures and allowed for a Soviet discovery of difference.

Conclusion

In the context of both the cultural Cold War and Khrushchev's focus on peaceful coexistence, the relationship with the United States was of vital importance for the Soviet Union. At the Moscow Youth Festival, the failure of the Soviet state to come up with a strategy to appeal to global audiences became apparent. In the mid-1950s, the American way of life was slowly turning into a global phenomenon and the socialist way of life was, as always, defined as the opposite of Western capitalist lifestyles. As a consequence, the Soviet side found itself struggling more than ever before to find a balance between the increased exposure to the United States and the ongoing control of images and perceptions of America in the Soviet Union. Selling peaceful coexistence as believable to an audience that had for over a decade considered war with America inevitable may seem like a difficult project, but the steps taken to increase interactions with the outside world on both the cultural and political level in the mid-to-late 1950s show how the strategy of peaceful coexistence started to take on tangible meaning in the Soviet Union.

Already in 1960, Frederick C. Barghoorn rightfully warned against exaggerating the meaning of interest in America:

> Interest in American comforts and luxuries should not [...] be interpreted as indication of a lack of pride and patriotism on the part of Soviet people. They are determined to have these luxuries themselves, and some of them may share the Kremlin's professed confidence that before many decades have passed the Soviet Union will actually outproduce even the United States, at first in heavy industry and possibly, eventually, in the field of consumers' goods.[122]

One of the mistakes the Kremlin made was to allow interest in America to become a threat to its policies and reforms. On the one hand, the admission that the Soviet Union lagged behind was an important one. Rallying Soviet people around the future goal of overtaking and surpassing America, as Khrushchev did in 1957, was in line with suggestions from various Soviet participants recounted here about what they could learn from the United States and how to improve the Soviet mission. But on the other hand, limiting access to and controlling interest in American propaganda created a paradox that only grew with increased contacts.

Although it is impossible to determine how many people read *Amerika* or listened to American radio broadcasts, the official reaction to these media and their efforts in trying to limit and eliminate them speak volumes about the perceived impact of American propaganda in the Soviet Union. Under Khrushchev, the political atmosphere underwent dramatic changes in the mid-1950s, but there were certain continuities in the way that Soviet authorities perceived their success in representing themselves to Americans, at home and in the United States. Throughout the years, the feeling of not reaching enough people became more pressing and lack of means to publicize the mission only increased, especially as

McCarthyism was no longer an obstacle. They tried, though, as we have seen, to present the Soviet Union as a land of abundance, well on its way to the construction of communism. But their means were limited and the methods too primitive for these events to have the effect the authorities wanted. Thus, the struggle to reconcile more exposure to American values with the strict ideological mission of the Soviet state grew sharper.

THE POSSIBILITIES OF PEACEFUL COEXISTENCE, 1958–1959

Khrushchev showed much more nuance in his understanding of world politics than Stalin, who had seen the Cold War as a prelude to another great war—this time against America—and cultivated a strong fear of a renewed conflict among the war-torn Soviet population. Drawing on Lenin's early NEP-era pronouncements, Khrushchev stated that a war between the imperialist and the socialist camps was not inevitable—they were capable of competing and coexisting at the same time.[1] In Khrushchev's version, as in Lenin's, socialism would indeed prevail, but when Khrushchev took armed conflict out of the equation he also removed the fear of another war—much to the relief of Soviet citizens.

Although the invasion of Hungary in November 1956 caused a setback in international relations, too much was at stake to allow the revival of Soviet-American friendly relations to fade out, and in 1958 an official agreement on which future official cultural exchanges were based became a reality.[2] In 1958, therefore, peaceful coexistence was taking on a very real form, but as became clear from Khrushchev's relationship with the West after the Secret Speech at the Twentieth Party Congress in 1956, coexisting with the United States also brought a unique set of problems domestically. For example, by emphasizing housing and the improvement of the everyday realities, increased interaction with foreigners put focus on the issues of consumerism and image control, which proved sensitive for the Soviet Union. Nevertheless, advocating for cultural exchanges while also helping the Soviet and the American people reach "correct conclusions" about each other came to be the essence of Khrushchev's cultural policy toward the United States in the late 1950s.

The intensity of Soviet cultural relations with the United States in the late 1950s reached its climax in 1959 with Khrushchev's visit to his rival country, an event that the Soviet side at the time saw as a "turning point" in Soviet-American cultural relations.[3] Like the

Moscow Youth Festival in 1957, the main goal of the visit was to advertise and celebrate the accomplishments of the Soviet Union, only now the focus group was the American public, so conspicuously absent in Moscow two years earlier. However, as in 1957, Khrushchev's American visit made a strong impression on the Soviet public, which enthusiastically responded to the trip in the name of improved international relations. Many Soviet people celebrated the newfound openness with the West because they hoped it would bring their living standards up to the level of the United States. But more than anything, in 1958 and 1959, both Soviet official rhetoric and popular attitudes were focused on the potential for the two superpowers to peacefully coexist. Both sides denounced the fear of another war that was cultivated in each country and assured the other that nobody wanted a new war. Given the prominence of such rumors in the postwar Soviet Union, it was certainly an important change in the official image of America to emphasize cooperation and coexistence with enemy number one. While the Soviet people remembered positive appraisals from the 1920s and 1930s about the United States when its industrial output was "a goal and standard of measurement,"[4] removing the fear of a new war was extremely successful in reinforcing people's faith in the Soviet international project. Focusing on the alliance brought attention to a period of successful cooperation, which in turn brought about relief among the population and increased the self-assurance of Soviet cultural organizations. Therefore, as many Soviet people expressed immense relief at not having to worry about a war between the superpowers, in 1958 and 1959 peaceful coexistence seemed meaningful as an international ideology.

Soviet-American Cultural Exchanges

Early in the summer of 1957, before the Moscow Youth Festival took place, Khrushchev started advocating publicly for an official cultural exchange agreement with the United States. He felt that the conclusion of such an agreement would confirm the Soviet Union's superpower status on a par with the United States, and he believed in the Soviet Union's ability to show off its accomplishments. By taking the initiative, Khrushchev also used this as a way of exerting control on the international arena; intertwined with all of this was his continued emphasis on peaceful coexistence.[5] Khrushchev pushed for the agreement even though it was becoming increasingly clear that competing with America was making Soviet socialism vulnerable to increased comparisons with Western capitalism. Nevertheless, Khrushchev was prepared to take this chance in order to correct impressions abroad of the Soviet Union as a backward country.[6]

The American authorities did not immediately jump on Khrushchev's offer to broker an official exchange agreement, but late in 1957 they agreed to start discussions, which lasted for three months and resulted in the Zarubin-Lacy Agreement of January 27, 1958.[7] Officially called the "Agreement between the United States of America and the Union of Soviet Socialist Republics on Exchanges in the Cultural, Technical, and Educational Fields," it entailed exchanges in multiple fields, such as science, technology, agriculture, radio and television, film, government, publication, tourism, and exhibitions. The agreement was a first of its kind for the US State Department, which had been sending delegations to the Soviet Union since 1957, and the Soviet side saw it as a marked success for its policy of peaceful coexistence.[8]

The Soviet cultural bureaucracy was prepared to take on the planning and execution of official cultural exchanges. Almost immediately after Stalin's death, his heirs in the party had created a Department for Ties with Foreign Communist Parties, which took over control of VOKS. This change meant that party control over VOKS was no longer a secret.[9] In 1957 and 1958, the Kremlin revolutionized the administrative structure of cultural relations with foreign countries, which led to a major reorganization of VOKS. VOKS had a reputation for being a "cover for police networks and state control" and, according to Eleonory Gilburd, the main impetus for this change was decentralization.[10] During a conference in Moscow on February 17–18, 1958, VOKS was discontinued and SSOD, or the Union of Soviet Societies for Friendship and Cultural Relations with Foreign Countries, was formally established.[11]

The new format assumed that each country would have a special friendship society on the Soviet side, with prominent Soviet cultural figures in charge of the meetings. The purpose of this change was to put more weight on domestic work and to counter perceptions of the friendship societies as powerless puppets of the Kremlin catering only to foreign fellow travelers. Recently, scholars have pointed out how, in the beginning, SSOD officials emphasized their intention to conduct "personal relations with foreigners,"[12] indicating that "ordinary people" and personal exchanges were better equipped to invoke positive images than official Soviet propaganda. This focus on "ordinary people" caught on in the media and lasted throughout the year 1959 but was ultimately abandoned, as the cultural bureaucracy was overwhelmed with responses from private individuals who wanted to participate in this project, asking for pen pals. Soviet archives contain many of these types of requests (also from Americans) and remain a solid testimony to the positive responses to this new strategy of opening up to the outside world. However, the Soviet bureaucracy had no way of controlling this type of interaction and nothing came of it.[13]

Another important change under Khrushchev was the establishment on March 4, 1957, of the State Committee for Cultural Relations with Foreign Countries (GKKS) under the aegis of the Council of Ministers.[14] GKKS was active for ten years, until 1967, with Iurii (Georgii) A. Zhukov as its first chairman.

This organization was meant to give cultural relations a more official look: now an all-union organ took the lead in the area of cultural cooperation with foreign countries, coordinating the activities of ministries and organizations.[15] One of the earliest observers of Soviet cultural diplomacy in the 1950s, Frederick C. Barghoorn, speculated that this change clearly showed how the Soviet side placed increased importance on the issue of cultural relations in Soviet foreign policy. More important, the establishment of a governmental agency on the Soviet side also made it possible for the Soviet cultural bureaucracy to deal with Western agencies such as the American State Department's East-West Contacts Staff at an official level.[16] Despite its organizational place with the Council of Ministers, however, GKKS was always in close cooperation with the Central Committee of the Communist Party, and in the remaining Khrushchev era, GKKS also worked closely with the Committee for State Security (KGB). It is therefore not unlikely that the Soviet authorities created the State Committee as a state body for external appearances.[17]

In 1958, however, with the signing of the Soviet-American cultural exchange treaty, it became clear that this change in the structure had been a necessary step in the process. Private individuals, mainly the Russian-born and New York–based impresario Sol Hurok but also Carlton Smith, director of the American National Arts Foundation, had worked since the mid-1950s to receive Soviet artists and performers in the United States, and arrange for American entertainers and performance companies to visit the Soviet Union. In addition to the original success of 1955, with, for example the Everyman Opera Company performing in front of large crowds in the Soviet Union and pianist Emil Gilels, and violinist David Oistrakh visiting the United States, many artists visited each country in the following years. The Boston Symphony Orchestra traveled to the Soviet Union in 1956, as did Isaac Stern, the world-famous violinist.[18] Rockwell Kent's 1957–1958 exhibition at the Pushkin Museum of Fine Arts was extremely popular,[19] as were the musical performances of the New York Philharmonic in 1959.[20] The American government had sponsored, at least partly, about half of these events,[21] but the formal exchange agreement brought with it new channels for cultural exchanges and radically changed Soviet-American interactions and the possibility of controlling images of the other.[22]

The year 1959 was the one that finally saw the establishment of a Soviet-American Friendship Society at SSOD in Moscow, but it kept a relatively low profile.[23] The GKKS was still in charge of maintaining the formal relationship with the US State Department, and the American department at SSOD, like VOKS earlier, kept in touch with the pro-Soviet American Russian Institutes in Chicago, San Francisco, and New York. Much of SSOD's work was on how to improve the image of the Soviet Union, at home and in the United States, but

SSOD was also interested in bringing American culture to the Soviet Union. In April 1959, Lydia Kislova, chief of the American department at SSOD, wrote to the painter Rockwell Kent, then chairman of the National Council of American-Soviet Friendship (NCASF), and asked him to recommend "novels and stories published recently in the USA for our library and probably for the translation into Russian for one of our goals is to acquaint the Soviet public with the American literature so highly estimated [esteemed] in our country."[24] Asking the NCASF for recommendations on American literature was of course a safe strategy, as it would certainly endorse only "appropriate" works of American literature for the Soviet audiences. The cultural exchange agreement, however, made sure that the American government now also had a say in the kinds of American culture available to Soviet audiences, and these years surely saw an influx of American artists, performers, tourists, academics, and students.

While hosting more and more Americans, the Soviet side remained deeply concerned about the widespread lack of interest in the Soviet Union they encountered in the United States. As America recovered from the damage inflicted by the communist witch-hunts upon its popular moods and opinions toward communism in general, Soviet authorities still had to work against strong anti-Soviet currents to get ordinary Americans interested in their country. In 1957, Zhukov reported that the Soviet embassy in Washington was concerned about the increased attacks on America in the Soviet press, as the American press was starting to report stories about them. After the *Washington Post* published an article by William Benton in August titled "What Ivan Thinks of Us," the embassy proposed to hold a press conference in order to correct the story and tell Americans what the Soviet public really knew about America. William Benton was no stranger to information activities; he was the founder of the US information offices and initiated the Voice of America broadcasts in his time at the State Department after the Second World War. Later, in his capacity as chairman of the Encyclopedia Britannica he was passionate about decreasing American ignorance of the Soviet other; he visited the Soviet Union often in the 1950s and 1960s and was well informed about the state of affairs in the country. On behalf of the State Committee for Cultural Relations, however, Zhukov decided against a press conference refuting Benton's article, arguing that the Americans would use such a meeting in order to justify their criticism of the Soviet state.[25]

A 1958 directive from the Soviet delegation to the United Nations in New York reported on the main problems Soviet cultural diplomats had to fight in the United States. Anti-Soviet propaganda was everywhere: "every hour on radio and in television, every day in film and the periodical press, every month and every year sees the publication of anti-Soviet books and numerous speeches and lectures about the Soviet Union."[26] According to the report, American anti-Soviet propaganda emphasized five themes: the absence of genuine democracy in the USSR; the shortage of consumer goods; deviations from the principles of Marxism in the practical building of socialism in the USSR; the foreign policy of the Soviet Union; and, finally, the use of the fine arts in propaganda.[27] Young Americans, according to Soviet diplomats, were convinced of the superiority of American-style democracy and repeatedly pointed to lack of freedom of speech, freedom of the press, and general democracy in the Soviet Union.

Nevertheless, the American press and population admired Soviet success in technology and in rebuilding the postwar economy. Since the *Sputnik* satellite launch in 1957, this admiration was mixed with fearful respect, but the media used the shortages of consumer goods to belittle these accomplishments: "American satellites may be only the size of an orange and Soviet citizens may have more satellites but the American people have enough oranges and other fruits in abundance."[28] Khrushchev had used this metaphor about American satellites being only the size of an orange to ridicule American accomplishments in outer space, but the American press found a way to turn it against him. Soviet officials worried that in the United States, people generally held the opinion that Soviet people were "poorly dressed, badly nourished, and live in bad apartments.... They keep saying that unemployed people in the United States live better than workers in the Soviet Union."[29]

It is clear that the Kremlin had high expectations of the official cultural agreement and expected it to provide better access to information about the Soviet Union in the United States. Thus, the Soviet delegation to the United Nations in New York recommended in 1958 that the general effort of Soviet propaganda in the United States should focus on the "exposure of false arguments," such as when the American media unfairly belittled Soviet accomplishments in outer space by pointing to Soviet shortages. The means and the methods to fight the American propaganda machine on its home territory, however, were limited. Although Radio Moscow broadcasts were available in the United States, few American listeners tuned in or even had the possibility of receiving the broadcasts. Instead, Soviet officials lamented, the 39 million television sets in the United States and the countless radios constantly broadcast anti-Soviet materials with the "methods of American advertising." The Soviet representatives judged that repetition seemingly was very effective in getting the anti-Soviet message through to ordinary Americans.[30] Soviet sources repeatedly emphasize the power of film and television as a way of reaching the American public: as early as 1955, writer Boris Polevoi had proposed an American film festival in the Soviet Union and a Soviet festival in the United States.[31] With the exchanges, however, there was finally an opportunity to expand the media focus of Soviet propaganda in the United States.

In the summer of 1958, when the report was written, the number one book on the *New York Times* best-seller list was John Gunther's *Inside Russia Today*, followed by J. Edgar Hoover's tale of American communists, *Masters of Deceit: The*

Story of Communism in America and How to Fight It. Milovan Djilas's *The New Class: An Analysis of the Communist System,* in which he criticized the communist system based on his experience as a member of the Central Committee of the Yugoslav Communist Party, was also much advertised and, according to the report, many other "anti-Soviet books" on subjects such as the Gulag were prominently displayed in American bookstores.[32] The Soviet representatives to the United Nations argued, however, that their responses to anti-Soviet books such as *Inside Russia Today* were not issued quickly enough. They should also publish many more books in foreign languages: "it would be most effective if we were to publish a book called *Inside America Today,* illuminating all the questions raised by Gunther in his book, but apply them to American realities."[33] Earlier, Polevoi had reported that there was great shortage of Soviet books in the United States. He also mentioned the issue of royalties and suggested that the government should pay several progressive authors their royalties as a way of supporting their continued writings.[34] The issue of royalties came up repeatedly in discussions about improving Soviet-American cultural relations, and it was a sensitive point for the Soviet authorities, who ignored international treaties on copyright and royalties and only sporadically and unpredictably paid American authors and publishers for the translation and publishing of their works.[35]

The report praised the propaganda efforts of Soviet cultural delegations but recommended the more effective use of visiting delegations.[36] The report writers speculated that it would be beneficial to include "a Jewish number" in their ensembles, as "many Jews live in America and often they hold influential positions." This, they claimed, would be seen positively in the United States, as American propaganda "often states that anti-Semitism prevails in the USSR." But more generally, they urged that all invitations to Soviet artists to perform in the United States should be accepted, since such performances generally got much attention among the American public.[37] The report was right on target; as of 1958 various folk ensembles and Soviet ballet troops performed to sold-out audiences and received very positive reviews in the United States. However, as the great success of the Bolshoi's first-ever American tour in 1959 showed, the American praise was focused on the artistic value of the performances; to the regret of Soviet cultural officials, Soviet ideology did not seem to rub off on American audiences.[38]

Thus, in spite of the general success of Soviet cultural delegations, the report from the UN delegation concluded that the delegates needed to be better prepared for the kinds of critical questions they would encounter in the United States. Apparently, "very often Americans pose provocative questions . . . their own propaganda makes fools of them and they do not think in terms outside of this propaganda." As examples of the subjects of sensitive questions that needed to be clarified in advance, the report writers mentioned the "era of Stalinism," the freedom of expression in the USSR, and the invasion in Hungary in 1956, and they concluded: "Avoiding answering such questions leaves a very bad impression and can be used to the advantage of American propaganda."[39] This was always a difficult issue, as Soviet delegates considered it rude of their hosts to ask questions that challenged the nature of the Soviet system. But echoing Boris Polevoi's 1955 report, more and more such pleas were coming through the Soviet cultural bureaucracy, which understood that avoiding sensitive topics and not countering misinformation was damaging to the Soviet image. The ideological answer was peaceful coexistence, which made it possible for the Soviet cultural officials to celebrate earlier successes of the Soviet-American relationship and increase respect for the Soviet Union as a superpower with a Cold War agenda, at least for a few years.

In 1958, shortly after the successful signing of the Soviet-American exchange agreement, but in the shadow of alarming events in the Middle East, Adlai Stevenson, two-time presidential candidate of the Democratic Party (in 1952 and 1956), visited the Soviet Union. Stevenson traveled as a tourist, so his travels were not a part of cultural exchange per se; nonetheless, his visit shows that in representing Khrushchev's Soviet Union, Soviet cultural officials now tried to fulfill the wishes of the travelers and did not systematically avoid sensitive sights and topics. Moreover, his writings about the trip show how pervasive the new ideological approach to the American enemy was getting.

The Soviet Union that Stevenson visited was a very different place from Stalin's postwar Soviet Union that John Steinbeck had visited in 1947, and, at first glance, the two men had little in common, one being a career politician and the other a left-wing writer. What they did have in common, however, was their long-term interest in the Soviet Union and the fact that both of them had visited the Soviet Union before the Second World War.[40] Both of them wrote articles about their postwar trips that were later published in book form (with photographs), and both visits left a long paper trail in Russian archives as Soviet cultural authorities reported on their daily activities and their "sputniks," or Soviet traveling companions, speculated on the course of their actions.[41]

Published eleven years apart, Steinbeck's *A Russian Journal* and Stevenson's *Friends and Enemies: What I Learned in Russia* are both fascinating reads, and not surprisingly, they are both as much about the people doing the travel as about the destination. The books are riddled with age-old cultural stereotypes, as both authors were searching for an understanding of not just the enemy, but also the way the enemy sees them. What is so remarkable is that even if these two visits took place at completely different times—one in the late Stalin era and the other during the climax of Khrushchev's openness to the West—the different contexts had little or no impact on the conclusions Steinbeck and Stevenson reached in their respective works, indicating that the American Cold War image of the Soviet Union was resistant to change. Still, compared to Steinbeck's 1947 experience, Stevenson's account illustrates some of the changes in exposure and treatment that came with the Khrushchev era, while it is also a testimony to the persisting power of Soviet ideology.

Adlai Stevenson traveled to the Soviet Union with two of his sons and a group of friends. He prepared well for all of his destinations, and he was especially interested in getting to know the Soviet republics in Central Asia. Stevenson's "collection of brief reports" about his journey through the Soviet Union were first published in the *New York Times* and then came out in book form. He claimed that his reason for writing the reports was curiosity about Soviet Union, a country that had "contradicted our ideas, organized a vast empire, raised our taxes, and challenged the United States to political, economic and military competition everywhere—all in forty years."[42] Much more than Steinbeck, who avoided mentioning his earlier trip to the Soviet Union, Stevenson drew on his experiences from his own trip thirty-two years earlier and came to the conclusion that "the people were more friendly, their ignorance and anxiety about America greater, and the industrialization more spectacular than I had expected."[43]

According to VOKS officials, Stevenson took many initiatives during his travels, asking to speak to performers after shows and taking spontaneous walks around towns he was visiting.[44] In sharp contrast to Steinbeck's experience, the authorities granted his wishes when possible, and overall there seems to have been much more tolerance toward Stevenson's requests during his stay than Steinbeck had experienced in the late 1940s.[45] Steinbeck, for example, wrote about the inefficiency of the Soviet cultural officials, who had him and his photographer, Robert Capa, linger for days in Moscow before deciding who was supposed to take care of them. For a couple of days, Steinbeck and Capa had no idea who had invited them and what their status was in the Soviet Union.[46] Stevenson's case was different. He was a world-famous politician, and it was consistent with the new emphasis on personal relations with foreigners that Stevenson was given near-royal treatment in the Soviet Union, including a surprise meeting with Premier Khrushchev himself. During that session Khrushchev reminisced about the 1955 visit to Crimea by Iowan farmer Roswell Garst as a part of an American agricultural delegation and suggested that Stevenson's two sons would "come back and marry Russian girls—'that would be a contribution to Russian-American relations!'"[47] An ironic request, seeing that even if Foreign Minister Viacheslav Molotov had lifted the Stalinist ban on marriage with foreigners five years earlier—in June 1953—Soviet authorities still harassed many Soviet and American spouses of intermarriage and generally made their lives very difficult.[48]

There was much general discussion of cooperation and coexistence during Stevenson's visit. The Soviets seemed satisfied with the recognition of the possibilities for improved Soviet-American relations, but Stevenson still asked questions about "uncomfortable" issues, such as why so many cities and areas in the Soviet Union were off limits to foreigners. Addressing this issue, Comrade Gordeev of the Altai region claimed that, although he could not speak for the rest of the country, Stevenson could visit every corner of his region. He felt obliged to mention, however, that "Soviet people, including tourists, are shown much less in the United States than Americans are shown in the Soviet Union."[49] Stevenson also spent a day in Gorky, a city that was closed to foreigners during most of the Cold War, where he was taken to see the car factories and other industrial production, which indicates that he was indeed shown more than the average visitor.

Stevenson's entourage was a lively one. His youngest son, John, carried two cameras and took many photographs. Their Soviet traveling companions permitted him to do so, but their disapproval was clear in reports of how John took pictures of poorly dressed children and specifically visited a third-class wagon of a train they traveled on in order to take photos of its passengers. In general, however, Soviet cultural officials wrote admiringly of Stevenson's commitment to increased cultural and educational exchanges between the two countries, noting how diligently he used his evenings to prepare for meetings with Soviet ministers and dignitaries. For example, when meeting with Zhukov at the State Committee for Cultural Relations with Foreign Countries, Stevenson passed on to him the same written statement about his experiences in the Soviet Union he had given American journalists. Reading the statement, the State Committee felt that the American correspondents who had reported on the trip had distorted and "omitted all the positive remarks" Stevenson had made about the Soviet Union. Zhukov therefore considered it urgent to publish the full text in *Izvestiia*.[50]

According to a report from Soviet cultural officials in Kazan and Gorky, members of the entourage spent their nights studying and listening to the Voice of America.[51] Stevenson, however, claimed that never once were they "able to hear more than the first few seconds of a Russian language broadcast from the Voice of America, the BBC or even the United Nations before the jamming drowned them out."[52] His conclusion was that the Soviet Union still went to great lengths to "keep them [the Soviet people] in ignorance of the United States and its motives."[53] Stevenson noted, however, that there was stark "contrast between the friendly people and the savage propaganda"[54] and saw hope in the "enthusiasm of people in Russia for more contact and communication with us."[55] To that effect, Stevenson and his sons sometimes even entertained "chance acquaintances" in their hotel rooms. They played jazz records for them and answered questions about the United States: "Their questions about phonographs, radio, TV, schools, automobiles, and every aspect of life in America, were searching and always accompanied by politeness and dignity."[56]

Overall, Stevenson was very impressed with the hospitality and courtesy of the Soviet people. In his account of the trip, he noted that "the Russians like us" and they did not want a renewed war any more than Americans did. He accounted for their interest in the American way of life by claiming that their curiosity reflected "obvious mistrust of the information the people were getting from their own sources."[57] But he also concluded that "the average Russian's naturally friendly attitude seems to have survived decades of anti-American propaganda. They know little about us, and their few vague ideas are sometimes sadly distorted. But their curiosity and eagerness are disarming."[58] Similarly, his Soviet hosts recounted how several times Stevenson "was astounded by the insufficient knowledge of the Soviet people about the United States of America and underlined the importance of the increased travel of Soviet people to the United States and of American people to the USSR."[59] Like Steinbeck, he was impressed with the unfailing hospitality and the endless feasts they were offered[60] and was fascinated by the slowly improving living standards, although both Steinbeck and Stevenson also noted the shortage and high prices of consumer goods.

Adlai Stevenson asked in the conclusion of his book whether coexistence was possible.[61] He hit on a common theme of misinformation and the lack of knowledge about the other in both nations:

> It is important, I believe, for us to make every possible effort to lessen their ignorance of our country and its democratic way of life. But likewise we need to study them hard and try by every means for better understanding and deeper appreciation of the conditions of life, attitudes, values and ideas, of the Russian people and their Communist masters.[62]

Stevenson's narrative focused on building confidence in the American political leadership and taking increased interactions as a good example of how to move forward with Soviet-American relations; Steinbeck's *Russian Journal* was more than anything an impressionistic literary/journalistic account from the gloomy late Stalinist Soviet Union, where there was no hope of cooperation with the number one enemy as the anti-Western, anti-American campaign was on the rise. But despite their different reasons for writing the books, they had the same motives for going to the Soviet Union in the first place: they wanted to get to know the enemy and correct misinformation about the United States. They both noted the Soviet people's ignorance about the United States, but simultaneously lauded their obvious interest in learning about the American enemy. They both emphasized the Soviet people's hatred of war and how, in Steinbeck's words, "they wanted the same things all people want—good lives, increased comfort, security, and peace."[63] In 1958, Stevenson similarly claimed that the Russians wanted "peace—and an apartment" and ultimately to attain "the American standard of living."[64]

Khrushchev had himself drawn attention to the quality of life by focusing on solving the Soviet housing crisis. Moreover, his own 1957 slogan to "overtake and surpass America" in the production of meat and butter literally directed Soviet attention to bread-and-butter issues.[65] Without intending to, these two issues, the standard of living in the Soviet Union and the American way of life, were now deeply embedded in Khrushchev's domestic social policy. And in 1959, the one year when "personal relations" between Soviet and American people were celebrated in the Soviet Union, these contentious issues—peace in tandem with a high (American) standard of living—contributed to the Soviet people's embracing of Khrushchev's policy of peaceful coexistence.

The Summer of 1959: A Turning Point

The most successful outcome of the first cultural exchange agreement was beyond doubt the mutual national exhibits in the summer of 1959, a Soviet National Exhibition in New York and the American National Exhibition in Moscow.[66] In New York, the Soviet Union celebrated socialist technology and accomplishments; while in Moscow, the Soviet administration put much effort into managing perceptions of the American National Exhibition. Increased co-operation meant that Soviet people had much easier access to American official propaganda, but Soviet cultural authorities relentlessly continued their mission of controlling images of America in the Soviet Union. Official cultural exchanges did not change the fact that the Soviet authorities did not trust its people to reach correct conclusions about the United States based only on American representations.

The American National Exhibition took place in Sokolniki Park in Moscow for six weeks in July and August 1959.[67] Early during the preparation stage, it became clear that Soviet Agitprop experts would respond with all their might to crank out counterpropaganda as American plans for the exhibit in Moscow unfolded.[68] Toward this goal, the now-renamed Soviet Exhibition of the People's Economic Achievement, or VDNKh, opened eighteen new pavilions in February 1959 with the goal of attracting a large mass of visitors in July and August.[69] Not long after the Americans built a Circarama screen that displayed scenes of American life in 360-degree circlevision in Sokolniki, Soviet authorities set up a similar screen in VDNKh to draw attention away from the novelty of the Disney feature.[70]

As the exhibition started, however, Soviet observers noted that it would not be wise to criticize it too much, and the Soviet authorities should keep in mind that "this exhibit has gotten high praise in the thirty-three countries it has visited. Therefore, any petty criticism on our behalf might be used to harm us."[71]

Khrushchev inspects the Soviet Exhibition of the People's Economic Achievement (VDNKh) in June 1959. Khrushchev placed much emphasis on showing off Soviet technological accomplishments as a way to counter American propaganda. *Sovfoto/Universal Images Group/REX/Shutterstock*

With its animated films and short documentary films about America,[72] an art exhibit,[73] a photography exhibit, an Ed Sullivan variety show, and a book exhibit, the American exhibition troubled the Soviet hosts. The book exhibit turned out to be one of the most sensitive issues, as the Soviets disapproved of the American books on Russia on display—claiming they represented anti-Soviet propaganda and were a breach of the agreement that called for representations only of one's own country.[74] The issue received so much publicity that Harold Chadwick "Chad" McClellan, manager of the American organizing committee, withdrew some books from the exhibit in order not to divert attention from its "real" purpose.[75]

Soviet organizers of the New York exhibition followed the preparations for the American exhibition in Moscow very closely. After American organizers withdrew provocative books from their exhibit, among them Adlai Stevenson's *Friends and Enemies*,[76] the Soviet planners recalled some items, such as *Negroes in America Fight for Freedom*,[77] from their planned New York display. Overall, however, Soviet planners were satisfied with the reception their exhibit got in the United States, even saying that although Americans still asked various and challenging questions, they were "more friendly than hostile" toward the Soviet Union.[78] A *New York Times* interview with Soviet guide Yuri Zonov revealed that most American visitors wanted to learn how people lived in the Soviet Union and "maybe 5 per cent of all the questions are about the sputnik."[79] Since the Soviet National Exhibition in New York City emphasized technology, the authorities— and the guides—would probably have preferred more questions about satellites and other technological accomplishments, but the average American visitor was more interested in the Soviet way of life.

While the Soviet authorities were satisfied with the outcome of the exhibition in New York, in the summer of 1959, their focus was on the American National Exhibition in Sokolniki Park. They tried to maintain control during the event, and over a three-day period (July 25–27) the Ministry of Internal Affairs (MVD) detained fifty-eight people who had been caught stealing from the stands at the American exhibition. Among the detainees were a senior lieutenant, an engineer, students, an actress, a nurse, and a member of the Komsomol.[80] Books and cosmetics seemed especially popular; the authorities were apparently right to worry about the attraction of the American items. The Americans had been prepared for the appeal of their products, however, and wanted each guest to receive a souvenir to keep. In May, the Soviet side noted that seven types of free souvenirs were to be handed out during the festival: a color-printed guide to the Exhibit, buttons with the American flag and the inscription USA EXHIBITION, a paper cup with the "refreshing drink" Pepsi Cola, an ice cream cup, 15 cm-long toy cars, powder, and lipstick (ten thousand lipsticks were made on site every day), but the Soviets vetoed the handing out of cosmetics and toy cars.[81] Consumer articles were still on display, though, and toward the end of the exhibit, on August 11, Harold McClellan expressed his overall satisfaction with the exhibition, which had been a great success, but he feared that "we had way too many cosmetics at this exhibit, which was soon identified with France and not with the USA."[82] Cosmetics and women's fashion was to a great extent associated with the West, and the association with France probably derives from the fact that in June 1959, only a few weeks before the American exhibition opened, thousands of Soviet people attended Christian Dior's show in Moscow, where the French designer Yves Saint-Laurent displayed his new collection.[83]

Still, targeting women ended up to be a smart move. The most lasting effect of the American exhibit turned out to be the spontaneous discussion Nixon and Khrushchev started in the American model kitchen about how modern technology could ease the plights of housewives all over the world. The "Kitchen Debate" drew much more attention to issues of convenience and consumerism—and the lack thereof in the Soviet Union—than Khrushchev cared or wished for. It was becoming increasingly clear that in addition to the space race, living standards and ways of life would play a role in the Cold War. The first full year of official exchanges did mark a change in Soviet-American cultural and diplomatic relations, because the focus of the Soviet cultural mission was now mainly on coexisting with the United States. The American National Exhibition showed the United States in a new light in the Soviet media, while always emphasizing socialism's ability to catch up with and surpass the United States. Yet displays of cars and shoes at the American exhibition apparently had a strong appeal, and the Soviet propaganda machine was hard pressed trying to mediate and control the responses of Soviet people to American consumerism.[84]

There is evidence that the exhibit had the desired effect on Soviet people, in that they compared their own life and living conditions to what they—or their friends—saw in Sokolniki. Ivan Aleksandrovich from Kazan did not visit the exhibit himself, but after hearing about it from his neighbor, he decided to write a detailed letter addressed to Harold McClellan, President Eisenhower, and Premier Khrushchev. In his letter, Ivan Aleksandrovich recounted the American propaganda about workers, how in the United States they received $100 per week allowing them to buy two suits or 420 kg of flour, and how American workers could own two cars. In fifteen pages, Ivan Aleksandrovich dissected the American propaganda and shared the details of his life as an ordinary Soviet citizen as a way of helping the authorities target their anti-exhibit propaganda. He also emphasized the need for personal exchanges in order for the Americans to start believing in the quality and satisfaction of Soviet life:

> We, the Soviet people, are happy if blue- and white-collar workers are financially taken care of and live very well in any country of the world. We want to live even better, we also wish the American people a better life, and if we are to become your friends, then there is never going to be a war. Send us your workers, pensioners, scientists and engineers, sportsmen, artists, farmers. We want them to see how we work and to observe our way of life, and we will come to you to see how your blue- and white-collar workers live, to see your way of life and then there will never ever be a war.[85]

Ivan Aleksandrovich then narrated in detail how he had lived during tsarist times and how he lived now—comparing everything from prices of white flour and general living circumstances. The increased comforts were of course all thanks to the Soviet project: "And if there are still people abroad who say that some of us, Soviet people, want to return to the earlier ways," they should rest assured that "nothing can affect us, because we do not want war, and we will never give up Soviet power or the banner of Lenin to anyone."[86]

Even if some people, like Ivan Aleksandrovich and his neighbor, countered the American propaganda with examples from their own good, Soviet life, the American National Exhibition confirmed to both the Soviet leadership and people that the United States provided comforts and goods that the Soviet people could only dream of. In the aftermath of the fateful summer and early fall of 1959, Soviet authorities started realizing that focusing on technological discoveries and education was not going to be sufficient—for neither American nor Soviet audiences. Shortly after Khrushchev's America trip, on October 16, 1959, the Central Committee and the Council of Ministers issued a resolution to increase the production and variety of consumer and household goods. The resolution stated explicitly that there was a shortage of television sets, pianos, washing machines, sewing machines, and refrigerators in the Soviet Union. In the 1950s, America remained a capitalist enemy, but one that forced the Soviet state to take into account the demand for consumer goods when designing domestic policy.

In addition to national exhibitions, 1959 was also a year of mutual official visits. Starting in January, Anastas Ivanovich Mikoyan, Khrushchev's deputy and close friend, visited Washington, New York, Chicago, and Los Angeles as a guest of Soviet ambassador to the United States Mikhail Menshikov, charged with the mission of easing relations with Americans.[87] In July, Politburo member Frol Romanovich Kozlov, Khrushchev's close deputy, opened the Soviet National Exhibition in New York City, and in the same month, US vice president Richard M. Nixon traveled to the Soviet Union to open the American National Exhibition in Sokolniki Park in Moscow, where he engaged in the Kitchen

Khrushchev squares off against Nixon during the storied Kitchen Debate at the 1959 American Exhibition in Sokolniki Park. This debate marked a turning point in the Cold War as it drew attention to convenience and consumerism—and the lack thereof in the Soviet Union. *Library of Congress, LC-DIG-ppmsca-19730*

Debate with Khrushchev.[88] And within two weeks after the exhibition closed, Premier Khrushchev embarked upon a tour of the United States.

Reflecting on these activities, the American department of the Union of Soviet Societies for Friendship and Cultural Relations with Foreign Countries (SSOD) concluded that the year 1959 was a "turning point" in Soviet-American cultural relations.[89] Described in official and private rhetoric as a "joyous occasion," Khrushchev's 1959 trip caused many people in the Soviet Union to send letters to the authorities. While many of the letter writers expressed themselves in a way that was similar to the official Soviet rhetoric, it is quite clear that the atmosphere of 1959 contributed to a comparatively open discussion about the nature of Soviet-American relations. For this reason, the year 1959 did indeed mark a turning point as the Soviet people articulated their thoughts on the new relationship between the superpowers. To a certain extent, this shift in public perceptions may have had more lasting significance than changes in Soviet-American relations at the official level, especially since the latter remained volatile.

SSOD credited the profound effects of 1959 mainly to Nikita Khrushchev's visit to the United States, which they estimated had "resulted in general changes in international relations and colossal influences on the minds of millions of ordinary Americans."[90] The SSOD report even stated that

> it would not be an overstatement to say that, for the first time since the war, the absolute majority of Americans heard the earnest truth about the Soviet Union, the absolute majority of Americans changed their minds about the USSR.... In hundreds of letters they expressed the admiration of the fruitful work, delivered by Comrade Khrushchev in the USA, and many asked to receive information about the Soviet Union, not believing the official American sources.[91]

It is safe to assume that SSOD strongly exaggerated Khrushchev's popularity in America, but surely, state and official visits and national exhibits got more media coverage and caught more people's attention than any delegation or tourist group could ever wish for, as the mass media in both countries feasted on these events. While the American media were naturally more skeptical, the Soviet press provided their readers mostly with upbeat coverage of peaceful coexistence and friendship between the two nations. Khrushchev's American trip was announced on August 4, 1959, and the visit immediately took on great visibility. When one flips through the summer and fall issues of *Pravda,* one certainly gets an impression of the significance of the visit. Even before the trip took place, the Soviet press was triumphant, describing the visit as a historic mission that would not have happened without Khrushchev leading the way with his rhetoric of coexistence. Much was at stake, and it seemed that world peace now depended on Khrushchev's positive reception in the United States.

Contrary to SSOD's estimates, however, 1959 likely provided a more important turning point in Soviet society than in the "minds of millions of Americans." Soviet coverage of the American trip gave Khrushchev's performance unanimous praise, but it dismissed the hostile welcome Khrushchev and his entourage received, for example, from East European immigrants in the United States as staged. The press generally described the American reception of the Soviet guests with great enthusiasm, emphasizing Khrushchev's competence in dealing with the Americans.[92] The Soviet press also embellished its discussion with letters from sympathetic Americans who were ashamed of the unfriendly welcome Khrushchev occasionally received—claiming that they were the "real" Americans whose opinions one could trust.[93]

All of the Soviet institutions involved in spreading "the truth about the Soviet Union" considered Khrushchev's visit to America a great success. Certainly, the mission of encouraging and spreading knowledge about the socialist system abroad was still often an uphill battle, as the American public remained relatively indifferent to Soviet culture and way of life. Yet, everyone who had been following developments in Soviet-American diplomatic relations since the Geneva talks considered the visit significant. With the 1956 invasion of Hungary still fresh in people's minds, many observers justifiably doubted the integrity of peaceful coexistence, but the "spirit of Geneva" and Khrushchev's insistence on friendlier relations made President Eisenhower decide, albeit reluctantly, to accept the Soviet leader as his guest, showing that Khrushchev was making some progress with his rhetoric.[94]

In 1959, therefore, the Soviet population was fixated on all things American and paid due notice to the unfolding events of the year.[95] Numerous Soviet people wrote letters and telegrams in relation to Khrushchev's travels and sent them to the leadership during a four-month period, from mid-August to mid-December. While most of the letters wrote only about the Khrushchev trip, wishing him good luck and godspeed, many also focused on the promising developments in Soviet-American relations. Even if many of the letters duly replicated the themes and formulations found in official Soviet propaganda, some people went beyond pure endorsement of the regime's goals, drawing on personal experiences and offering advice. What all of the letters have in common is a certain command of the languages of de-Stalinization, crystallized in praising the return to pure Leninism and the complete silence on Stalin as well as an interest in the Soviet status as a superpower.

The act of public letter writing in 1959 has to be analyzed within the context of de-Stalinization. The risk of expressing an opinion in a letter to the authorities was nowhere near as high as it had been under Stalin; the letter writers of the late

1950s acted within this different atmosphere. In form, the letters were public—these were not private communications between lovers, friends, or family members—and the writers, full of optimism and good advice, all seem aware of the public nature of the act of writing to Khrushchev.[96] Because many of the letters were published in late 1959 in a popular book with a press run of 250,000 copies titled *Face to Face with America: The Story of N. S. Khrushchov's Visit to the USA, September 15–27, 1959*,[97] their authors immediately entered a public space. Some, however, especially those who gave explicit advice based on experience with Americans or articulated opinions about Soviet policy and relations with America, were not published and other letters were published only in part.[98]

A large majority of the letter writers directly addressed Khrushchev ("Dear Nikita Sergeevich"), but some also wrote to President Dwight D. Eisenhower ("Mister President"), Vice President Richard M. Nixon, or Harold McClellan, organizer of the American National Exhibition. It is not always clear what motivated the letter writers to write to the authorities; many people probably took it upon themselves to craft a letter but since some of the telegrams came from groups such as factory workers and collective farmers, it is likely that at least a part of the letters were engineered by Communist Party officials. There is no way of knowing how many letters and telegrams Soviet citizens sent to the various media and governmental organs on the occasion of Khrushchev's American visit, but it is safe to assume that hundreds, if not thousands, of people picked up a pen on this occasion.[99]

People from all walks of life wrote to Premier Khrushchev and President Eisenhower. The presentation of self is generally through conventional social stereotypes such as that of mother, veteran, peasant, worker, or engineer.[100] These people were not dissidents, and their goals were not to malign the Soviet authorities. Rather, mostly these were ordinary Soviet citizens, who used the new rhetoric of peaceful coexistence to elaborate on issues of interest to them. Some letter writers claimed, in good socialist fashion, to represent a Soviet collective and to speak on behalf of millions of people, such as a twenty-two-year-old man from Tambov who wrote: "I cannot hold back the emotions which fill my soul at present and which I can confidently say fill the hearts of millions of people like me."[101]

People of different generations wrote to Khrushchev, but the majority of people identified themselves as elderly pensioners or invalids. The pensioner frequently took out his or her pen to contrast the country's earlier backwardness with the technological achievements of the late 1950s or to reminisce about the horrors of the Great Patriotic War.[102] The common experience they usually draw upon is the war, and the letter writers' enthusiasm for improved Soviet-American relations often reflects their sincere hopes never to experience another war. At a Kremlin press conference on August 5, at which Khrushchev answered questions about the invitation and the purposes of the trip, he also reminded the Soviet people of the wartime alliance with the United States, emphasizing that the two superpowers were indeed capable of cooperating and working together.[103] Many Soviet people seized this opportunity to share their experiences and finally incorporate the American ally into the myth and memory of the Great Patriotic War.

The most tame letters to Khrushchev are devoted to wishing him well or, after his return, congratulating him on the successful outcomes of the trip. These letters are laden with praise and admiration for the Communist Party, the Soviet government, and Premier Khrushchev, and, not surprisingly, the authors rely on the official formulations and tropes presented in the mass media. The more passionate letters also draw on official rhetoric, but go into more detail about the events of 1959 as well as the processes leading up to them. Here, the letters recount their appraisals of the year 1959, both positive and critical, as well as detailed descriptions of earlier encounters with American culture. One even finds optimism about "catching up with and surpassing America," and advice on how to best achieve that goal.

Khrushchev's rhetoric signaled to Soviet people that it was now acceptable to reflect on their own personal experiences with Americans, such as living and working in the United States, and to give advice on the development of Soviet-American relations. The letters therefore describe a range of extreme to everyday situations, but it is striking how often people drew upon their wartime experiences and everyday life in the newfound, post-Stalin socialist reality. Generally, there is a feeling of living through historic times: not just in terms of the importance of the Soviet socialist project, but also in terms of the perceived acceptance and recognition of the post-Stalin Soviet Union as an equal player on the world stage.[104] Finally, after years of isolation, Soviet participation and acceptance in broader international life seemed like a real prospect—and so did reconciliation with the former American ally.

Breaking the Ice of the Cold War

Celebrating them as clear signs of the supremacy of the Soviet way of life, many letter writers praised the "twin achievements" of Soviet scientists.[105] The two achievements were the launching of *Lunik*, the Soviet space rocket to the moon, and the construction of *Lenin*, an atomic icebreaker: "The sending of our space rocket to the moon, the trials of the atomic ship which bears the great name of Lenin, arouse a feeling of pride in our country, our Communist Party, thanks to which backward Russia has become the advanced Union of Soviet Socialist Republics."[106] Indeed, Premier Khrushchev's successful promotion of peace in America was a monumental move toward world peace and melting "the ice of the 'Cold War.'"[107] In this metaphor, Khrushchev introduced the simple logic of peace and friendship to all hostile Americans that would solve all tensions and end the Cold War. Relying on the language and propaganda of de-Stalinization, not only *Lenin*, but also Khrushchev, became an icebreaker of colossal significance.

As evident in the emphasis on the twin achievements of *Lunik* and *Lenin*, some letter writers appropriated the official language and policy so easily accessible in the Soviet media. Two days before Khrushchev arrived in the United States, *Pravda* celebrated the success of *Lunik* on the front page and of *Lenin* on the third page. Carefully calculated to strengthen the image of the Soviet Union as a worthwhile competitor in the area of technology, the timing of these stories was no coincidence.[108] Earlier, in 1957, the success of *Sputnik* had justifiably increased Soviet people's confidence in the technological sphere, and the letters often reflect great faith in Soviet technology. Now *Lunik* and *Lenin* helped to validate the patriotic feeling that no one, not even the United States, could beat the Soviet Union in the space race.

When discussing the United States, the Soviet people often distinguished between ordinary Americans and American policy—expressing sympathy for individuals but not for the government.[109] An anonymous writer using the pen name "Leningrader" suggested that Khrushchev should praise "Americans themselves, while, as for the technological level in U.S.A, you had expected to see something quite different from what you actually saw, that all you did see makes you say in good Russian: 'It seems the devil is not so bad as the cold warriors painted him.'"[110] The "Leningrader" continued:

> I realize very well how silly it is for a passenger to be a back-seat driver. Still, what I want to do is not advise you—oh, no!—but simply ask you not to feel admiration for anything in America. To see the flaws in everything, even the best, and to say with an air of disdain when you see something we don't have: "Yes, perhaps we ought to use that."[111]

This sort of advice on how to deal with the perceived preeminence of American progress in both technology and comfortable lifestyle went hand in hand with the Soviet party line of the late 1950s. The Soviet line was to accept that—for now—the Soviet Union was lagging behind America, but in order to catch up, the Soviet people would cherry-pick whatever they felt America had to offer them and would eventually surpass it.

The official propaganda aim was to show how grateful and satisfied the Soviet people were with their way of life and how they could not live without peace and friendship with other nations, and people seemed well aware of this: "Why do we live so well? Because the party and the government are constantly concerned with our well-being, with the well-being of all us ordinary Soviet people. . . . We live wonderfully. We need peace."[112] Expressing blind adoration of the Communist

Party was a standard feature of the letters written in support of the tour, as was congratulating Khrushchev on following Lenin's teachings.[113] Tracing the socialist project back to Lenin fits the need that many authors, especially women, had to identify themselves as "simple" people and then recount their advancements in life, which the Communist Party had made possible for them, echoing the focus on social mobility in the Soviet Union.[114]

Many also compared life in prerevolutionary times with life under Soviet power. People writing about survival issues were often very patriotic and usually repeated the official propaganda of the Soviet media, proud to be Soviet and proud of the Soviet "way of life."[115] Typically, they recalled the suffering of the Great Patriotic War to place emphasis on how Soviet socialism had since succeeded in providing the Soviet people with a better life. Their lives had turned out much better than they had dared to hope, and for that they expressed their deepest gratitude to Comrade Khrushchev. Indeed, thanking Khrushchev for "everything" he had done, for his "dignity" and "for the difficult, tremendous job you are doing," were common formulations.[116] Some also revealed their need for a father figure in the leadership role, reminding Khrushchev to take care of himself "for us, for the people."[117] Khrushchev's speeches in America were published on the front page of *Pravda* every day during the visit and many reacted to them with enthusiasm and flattery. Tamara Nikonova from Minsk wrote: "never in my life did I read anything more interesting, wonderful, and sharp-witted."[118]

On July 25, *Pravda* published Nixon's opening speech at Sokolniki. Nixon's claims about the well-being of American workers attracted much attention in the Soviet Union, and, over the next few days, *Pravda* deconstructed the speech, word by word. Nixon had stated that American workers could easily own a television set and afford a car, but the Soviet press countered his arguments by, for example, citing Americans who did not recognize the comfort of the American way of life presented in Moscow at the exhibition.[119] Several letter writers took it upon themselves to echo the counterpropaganda in *Pravda*. Semyonov from Leningrad had read Nixon's speech and boldly claimed that "it made no impression on our people at all."[120] Others were more nuanced, such as V. A. Zavadsky from Orel, who found the achievements Nixon spoke of to be "marvelous" but explained that the Soviet people felt no greed or envy—"we have firm faith in our government and our Party and in our toil-hardened hands. If we haven't got fifty million cars today, we'll have as many as we need tomorrow. If we haven't got fifty million TV sets today, we'll have a hundred million tomorrow. And so on and so forth."[121] If they had not visited the American National Exhibition themselves, most everyone in the Soviet Union was aware of it, and many of the letters mentioned the American exhibition in Sokolniki in passing. Adopting the tone of Soviet counterpropaganda to describe the exhibition a typical response would negate the impact of the exhibit, exemplified in the letter by A. N. Krainev, a Soviet factory worker: "our workers thought it was not at all what we expected. Either you are afraid to show what you've got, above board and frankly, or for some reason you simply don't want to. It is a fact, though, that we thought your exhibition weak. We've got to be frank and let you know that we expect more in the future."[122]

Not surprisingly, the editors of *Face to Face with America* claimed that the letters published in the book testified to the "political maturity of the Soviet people, their active participation in matters of great state importance. What they say is but one more proof of the real democracy of our socialist system, of the unbreakable bonds between the Party and the people."[123] Until recently, the Cold War historiography of the Khrushchev period sought to emphasize the initial willingness of the regime to reform itself and overcome the crimes of the Stalin era. Clearly, people allowed themselves to reflect upon current events in the Soviet Union and abroad, but as it became increasingly clear that those who were over-enthusiastic about Khrushchev's Secret Speech or interpreted it "incorrectly" risked repression, playing it safe was perhaps preferable.[124] It was only in 1959 that the state dramatically reduced political persecution and called upon people to take responsibility for themselves—and others. Thus, "the real democracy of the socialist system," as the editors phrased it, was neither a stable nor a trusted thing in those years, and this partly helps explain the public presentation of peaceful coexistence.

The Soviet authorities decided to publish some of the letters because they emphasized the general accomplishments of the Soviet state in general, and in particular, the two accomplishments, *Lunik* and *Lenin*, designed to minimize the effects the visit to the West might have in the Soviet Union. The published letter writers thus supported the new developments in the same way they would have supported any new initiative by the Soviet authorities and did not go very far in embracing the opportunity to renew their friendship with Americans.

Imagining Coexistence

Soviet views about the United States relied on both prewar images and wartime experiences, but in Stalin's time they had also been dependent on alternative sources of information, such as Voice of America radio broadcasts. In the summer of 1959, however, the exposure to America on Soviet grounds and in the Soviet media greatly influenced some Soviet people who openly referred to their previous experiences with Americans because they were now in coordination with the official strategy of emphasizing personal exchanges and coexistence. Several people crafted letters that went as far as they deemed possible with the new language of the Khrushchev period and offered independent thoughts on how far the policy of peaceful coexistence could take the two countries. The most enthusiastic letter writers thus went well beyond the language of *Pravda*, elaborating on the pressing aspects of Soviet-American relations and speculating on the nature and development of the Cold War. They hardly mentioned the scientific superiority of the Soviet Union but focused on how the Soviet and American people might happily coexist in the future.

Letters detailing advice or strong opinions were not published in *Face to Face with America*, most likely because they often revealed intimate knowledge of the United States, and mediating the responses of readers to such information would have been an impossible task. In a way, it is extraordinary that so many would detail their personal interactions with Americans, since Soviet people always had to keep in mind what the recipients wanted to hear and what the consequences could be if those on the receiving end did not approve of the content. As there is no indication that the Soviet authorities contacted the letter writers in question, one may assume that writing these letters did not have serious consequences, but only a few years earlier, positive utterances about the United States had often cost people their freedom.[125]

Fearlessly, several people now spoke openly of not just their wartime experiences but also earlier contacts and even long-term stays in the United States. Going as far back as to 1905, people now recounted stories of earlier lives and time spent in the United States—ranging from political immigrants to workers—emphasizing the qualities of the American people they knew and how to best deal with them. A man identifying himself only as Tsukerman had lived in the United States in the late 1920s, in the early years of Soviet-American trade relations. He claimed that while important American firms, such as General Electric and Hercules Powder, had shown interest in trading with the Soviet Union, the State Department had already then been very skeptical of Soviet motives and treated them as a "potential enemy." He told this story in order to provide parallels between now and then; like Khrushchev in 1959, he and his coworkers had worked hard to refute State Department propaganda in the 1920s. He was also of the opinion that since the Second World War had proven Soviet loyalty to Americans, they had no reason to be skeptical of the Soviet rhetoric about coexistence.[126]

Another man, Nikolai Andreevich, had lived in the United States for seven years as a political émigré after the 1905 Revolution;[127] he later returned and associated closely with Americans who came to the Soviet Union during the Great Depression, assisting in "the restoration of the national economy; when we invited foreigners, including Americans, to help us." He claimed that since he had mingled with American workers and students, this gave him "a basis to form a few ideas about the average (middle, as they say) American, representative of the American people."[128] According to Nikolai Andreevich, American people were generous, responsive, cheerful, optimistic, cordial, and free of pettiness: "I could tell you many interesting things about my personal and business contacts with them," Nikolai Andreevich said, but he assumed that someone had already briefed Khrushchev on such things. On the other hand, for Khrushchev to have the best possibility of "seeing America and her 'natural greatness,' as they say, from within, the way she actually is," Nikolai Andreevich recommended that Khrushchev visit an old friend, a participant in the October Revolution and "a close friend of Lenin himself:" Albert Rhys Williams. Williams, a Congregational minister from Boston and a member of the American Socialist Party, had visited Russia in the aftermath of the 1917 February Revolution.[129] He had throughout the years been a staunch supporter of the Soviet project and had spent five months in Moscow as a guest of the Soviet Writers' Union in 1959, thus making him one of the Americans who were visible and accessible in the Soviet Union in that year. Williams would be the right man, said Nikolai Andreevich, to tell Khrushchev about America—"in a way no other man could."[130]

Nikolai Andreevich felt safe in painting a positive picture of the ordinary American—but for an "accurate" picture of America, he recommended a meeting with a socialist American. Clearly, friends of the Soviet Union—fellow travelers or people who sympathized with socialism—would be able to present America "the way she actually is," which here indicated a country where racial and social inequality were carefully hidden from the visitor unless accompanied by the right kind of guide. This recommendation indicates the lasting impact of the dual-America image, where a socialist America represented the progressive and acceptable America, which in turn also relied on the tangible contacts Soviet and American people had had in the prewar years.

People also offered to travel with Khrushchev to represent ordinary Soviet people and thus connect personally to Americans. To increase their chances, some offered special knowledge or qualifications that might be helpful to Khrushchev en route. For example, a young man claimed that if only he had mastered the English language, he would have had the courage to volunteer his services as an interpreter during the trip, but clearly indicating that he would still like to see how ordinary people lived in the United States. He claimed that he could observe life in America "without envy," as he had intimate knowledge of the "different levels of our relationship in the past twenty years."[131] In order to appeal to ordinary Americans, people also sent photographs of themselves for Khrushchev to hand out.[132] A woman, A. I. Chistiakova, wrote a sentimental story of a photograph depicting a Soviet and American soldier in Berlin at the end of the Second World War, and a reader at the Council of Ministers marked her letter as "deserving of attention." She wrote: "if our countries can fight together against the general enemy of fascism, how can they not together strengthen peace?" Chistiakova concluded that, in her opinion, this photograph would come in handy for reminding American statesmen of the former alliance and reconfirm the need for peace and friendship, but since this photograph of her childhood friend and his American friend was very dear to her, she asked for it to be returned after the trip.[133]

Many of the letter writers pointed to the Second World War as a defining event, but since the official rhetoric no longer mentioned the inevitability of a renewed global conflict, there was now a more optimistic tone about the nature of Soviet-American relations in the letters. And even the Cold War seemed to be changing, perhaps even disappearing.[134] The Soviet people were clearly acting on this phenomenon when they offered photographs of ordinary Soviet citizens or Soviet and American allied soldiers, hoping that friendly personal relations would set an example for superpower politics. Nevertheless, this realization was possible only because the deep rooted fear of a renewed war was no longer present. Literally providing Khrushchev with soft weapons such as photographs, drawings, and poems thus represented a form of active participation in the campaign for peaceful coexistence.

Even with the fear of war absent from the letters, some still expressed worries about doomsday and other unspeakable outcomes should peaceful coexistence between the United States and the Soviet Union fail. For example, a letter addressed to President Eisenhower by O. I. Kulikova from Stalinabad, a seventy-three-year-old pensioner in Tajikistan, recounts the events leading up to the latest developments in international relations. Kulikova wrote about Soviet-American cooperation during the war. She recounted Cold War tensions between the two former allies, claiming that it would be a waste of time to assign blame as better times were ahead: "the faith of humanity is in your hands."[135] This is a common feature of many of the letters—Khrushchev had offered Americans peaceful coexistence, and it was up to them to accept it: "Comrade Khrushchev will do everything he can in order to assure success and benefit humankind." The fact that Eisenhower had agreed to meet with Premier Khrushchev in the United States raised hopes that Eisenhower would react positively to Khrushchev's offer of peaceful coexistence: "Only you two can say: peace—and there will be peace." But, should Eisenhower fail to accept the extended hand of friendship, then all hell would break loose: "Your Cold War will change into a warm one, you will drown humankind with tears of blood, people caught in the crossfire will curse you and compare you to Hitler, and God will prepare darkness for you." Kulikova not only predicted a day of judgment and an afterlife in hell, but she also asked him to listen to her, a "simple woman," because after all, he was her "brother in faith" and she was his older sister.[136]

A few of the letter writers touched upon religion as something they had in common with Americans. Thus Ia. Pedchenko, a kolkhoz worker from Ukraine, pointed out that the "creator of life" loved all people equally and should be

Eisenhower and Khrushchev pose in front of Aspen Lodge at Camp David on September 25, 1959. Khrushchev's tour of the United States gave him the opportunity to spread the rhetoric of peaceful coexistence to Americans. *US Navy, Dwight D. Eisenhower Presidential Library & Museum*

glorified. Pedchenko focused on the "primitive" and "beastly" nature of the Cold War conflict: "we, Mr. President, live in an epoch of civilization, in an era of the dawn of reason of humankind." He continued, "you both need to direct all of your thoughts and energy to establishing peace and friendship between our great nations, peace and friendship in the whole world. The countries and their people are children of one peaceful planet."[137] This idea to turn coexistence into a global project also goes hand in hand with the long-term tasks of Soviet cultural and political organizations—the Soviet mission was always to spread a civilized, modern, classless way of life to other countries. Due to Khrushchev's planned trip and the media attention it would attract, Soviet propaganda might now get through to an audience in the United States for the very first time since the Cold War started. Until the mid- to late 1950s, this had been unthinkable, as Americans had not exactly been receptive to Soviet propaganda and America as such stood for the bourgeois greed and imperialist aggression against which the Soviet cultural mission had campaigned.

Another letter writer also voiced his belief in personal exchanges as a way of correcting the Soviet image abroad and sent "a friendly note" to all the people of the United States:

> We have heard much about America and about the American people, and the Russian people have always been sympathetic to your people. But from the American side the wind has always been cold toward the Soviet Union. American people think we are a red plague. They look at communists as their bloody enemy. But you, American people, are profoundly mistaken in this. Communist—it is the greatest word in the world.[138]

Many letter writers expressed a similar sentiment. If the American people could only see for themselves how the Soviet people lived and worked, they would immediately stop fearing them and support their search for peace in the world.

Khrushchev's visit to America was the impetus for these letter writers, but many people also used the opportunity to inform Khrushchev about their personal lives and request something for themselves or for family members. Dzhavakov from Rustavi[139] wrote on behalf of his wife, who had an aunt and an uncle living in America. He decided to write to see if Khrushchev would take his eighty-seven-year-old grandfather-in-law with him to America so he could see his children one last time. He claimed that while some might think this could harm Khrushchev's mission—the old man's son and daughter having migrated to the United States—he thought otherwise and offered his opinion of why this would "have the opposite effect." He claimed that "this will be of interest and in all of America, news spreads fast." Dzhavakov went on to assure Khrushchev that his father-in-law was "still very strong, and he could drink Kaganovich under the table." Furthermore, he knew "many old soldiers' songs" and spoke good Russian. Moreover, Dzhavakov made sure to ask that his grandfather-in-law, "father of two American citizens," be returned to them unharmed and intact. "We have no one besides him."[140]

This and other such letters reveal much about the Soviet people's belief in the value of personal interactions. They gave the abstract term "friendship between nations" a personal twist as they thought up ways of making the American people sympathize with ordinary Soviet people. The letter writers often showed strong faith in personal relations and cultural exchanges, and many based this belief on former experiences with Americans. Unthinkable under Stalin, this sort of advice shows that people embraced the new attitude toward the United States and, by relating positive experiences and relations with Americans, they wanted to show that they supported Khrushchev's goal to improve the superpower relationship.

It is still likely that most of the letter writers exercised strong self-censorship.[141] What shines through, however, is vigorous self-fashioning accommodating the softer ideological approach to the United States and adapting to the relative relaxation of the Thaw. The style of the letters takes after the changed tone of the Soviet press and other official language, which people seem to have intuitively co-opted as their own. Considering how many elderly people wrote to Premier Khrushchev on the eve of his trip to America, it is also likely that they were relieved not to have to worry about another war—they wanted to have peace of mind as well as peace and friendship between the two nations. The return to Leninism also marked a return to the times when the United States was—in some areas—seen as a model in production and industry, and Khrushchev's emphasis on improved social conditions in the Soviet Union is also reflected in the letters in the longing for the time when the Soviet Union would eventually catch up with and surpass America.

Conclusion

It was generally believed that Premier Khrushchev's visit would be reciprocated by President Eisenhower. The impending visit was broadly discussed in the Soviet Union—and in the letters—as an opportunity to display both technological progress and traditional hospitality to the outside world. But on May 1, 1960, Francis Gary Powers flew an American U-2 spy plane over Soviet airspace and, after the Soviets downed the plane, the superpowers immediately abandoned the friendly facade. Khrushchev tried to get Eisenhower to apologize publicly at the Big Four Summit in Paris just days later, but failed. Their talks scheduled for Paris were canceled and so was Eisenhower's impending visit to the Soviet Union.[142] The Cuban Missile Crisis in 1962 dealt Khrushchev's peaceful coexistence with the United States the final blow.

In 1959, however, the possibilities seemed endless, and the letter writers embraced peaceful coexistence. They wholeheartedly supported the idea that, if only Americans would realize that the Soviet people were peace-loving, ordinary people, the "two great nations" would be able to understand each other—with the help of personal exchanges and individual contacts. Moreover, it was now relatively safe to address recently lifted taboos of real political significance, such as working abroad, emigration, production and industry, the nature of consumerism, and religion. This was only possible because of the considerably changed atmosphere in the Soviet Union, which paved the way for people's hopes for a permanent relaxation of superpower relations.

Memories of the year 1959, particularly memories of Sokolniki and of Khrushchev in America, became important reference points as the Soviet people later looked back on their rediscovery of America and the West. Khrushchev thus succeeded in changing the ideological approach to the United States in the Soviet Union, bringing new ways of experiencing America to the forefront. The Stalinist image of the former American war ally as a warmonger and potential aggressor receded when Khrushchev invited Americans to display their comfortable and modern lifestyle in Moscow and openly celebrated the wartime alliance as an example of the two countries' proven capabilities to work together.

The repeated references to the Second World War suggest that at least some people were relieved that they were allowed to include the alliance with the United States in their recollections of the Great Patriotic War. They also indicate that hopes for reconciliation between the two countries were earnest—people wanted to live without the fear of a war between the Soviet Union and the United States. When relations cooled again, these re-established memories of the United States could not easily be extinguished. Despite the failure of peaceful coexistence at the highest level, Soviet-American cultural relations of the post-Stalin period and above all, the changes in attitudes toward the United States, had a deep impact on the Soviet people and their perceptions of the Soviet superpower status.

Under Stalin, the anti-American campaign set the tone for how the government wanted Soviet citizens to discuss and experience America in the Soviet Union, but Khrushchev softened this approach by advocating for peaceful coexistence with the United States—and the West in general—in the mid-1950s. In this period, cultural relations with the United States almost completely died out, then went through a period of recovery and rehabilitation. This sequence of events involved advances, retreats, hesitation, and rapprochements from both sides; but the most important change came when Soviet cultural officials realized that their mission of "telling the truth" about Soviet socialism was fundamentally flawed. Soviet cultural officials repeatedly tried to point out that the Soviet state's propaganda was ineffective, and with the change in leadership after Stalin's death, some efforts were made to improve their methods, such as introducing the idea of personal exchanges and emphasizing face-to-face contact with the enemy in the 1950s. But although cultural officials repeatedly reported an urgent need for better information about daily life in the Soviet Union, they lacked the courage to state—or simply did not see—the real problem: Red Square marches and pictures of party congresses did not appeal to the majority of Americans. In fact, such images did not even appeal to many people in the Soviet Union, and those privileged enough to get a spot on a delegation to the United States were embarrassed when they found out that their knowledge of the enemy was outdated.

The Soviet state worked hard to limit the influence of undesirable information about the United States and the "American way of life," but no amount of Soviet propaganda could cover up the fact that the Soviet Union could not match American images of plenty. The Soviet state's decision to prosecute and repress people who allegedly spoke favorably about the United States—and thereby critically of the USSR—is extremely telling: inherent in the anti-American campaign and the creation of the American enemy was the fear of losing people's faith in the project of building true socialism. The nature of Soviet control over culture and propaganda meant that the authorities rarely worried about those who remained silent, but they saw those who spoke out as a threat.

With increased cultural contacts, Soviet authorities had to overcome some of this anxiety, but their ideological focus is revealing in terms of how they viewed the superpower relationship and how they consequently treated their people. Under Stalin, the narrative was dominated by fear and animosity, while under Khrushchev, optimism and self-assurance led to a softening in the ideology. Soviet authorities were concerned about the questions Soviet citizens posed about America during party meetings, interpreting them as a lack of support for the Soviet leadership. Later, they worried about the content of American propaganda, especially the journal *Amerika* and the Voice of America broadcasts, where discussions of American living standards and freedom of speech seemed to strike a responsive chord among some people. In sum, they were anxious about their ability to counter American propaganda and control the alternative sources of information available in the Soviet Union. Most of all, Soviet authorities worried when people compared the United States favorably with the Soviet Union, for this suggested to them that foreign influences corrupted their people, not only culturally but politically.

Without a doubt, many people accepted the official Soviet rhetoric about America, in part or in full. Especially, the focus on the "dual America" was successful and remained important in the way Soviet citizens understood the United States. But perhaps most telling of this partial acceptance is the way Soviet people celebrated the wartime alliance in 1959. Apparently, it was a welcome relief to many when the official Soviet propaganda allowed for—and even advocated for—the inclusion of the former American ally in the narrative of the Great Patriotic War. It was a narrative that succeeded on many levels. In addition to the positive reception among the population, the Kremlin could also use the renewed focus on the wartime alliance to emphasize Soviet accomplishments in the Second World War, and to remind the world that the Soviet Union had earned its superpower status through the extraordinary war effort.

Various actors helped shape Soviet ideology and propaganda about the United States in the postwar period, but one should not underestimate the effect of the change in leadership at the highest level: the transition from Stalin to Khrushchev. In particular, the way that Stalin ruled in the postwar era and the control he exerted was so significant that even if some of his policies continued into the Khrushchev period, the difference in degree, the organizational restructuring, and the overall changes in the way the Soviet Union acted in the international arena were noticeable and keenly felt by both "ideological workers" and ordinary Soviet people. During this whole time, the two superpowers were competing Cold War rivals and the United States remained the USSR's enemy number one, but with competition and open confrontation came increased knowledge and slow change, exemplified most officially in the 1958 exchange agreement.

Beyond Peaceful Coexistence with the United States

The Soviet downing of an American U-2 spy plane in 1960 and the Cuban Missile Crisis in 1962 strained official Soviet-American relations, but some of the beneficial results of 1959 could not be reversed. For one, Khrushchev's efforts to improve international relations lived on, with the Soviets advocating for peaceful coexistence in the arena of international law, only to be utterly delegitimized with the crushing of the 1968 Prague Spring.[1] The *shestidesiatniki*, the generation that came of age during the 1960s, did not know America, but they believed in her. Even without direct access to the country, America became a part of the Soviet consciousness.[2] The repression of attitudes continued, however, and so did efforts to control American cultural influences.[3] But still, the way the Soviet state treated the American enemy contributed to the "Imaginary West," one of the most important imaginary worlds for the last Soviet generation.[4]

Despite strained political relations in the 1960s, interest in American culture grew with increased flow of American artists and cultural artifacts to the Soviet Union. Ernest Hemingway became an underground hero, and Harper Lee's *To Kill a Mockingbird* was published in Russian—indicating a more nuanced approach to the Soviet stand on racial issues in the United States, which had relied on Harriet Beecher Stowe's *Uncle Tom's Cabin*—and American rock and pop music circulated more than ever in illegal copies, as did jeans and T-shirts.[5] In the words of satirical writer Vladimir Voinovich:

> Every day Soviet newspapers, radio and television broadcasts curse the United States of America. They paint a bleak picture of the unemployed, racial discrimination, crime, devaluation, and impoverishment. But precisely because of such propaganda, an enormous number of Soviet people believe that there are no such serious problems in America. They think that money there grows on trees and that one can, without doing anything, live luxuriously, gamble in a casino, and drive around in Cadillacs.[6]

Voinovich's observation shows how, in some cases, the anti-American campaign generated an alternative view of America as the Promised Land; how, inadvertently, Soviet anti-American propaganda contributed to positive images of the number one enemy. Furthermore, the Cold War competition only confirmed the persistence of ambivalent attitudes about the United States in the Soviet Union, well documented in the following Soviet anecdote:

A teacher was quizzing her pupils on the difference between decadent, Capitalist America and Socialist Russia.

"Tell us, Ivan," she asked. "What is the United States like?"

"The United States is a Capitalist country where millions of people are unemployed and where millions of others are starving," he recited.

"That is very good, Ivan. Now, Sasha, you tell us what is the goal of the Soviet Union?"

"To catch up with the United States."[7]

By the late 1970s, the majority of the Soviet people held negative attitudes toward American foreign policy. However, the same majority believed in the success of the capitalist social system and economy, and most people embraced the ideals of American materialism.[8] After Mikhail Gorbachev came to power in 1985, the official anti-American rhetoric softened considerably, and in 1991 Boris Yeltsin officially declared that Russia was to embark upon a pro-Western path. Economic difficulties, however, brought disillusionment. Some people had expected the United States to provide economic aid and therefore blamed Americans for Russia's slow development.[9] Still, Russians initially responded with sympathy and shock to the terrorist attacks on New York and Washington on September 11, 2001. But within a few months, the Russian media adopted an aggressive tone toward the United States and its military response in Afghanistan and later Iraq, and they soon echoed some of the most common anti-American themes from the Soviet period, such as arrogance and greed.[10]

Under Putin, Russia has once again resorted to "top-down" anti-Americanism, which is actively promoted in the state-controlled media, youth organizations, and film—to name a few outlets.[11] Contemporary anti-Americanism is generally seen as a project that originates with the ruling elite, but Vladimir Shlapentokh claims that just as in Soviet times, people's overall welfare is dependent on where they stand in relation to this top-down ideology.[12] Putin's anti-Americanism is therefore important as a distraction. It is in the interest of the government to have the population focused on an outside enemy instead of criticizing domestic developments.[13] Following a familiar pattern, the Putin era has come down hard on dissent and made it a priority to eliminate both internal and external enemies.[14] By virtue of the state-owned and Kremlin-dominated media, in the 2000s, anti-Americanism was once again a widespread phenomenon in Russia.

The Meeting on the Elbe Revisited

After a period of relative coldness, the spring of 2010 saw a relaxation of Russian-American relations. In April, Presidents Barack Obama and Dmitri

Medvedev signed a nuclear proliferation treaty announcing the reduction of strategic nuclear missile launchers by half. In April and May, both presidents commemorated the sixty-fifth anniversary of the end of the Second World War, or the Great Patriotic War as it is still known in Russia. On April 25, they issued a joint announcement on Elbe Day, to commemorate the day Soviet and American soldiers met to split up the German army in 1945; and on May 9, Russian Victory Day, American soldiers participated for the first time in a Red Square military parade to celebrate the end of the Second World War in Europe. Finally, Medvedev visited the United States and the White House for two days in June 2010, mainly to celebrate what was being portrayed as the "resetting" of the Russian-American relationship after notable deterioration in the post–Cold War period.[15]

What President Obama labeled "resetting" of Russian-American relations in 2010, Moscow had called a "revival" of Soviet-American relations in 1955.[16] In both cases, however, the war alliance was used as a positive example of the two nations' capabilities to work together toward a common goal. On the sixty-fifth anniversary of Elbe Day, April 25, 2010, Presidents Barack Obama and Dmitry Medvedev issued a joint statement:

> April 25, 2010 marks the 65th anniversary of the legendary meeting of Soviet and American troops at the Elbe River, which became a striking symbol of the brotherhood-in-arms between our nations during World War II.
>
> We pay tribute to the courage of those who fought together to liberate Europe from fascism. Their heroic feat will forever remain in the grateful memory of mankind.
>
> The atmosphere of mutual trust and shared commitment to victory, which accompanied the historic handshake at the Elbe, is especially called for today when Russia and the United States are building a partnership for the sake of a stable and prosperous world. We are convinced that, acting in the "spirit of the Elbe" on an equitable and constructive basis, we can successfully tackle any tasks facing our nations and effectively deal with the challenges of the new millennium.[17]

Here is a prime example of how both leaders used the war alliance as proof that the two countries could and should cooperate, or at least coexist, in a partnership. The soldiers who fought the war were celebrated, as was "the historic handshake at the Elbe," and the "spirit of the Elbe"—or *dukh El'be*—once again entered official rhetoric on both sides of the Atlantic.

In 2010, the mainstream media and the political rhetoric were focused on the fact that it was the first time ever that American soldiers had marched on Red

Square. While this was indeed significant, neither the media nor the political leaders mentioned the reunions that took place between Soviet and American soldiers during the Cold War or any of the Soviet and Russian commemorations of the allied powers in general and the Soviet-American relationship more specifically. As was to be expected, the media focused on the sensationalist aspects of the story, of which there were plenty. For example, neither President Obama nor British prime minister Gordon Brown could attend the celebrations in Moscow and offered respectively to send Vice President Joe Biden and Prince Charles in their place—an offer that Prime Minister Vladimir Putin declined.[18]

Leading up to the event, Moscow mayor Yuri Luzhkov's plans to include posters of Stalin in the decorations for the celebrations around Moscow led to a domestic and international outcry, and in the end the Kremlin stepped in and banned Stalin posters.[19] It was clear that with all eyes on the joint Russian-NATO march on Red Square, Russian leaders did not want a Stalin scandal to take the attention away from the parade itself. Indeed, the international media loved the Red Square parade and celebrated the historic reunion of Soviet/Russian and American soldiers in May 2010. Sadly, however, the coverage of the event was so insular that it almost seemed as if Russians had never had any contact with the outside world, with headlines such as "Victory Day parade is a sign of Russia opening to the West"[20] and "Russia offers olive branch as NATO joins parade."[21] Reuters also remarked that "most of the Soviet war veterans attending the parade seemed unconcerned by the presence of NATO soldiers, though they did not applaud when they marched past." One of the Soviet veterans claimed: "Let them see how we celebrate a solemn parade, I am absolutely not against it. I met English troops myself on the Elbe on May 4, 1945."[22] Clearly, images of Russia as a closed country and as an adversary were not very far away in the international media.

But while the 2010 parade was a unique event, and portrayed a much fuller version of victory in the Great Patriotic War than the usual Soviet and post-Soviet celebrations had allowed, the Soviet-American wartime alliance had been commemorated for quite a long time in the Soviet Union, starting with celebrations of the Soviet-American meeting on the Elbe as early as the mid-1950s, and sometimes in the context of the allied powers in general. For the fiftieth anniversary of the end of the Great Patriotic War in 1995, Russia issued a 3 ruble coin to commemorate the Meeting on the Elbe. The coin is a rather neutral memorial, but then, within three years of each other, two prominent artists, the Georgian Zhurab Tsereteli and an Israeli, Frank Meier, each produced sculptures of the famous "big three" at Yalta: Churchill, Roosevelt, and Stalin. These "big three" sculptures were of course rather contentious, as many people did not like the idea of putting up sculptures of Stalin, even if it was based on one of the most famous photograph sessions of the twentieth century. Those in favor argued, though, that it would be worse not to include him.[23]

In the mid-2000s, around the time when the "big three" sculptures were first erected, there was a strong rumor that a similar sculpture, one including Stalin, would be put up in Victory Park in Moscow. Instead, a "Monument to the Anti-Hitlerite Coalition Countries" was erected. Celebrating the whole allied coalition and focusing on the soldiers, not the leaders, the monument shows a French soldier, a Soviet Red Army soldier, an American GI, and a British soldier. The French and the British soldiers are positioned behind the Soviet and the American soldiers, with the Soviet soldier slightly taller than the American. This monument was unveiled in 2005, on the sixtieth anniversary of victory in the Great Patriotic War, and out of all the memorials celebrating the alliance in Russia, it is the biggest, most permanent, and most important in terms of its location and presentation. Also in 2005, Putin made an attempt to reconcile European and Russians views of the victory, which was seen as a significant gesture.[24]

Whereas the 2010 parade on Red Square was significant in that it was the first time the actual Victory Day celebration included the allies in a military parade, the alliance had been celebrated for quite a while in Russia, not only as a disguise for erecting Stalin sculptures but also to remember the soldiers who fought for victory in the war. Perhaps not surprisingly, Russia was unique in terms of celebrating the memory of the alliance, both as a part of peacefully coexisting with the outside world, and as a part of a national celebration of victory in the Great Patriotic War—that is, until 2010 when President Obama also embraced the war alliance in his "resetting" of Russian-American relations. However, the absolute silence about former reunions of Soviet and American Elbe soldiers, and the attempts made by Khrushchev in the mid-1950s to use the war alliance to improve relations with the United States was striking. Combined with the fact that the Western media acted as if Russia were an isolated country whose people had little or no contact with the outside world, the way that the alliance and the Russian-American relationship was used by politicians and portrayed in the media is a lasting testimony to the persistence of attitudes about the former Cold War enemies.

Finally, in addition to the renewed rhetoric of the "spirit of the Elbe," a Russian film titled *Meetings on the Elbe River: Love on the Ashes of War* (*V dalekom sorok piatom: Vstrechi na El'be*) premiered in 2015. The film was directed by Mira Todorovskaya, the widow of the belated Petr Todorovsky, a veteran of the original Elbe meeting and whose recollections inspired the film. Todorovsky was himself a renowned filmmaker, best known for his films *Intergirl* (*Interdevochka*) and *Wartime Romance* (*Voenno-polevoi roman*), but he did not live to see the project finished. In this new film, the focus is on the various relationships that were built in the aftermath of the Elbe meeting, but according to his widow, Todorovsky had all his life wanted to convey the feeling of what it felt like when the war was over, how one "acutely and clearly smelled life" after the devastating experience of war. His goal was not to only talk about the war but about what was "so keenly missing from the battlefield," namely love.[25]

In the production phase of the film, Todorovskaya received information that the Russian Military-History Society (RVIO—*Rossiiskoe voenno-istoricheskoe obshchestvo*), based at the Russian Ministry of Culture, had concluded that her script did not reflect the historical truth.[26] Todorovskaya claimed that later, a member of RVIO had told her that he was forced to make such a decision[27] but it is still clear that as the Kremlin continues to rely on the uses of history for political purposes, it also wants to maintain control over the memory of the Second World War and the anti-Hitler coalition. On December 29, 2012, Putin had resurrected the old imperial Russian Military-History Society by Order No. 1710, "with the goal of consolidating the resources of the State and the Society for the study of Russia's military past, facilitating the study of national military history and counteracting attempts to distort it, as well as to popularize the achievements of military-historical study, encourage patriotism, and raise the prestige of military service."[28] In May 2014, the RVIO held a conference with the title "The Cooperation of the Anti-Hitler Coalition: An Important Factor in the Victory in World War II," to celebrate the seventieth anniversary of the opening of the Second Front;[29] a quick look at the list of presentations shows a patriotic and rather selective understanding of the role the various allies played in the victory over Nazi Germany.

Be that as it may, for more than seventy years the wartime alliance and the meeting on the Elbe have played important roles in political and personal efforts to celebrate the abilities of the Soviet Union/Russia and the United States to work together. In the fall of 2015, *Meetings on the Elbe River: Love on the Ashes of War* was screened in Washington, DC, as part of the commemoration of the seventieth anniversary of the Allied victory in the Second World War. The US-Russia Business Council issued a statement expressing its pleasure that they were able to pay tribute to this historic period of friendship between the former allies.[30] Certainly, May 1945 offered a shared experience of a break between the bloody, horrible war and the Cold War. For a brief moment, the survivors believed in a shared future without conflict. And since then, the Kremlin has held on to the legacy of the Elbe meeting as the most fitting narrative of the possibilities for Russia and the United States to coexist and cooperate. But it is telling of the ambivalence of attitudes that artistic contributions and efforts to celebrate this brief moment of friendship in the Soviet Union and Russia have continually been met with distrust from the Kremlin, which is apparently still anxious to control, contain, and appropriate attitudes toward the United States.

NOTES

A NOTE ON CITATIONS

I provide the title and date or sender/receiver of the archival documents when available. Exceptions are the review files (nadzornye proizvodstva), where I list only their location (fond, opis', delo, list; Eng., collection, subgroup, file, leaf). The 1959 letters to Khrushchev and Eisenhower follow the same principle as the review files.

INTRODUCTION

1. Mark Scott, *Yanks Meet Reds: Recollections of US and Soviet Vets from the Linkup in World War II* (Santa Barbara: Capra Press, 1988), 28. Official celebration of the Elbe linkup was on April 30, 1945. See Harold Denny, "Red Army Honors Hodges on Link-Up: Russians Serve an Elaborate Dinner to Celebrate Meeting of US and Soviet Forces," *New York Times*, May 1, 1945, 4. For further recollections of the Elbe linkup, see Delbert E. Philpott and Donna Philpott, *Hands across the Elbe: The Soviet-American Linkup* (Paducah, KY: Turner Publications, 1995).
2. For a recent work that emphasizes Cold War interactions, see Sari Autio-Sarasmo and Katalin Miklóssy, *Reassessing Cold War Europe* (London: Routledge, 2011).
3. For an incomplete list see Nicholas J. Cull, *The Cold War and the United States Information Agency: American Propaganda and Public Diplomacy, 1945–1989* (Cambridge: Cambridge University Press, 2009); Lisa E. Davenport, *Jazz Diplomacy: Promoting America in the Cold War Era* (Jackson: University Press of Mississippi, 2009); Laura A. Belmonte, *Selling the American Way: US Propaganda and the Cold War* (Philadelphia: University of Pennsylvania Press, 2008); Kenneth Osgood, *Total Cold War: Eisenhower's Secret Propaganda Battle at Home and Abroad* (Lawrence: University Press of Kansas, 2006); Walter L. Hixson, *Parting the Curtain: Propaganda, Culture, and the Cold War, 1945–1961* (New York: St. Martin's Griffin, 1997); and Stephen J. Whitfield, *The Culture of the Cold War*, 2d ed. (Baltimore: Johns Hopkins University Press, 1996).

4. Sheila Fitzpatrick, *On Stalin's Team: The Years of Living Dangerously in Soviet Politics* (Princeton, NJ: Princeton University Press, 2015); and Nikolai Mitrokhin, "The Rise of Political Clans in the Era of Nikita Khrushchev," in *Khrushchev in the Kremlin: Policy and Government in the Soviet Union, 1953–1964*, ed. Jeremy Smith and Melanie Ilic (London and New York: Routledge, 2011), 26–40.

5. Michael David-Fox, "The Iron Curtain as Semipermeable Membrane: Origins and Demise of the Stalinist Superiority Complex," in *Cold War Crossings: International Travel and Exchange across the Soviet Bloc, 1940s–1960s*, ed. Patryk Babiracki and Kenyon Zimmer (College Station: Texas A&M University Press, 2014), 14–39. Here p. 19.

6. See Michael David-Fox, *Showcasing the Great Experiment: Cultural Diplomacy and Western Visitors to the Soviet Union, 1921–1941* (New York: Oxford University Press, 2012); and Michael David-Fox, *Crossing Borders: Modernity, Ideology, and Culture in Russia and the Soviet Union* (Pittsburgh, PA: University of Pittsburgh Press, 2015).

7. Certainly, even earlier narratives of the United States existed in Russia but they will not be recounted here. For an excellent analysis, see Milla Fedorova, *Yankees in Petrograd, Bolsheviks in New York: America and Americans in Russian Literary Perception* (DeKalb: Northern Illinois University Press, 2013).

8. See, for example, Alan M. Ball, *Imagining America: Influence and Images in Twentieth-Century Russia* (Lanham, MD: Rowman & Littlefield, 2003), x.

9. For a discussion about Korolenko and perceptions of America, see Olga Peters Hasty and Susanne Fusso, *America through Russian Eyes, 1874–1926* (New Haven: Yale University Press, 1988), 83–85. See also Vladimir Korolenko, *Puteshestvie v Ameriku* (Moscow: Zadruga, 1923); Vladimir Korolenko, *In a Strange Land* (New York: Bernard G. Richards, 1925); Charles A. Moser, "Korolenko and America," *Russian Review* 28, no. 3 (1969): 303–14; Jane E. Good, "'I'd Rather Live in Siberia': V. G. Korolenko's Critique of America, 1893," *Historian* 44, no. 2 (1982): 190–206; Charles Rougle, *Three Russians Consider America: America in the Works of Maksim Gor'kij, Aleksandr Blok, and Vladimir Majakovskij* (Stockholm: Almqvist & Wiksell International, 1976); Filia Holtzman, "A Mission That Failed: Gor'kij in America," *Slavic and East European Journal* 6, no. 3 (1962): 227–35; Ernest Poole, "Maxim Gorki in New York," *Slavonic and East European Review American Series* 3, no. 1 (1944): 77–83; and Mark Twain, "The Gorki Incident: An Unpublished Fragment (1906)," *Slavonic and East European Review American Series* 3, no. 2 (1944): 37–38. On Mayakovsky see Charles A. Moser, "Mayakovsky and America," *Russian Review* 25, no. 3 (1966): 242–56; and Charles A. Moser, "Mayakovsky's Unsentimental Journeys," *American Slavic and East European Review* 19, no. 1 (1960): 85–100.

10. Fedorova, *Yankees in Petrograd*, 7.

11. Kevin J. McKenna, *All the Views Fit to Print: Changing Images of the US in Pravda Political Cartoons, 1917–1991* (New York: Peter Lang, 2001), 4.

12. Ball, *Imagining America*, 37–38. S. Shvedov, "Obraz Genri Forda v sovetskoi publitsistike 1920–1930-kh godov: vospriiatie i transformatsiia tsennostei chuzhoi

kul'tury," in *Vzaimodeistvie kul'tur SSSR i SShA XVIII–XX vv.*, ed. O. E. Tuganova (Moscow: Nauka, 1987), 133–42; Jeffrey Brooks, "The Press and Its Message: Images of America in the 1920s and 1930s," in *Russia in the Era of NEP: Explorations in Soviet Society and Culture*, ed. Sheila Fitzpatrick, Alexander Rabinowitch, and Richard Stites (Bloomington: Indiana University Press, 1991), 231–52.

13. Richard Stites, *Revolutionary Dreams: Utopian Vision and Experimental Life in the Russian Revolution* (New York: Oxford University Press, 1989), 148. See Kathy M. Iwasaki, "The Memoir as Text: Impressions of American Engineers in the Soviet Union, 1928–1932" (M.A. thesis, UNC–Chapel Hill, 1990).

14. Recounted in Eric Shiraev and Vladislav Zubok, *Anti-Americanism in Russia: From Stalin to Putin* (New York: Palgrave, 2000), 12.

15. Jeffrey Brooks, *Thank You, Comrade Stalin! Soviet Public Culture from Revolution to Cold War* (Princeton, NJ: Princeton University Press, 2000), 37.

16. Ben Hellman, "Samuil Marshak: Yesterday and Today," in *Russian Children's Literature and Culture*, ed. Marina Balina and Larissa Rudova (New York and London: Routledge, 2008), 217–39.

17. Stites, *Revolutionary Dreams*, 149.

18. Recounted in Ball, *Imagining America*, 59–60.

19. Jonathan A. Becker, *Soviet and Russian Press Coverage of the United States: Press, Politics, and Identity in Transition* (New York: Palgrave Macmillan, 2002), 71.

20. McKenna, *All the Views Fit to Print*, 33–39. Quote on p. 39.

21. David Brandenberger, *National Bolshevism: Stalinist Mass Culture and the Formation of Modern Russian National Identity, 1931–1956* (Cambridge, MA: Harvard University Press, 2002), 183. See also Amir Weiner, "The Making of a Dominant Myth: The Second World War and the Construction of Political Identities within the Soviet Polity," *Russian Review* 55, no. 4 (1996): 638–60.

22. Elena Zubkova, *Russia after the War: Hopes, Illusions, and Disappointments, 1945–1957*, trans. and ed. Hugh Ragsdale (Armonk, NY, and London, England: M. E. Sharpe, 1998), 18.

23. Ibid.

24. Dmitry Shlapentokh and Vladimir Shlapentokh, *Soviet Cinematography, 1918–1991: Ideological Conflict and Social Reality* (New York: A. de Gruyter, 1993), 121.

25. Robert Huhn Jones, *The Roads to Russia: United States Lend-Lease to the Soviet Union* (Norman: University of Oklahoma Press, 1969), 265 and 269. One of President Franklin D. Roosevelt's suppositions about Lend-Lease was that it would guarantee Stalin's cooperation in the postwar period.

26. Interview with Eduard Ivanian, historian at the Institute for US and Canada Studies in Moscow, November 27, 2002.

27. Oleg Anisimov, "The Attitude of the Soviet People toward the West," *Russian Review* 13, no. 2 (1954): 79–90. Here p. 86.

28. Richard Stites, "Frontline Entertainment," in *Culture and Entertainment in Wartime Russia*, ed. Richard Stites (Bloomington: Indiana University Press, 1995), 126–40. Here pp. 133–34.

29. Choi Chatterjee, Lisa A. Kirschenbaum, and Deborah A. Field, *Russia's Long Twentieth Century: Voices, Memories, Contested Perspectives* (London and New York: Routledge, 2016), 155.

30. See Stites, *Russian Popular Culture: Entertainment and Society since 1900* (Cambridge: Cambridge University Press, 1992), 104 and 118–19.

31. John Steinbeck, *A Russian Journal* (New York: Penguin Books, 1999), 121–23.

32. The term "propaganda" had a different trajectory in the United States in the twentieth century, where it was eventually seen as an "instrument of coercion" and a "treacherous and deceitful practice." Osgood, *Total Cold War*, 7.

33. David Brandenberger, *Propaganda State in Crisis: Soviet Ideology, Indoctrination, and Terror under Stalin, 1927–1941* (New Haven and London: Yale University Press, 2011), 2.

34. Ibid.

35. See, for example, L. Gudkov, ed., *Obraz vraga* (Moscow: OGI, 2005); and Silke Satjukow and Rainer Gries, eds., *Unsere Feinde: Konstruktionen des Anderen im Sozialismus* (Leipzig: Leipziger Universitätsverlag, 2004). For an overview of enemy images in political cartoons, see, for example, Frank Althaus and Mark Sutcliffe, *Drawing the Curtain: The Cold War in Cartoons* (London: Fontanka, 2012). For the view from the other side, that is, American images of Russia, see Victoria I. Zhuravleva, *Ponimanie Rossii v SShA: obrazy i mify 1881–1914* (Moscow: RGGU, 2012).

36. See David R. Shearer, *Policing Stalin's Socialism: Repression and Social Order in the Soviet Union, 1924–1953* (New Haven: Yale University Press, 2009).

37. David Caute, *The Dancer Defects: The Struggle for Cultural Supremacy during the Cold War* (Oxford: Oxford University Press, 2003), 219–20.

38. Vladislav M. Zubok touches upon this "contrast in consumerist capacities between the West and the East" in his introduction to *Cold War Crossings*, 1–13. Here p. 3.

39. See, for example, Vladislav M. Zubok, *A Failed Empire: The Soviet Union in the Cold War from Stalin to Gorbachev* (Chapel Hill: University of North Carolina Press, 2007); and Melvyn P. Leffler, *For the Soul of Mankind: The United States, the Soviet Union, and the Cold War* (New York: Hill and Wang, 2007).

40. See, for example, Brooks, *Thank You, Comrade Stalin!*; David L. Hoffmann, *Stalinist Values: The Cultural Norms of Soviet Modernity, 1917–1941* (Ithaca, NY: Cornell University Press, 2003); Clive Rose, *The Soviet Propaganda Network: A Directory of Organisations Serving Soviet Foreign Policy* (London: Pinter Publishers, 1988); and Peter Kenez, *The Birth of the Propaganda State: Soviet Methods of Mass Mobilization, 1917–1929* (Cambridge: Cambridge University Press, 1985).

41. A more detailed view of the organizational structure is provided in chapter 3.

42. David-Fox, *Showcasing the Great Experiment*, 14 and 16. See also Paul Sharp, "Revolutionary States, Outlaw Regimes and the Techniques of Public Diplomacy," in *The New Public Diplomacy: Soft Power in International Relations*, ed. Jan Melissen (New York: Palgrave Macmillan, 2005), 106–23.

43. David-Fox, *Showcasing the Great Experiment*, 17.

44. Brandenberger, *Propaganda State in Crisis*, 2.

45. Vladislav Zubok, *Zhivago's Children: The Last Russian Intelligentsia* (Cambridge, MA: Belknap Press of Harvard University Press, 2009), 89.

46. Zubok, *Zhivago's Children*, 73; Eleonory Gilburd, "The Revival of Soviet Internationalism in the Mid to Late 1950s," in *The Thaw: Soviet Society and Culture during the 1950s and 1960s*, ed. Denis Kozlov and Eleonory Gilburd (Toronto: University of Toronto Press, 2013), 362–401. Here p. 363.

47. Akira Iriye, "Culture," *Journal of American History* 77, no. 1 (1990): 99–107. Here p. 100. See also his "Culture and Power: International Relations and Intercultural Relations," *Diplomatic History* 3, no. 2 (1979): 115–28. More recently, Nigel Gould-Davies, "The Logic of Soviet Cultural Diplomacy," *Diplomatic History* 27, no. 2 (2003): 193–214 has discussed Soviet cultural diplomacy, and Jessica C. E. Gienow-Hecht, "'How Good Are We?' Culture and the Cold War," in *The Cultural Cold War in Western Europe, 1945–1960*, ed. Giles Scott-Smith and Hans Krabbendam (London: Frank Cass, 2003), 269–82, looks at cultural diplomacy in general terms.

48. For a recent overview of this trend, see Jan Plamper, "Beyond Binaries: Popular Opinion in Stalinism," in *Popular Opinion in Totalitarian Regimes: Fascism, Nazism, Communism*, ed. Paul Corner (Oxford: Oxford University Press, 2009), 64–80.

49. Especially Brandenberger, *Propaganda State in Crisis* and Zubok, *A Failed Empire*.

CHAPTER I

1. "O meropriiatiiakh Soiuza sovetskikh pisatelei po usileniiu antiamerikanskoi propagandy," Rossiiskii gosudarstvennyi arkhiv sotsial'no-politicheskoi istorii, here-after RGASPI, f. 17, op. 132, d. 234, ll. 54–55.

2. Eric Shiraev and Vladislav Zubok, *Anti-Americanism in Russia: From Stalin to Putin* (New York: Palgrave, 2000), 14.

3. An investigation of the documents of the Agitprop Department of the Central Committee of the CPSU (found in RGASPI, f. 17, op. 125 and 132) reveals the strategy and planning behind the anti-American propaganda in the immediate postwar years. See also Vladimir Pechatnov, "Exercise in Frustration: Soviet Foreign Propaganda in the Early Cold War, 1945–47," *Cold War History* 1, no. 2 (2001): 1–27; and N. I. Nikolaeva, "Obraz SShA v Sovetskom obshchestve v poslevoennye gody, 1945–1953," in *Amerikanskii ezhegodnik*, ed. Nikolai N. Bolkhovitinov (Moscow: Izd-vo Nauka, 2002), 244–70.

4. This definition was noted, for example, in a document from the Communist Party oblast committee of the state of Buryat-Mongolia, October 8, 1948, RGASPI, f. 17, op. 132, d. 15, ll. 83–85.

5. Werner G. Hahn, *Postwar Soviet Politics: The Fall of Zhdanov and the Defeat of Moderation, 1946–53* (Ithaca, NY: Cornell University Press, 1982), 57–78; Kees Boterbloem, *The Life and Times of Andrei Zhdanov, 1896–1948* (Montreal and Kingston: McGill–Queen's University Press, 2004), 254; D. G. Nadzhafov, *Stalin i kosmopolitizm: Dokumenty Agitpropa TsK KPSS, 1945–1953* (Moscow: Materik, 2005), 7; and Sheila Fitzpatrick, *On Stalin's Team*, 192.

6. Nadzhafov, *Stalin i kosmopolitizm*, 31.

7. For Stalin's high approval of Andrei Zhdanov see Sheila Fitzpatrick, *On Stalin's Team*, 178 and 194.

8. Vladislav Zubok and Constantine Pleshakov, *Inside the Kremlin's Cold War: From Stalin to Khrushchev* (Cambridge, MA: Harvard University Press, 1996), 119.

9. Yoram Gorlizki and Oleg Khlevniuk, *Cold Peace: Stalin and the Soviet Ruling Circle, 1945–1953* (New York: Oxford University Press, 2004), 32. Fitzpatrick, *On Stalin's Team*, 191.

10. Gorlizki and Khlevniuk, *Cold Peace*, 34 and 43.

11. Nadzhafov, *Stalin i kosmopolitizm*, 107–8.

12. Gleb Struve, "Anti-Westernism in Recent Soviet Literature," *Yale Review* 39, no. 2 (1949): 209–24.

13. Frederick C. Barghoorn, "The Image of Russia in Soviet Propaganda," in *Soviet Imperialism: Its Origins and Tactics*, ed. Waldemar Gurian (Notre Dame, IN: University of Notre Dame Press, 1953), 137–65. Here pp. 141–42.

14. Peter Kenez, *Cinema and Soviet Society: From the Revolution to the Death of Stalin* (London and New York: I. B. Tauris, 2001), 1. Soviet culture emphasized mass mobilization and indoctrination, and Vadim Volkov argues that words such as enlightenment, education, civilization, literature, and spirituality were used in Russian as synonymous with culture. Vadim Volkov, "The Concept of kul'turnost': Notes on the Stalinist Civilizing Process," in *Stalinism: New Directions*, ed. Sheila Fitzpatrick (London: Routledge, 2000), 210–30. Here p. 212.

15. Shlapentokh and Shlapentokh, *Soviet Cinematography,* 121. David Brandenberger has shown how Stalin's plan for postwar patriotism, embracing both a focus on a russocentric glorious past while embracing the accomplishment of the Soviet war, created the foundation for the Soviet state until its collapse in 1991. Brandenberger, *National Bolshevism*, 192–93 and 196.

16. Konstantin Azadovskii and Boris Egorov, "From Anti-Westernism to Anti-Semitism: Stalin and the Impact of the 'Anti-Cosmopolitan' Campaigns on Soviet Culture," *Journal of Cold War Studies* 4, no. 1 (2002): 66–80. Here p. 67–69.

17. Zubkova, *Russia after the War*, 68.

18. For more on enemy images in the Soviet Union, see Lev Gudkov, "Ideologema 'vraga': 'vragi' kak massovyi sindrom i mekhanizm sotsiokul'turnoi integratsii," in *Obraz vraga*, ed. L. Gudkov (Moscow: OGI, 2005), 7–79.

19. Zubkova, *Russia after the War*, 19.

20. Gorlizki and Khlevniuk, *Cold Peace*, 185, n. 115. See also Robert C. Tucker, "The Cold War in Stalin's Time: What the New Sources Reveal," *Diplomatic History* 21, no. 2 (1997): 273–81. Here p. 276.

21. Tucker, "The Cold War in Stalin's Time," 275–76.

22. Ibid. For a good overview of new research on postwar Soviet anti-Semitism see David Brandenberger, "Stalin's Last Crime? Recent Scholarship on Postwar Soviet Antisemitism and the Doctor's Plot," *Kritika: Explorations in Russian and Eurasian History* 6, no. 1 (2005): 187–204.

23. Tony Shaw and Denise J. Youngblood, *Cinematic Cold War: The American and Soviet Struggle for Hearts and Minds* (Lawrence: University Press of Kansas, 2010), 47.

24. John N. Washburn, *Soviet Theater: Its Distortion of America's Image, 1921 to 1973* (Chicago: American Bar Association, 1973), 22. See also chapter 19 in Michel Gordey, *Visa to Moscow* (New York: Knopf, 1952), 147–52.

25. *Russkii vopros*, directed by Mikhail Il'ich Romm (Moscow, 1947).

26. David Caute, *The Dancer Defects: The Struggle for Cultural Supremacy during the Cold War* (Oxford and New York: Oxford University Press, 2003), 135.

27. Andrei Kozovoi, "The Cold War and Film," in *The Routledge Handbook of the Cold War*, ed. Artemy M. Kalinovsky and Craig Daigle (Oxford and New York: Routledge, 2014), 340–50. Here p. 342.

28. The play opened in Berlin in 1947. See "Russian Play Drops Anti-American Attacks in Version for the Soviet Zone of Germany," *New York Times*, November 12, 1947, 34. The title of the play was translated as "Colonel Kusmin" in the *New York Times* article. For a detailed analysis of the movie see Isabelle de Keghel, *"Meeting on the Elbe (Vstrecha na El'be)*: A Visual Representation of the Incipient Cold War from a Soviet Perspective," *Cold War History* 9, no. 4 (2009): 455–67.

29. *Vstrecha na El'be*, directed by Grigorii Aleksandrov (Moscow, 1949).

30. See Harrison E. Salisbury, "Soviet Films Depict US as Spy and as an Enemy of World Peace: Muscovites See Americans Portrayed as Mata Haris, Thieves of Russian Science, and as Super-Knaves in Germany," *New York Times*, March 18, 1949, 33.

31. *Pravda*, April 1949, passim.

32. Zubkova, *Russia after the War*, passim. See also chapter 2 for more details on the fear of a renewed war.

33. For detailed information about *The Russian Question* see Caute, *The Dancer Defects*, 88–116.

34. For more about rumors in postwar Soviet society, see Timothy Johnston, *Being Soviet: Identity, Rumour, and Everyday Life under Stalin, 1939–1953* (Oxford: Oxford University Press, 2011).

35. Caute, *The Dancer Defects*, 89. The 1946 trip is discussed in chapter 3.

36. Nikolai A. Gorchakov, *The Theater in Soviet Russia*, trans. Edgar Lehrman (New York: Columbia University Press, 1957), 385. For a non-exhaustive list of anti-American plays, see 453: *Velikaia sila* (*Great Force*) by Boris Romashev; *Zakon chesti* (*Law of Honor*) by A Shtein; *Dva lageria* (*Two Camps*) by August Iakobson; *Tsvet kozhi* (*Color of Skin*) by Bill-Belotserkovsky; *Mir* (*Peace*) by Eugene Dolmatovsky; *Liudi dobroi voli* (*People of Good Will*) by G. Mdivani; *Missuriiskii val's* (*Missouri Waltz*) by Nikolai Pogodin; *Zemliak prezidenta* (*Man from the President's Home Region*) by Anatolii Surov; *Chuzhaia ten'* (*Alien Shadow*) by Konstantin Simonov; *Zagovor obrechennykh* (*The Conspiracy of the Doomed*) by Nikolai Virta; *Ia khochu domoi* (*I Want to Go Home*) by Sergei Mikhalkov; *Osobniak v pereulke* (*Lone House in the Alley*) by the Tur brothers and L. Sheinin; and *Mladshii partner* (*Junior Partner*) by Arkady Perventsov.

37. From Konstantin Simonov to Georgy Malenkov, March 19, 1949, RGASPI, f. 17, op. 132, d. 235, ll. 27–29.
38. See Dina Fainberg, "Unmasking the Wolf in Sheep's Clothing: Soviet and American Campaigns against the Enemy's Journalists, 1946–1953," *Cold War History* 15, no. 2 (2015): 155–78.
39. Aleksander M. Egolin was deputy editor of *Zvezda* from 1946 and deputy chief of Agitprop from 1944 to 1947. As of January 1948, he was director of the Institute for Global Literature at the Academy of Sciences (IMLI AN SSSR). See Nadzhafov, *Stalin i kosmopolitizm*, 683.
40. Egolin, "Zakliuchenie Khudozhestvennogo Soveta Ministerstva Kinematografii SSSR o fil'me 'Russkii vopros'," RGASPI, f. 17, op. 125, d. 639, ll. 5–7.
41. Ibid.
42. Ibid.
43. Caute, *The Dancer Defects*, 112.
44. Shaw and Youngblood, *Cinematic Cold War*, 41. See also Maya Turovskaya, "Soviet Films of the Cold War," in *Stalinism and Soviet Cinema*, ed. Richard Taylor and Derek Spring (London and New York: Routledge, 1993), 131–41; and Kozovoi, "The Cold War and Film."
45. Kenez, *Cinema and Soviet Society*, 227.
46. Shaw and Youngblood, *Cinematic Cold War*, 41–42.
47. Evgeny Dobrenko, "Late Stalinist Cinema and the Cold War: An Equation without Unknowns," *Modern Language Review* 98, no. 4 (2003): 929–44. Here p. 940.
48. Andrei Kozovoi, "'This Film Is Harmful'": Resizing America for the Soviet Screen," in *Winter Kept Us Warm: Cold War Interactions Reconsidered*, ed. Sari Autio-Sarasmo and Brendan Humphreys (Helsinki: Aleksanteri Cold War Series, 2010), 137–53. Here pp. 139–40.
49. Ibid., 140.
50. Ibid., 140–41. See also D. Shepilov to Stalin, July 19, 1949: "Dokladnaia zapiska agitpropa TsK I. V. Stalinu o sozdanii kinofil'mov na antiamerikanskuiu temu," RGASPI, f. 17, op. 132, d. 251, l. 54. Also in Nadzhafov, *Stalin i kosmopolitizm*, 452–53. For more information about Shepilov see Dmitrii Shepilov, *The Kremlin's Scholar: A Memoir of Soviet Politics under Stalin and Khrushchev*, ed. Stephen V. Bittner, trans. Anthony Austin (New Haven: Yale University Press, 2007).
51. Kozovoi, "'This Film Is Harmful'," 141.
52. See the January and February (1949) issues of *Kul'tura i zhizn*, which was the Agitprop newspaper.
53. The following documents detail the campaign for the strengthening of anti-American topics in the arts: RGASPI, f. 17, op. 132, d. 234, ll. 26, 27–28, 29, 50–51, 52–53, 56–57, 58–62, 65–66, 67–68, 69–71, 72–74, 75, 76, 78–81, 82. They cover over half of 1949, starting at the end of March and continuing until mid-October. These documents detail topics and themes of plays, circus skits, variety shows, and ballet performances. The year 1949 definitely marked a highlight in efforts

to strengthen anti-Americanism in the arts. For more on the strengthening of anti-Americanism, see the 1949 "Plan meropriiatii po usileniiu anti amerikanskoi propagandy na blizhaishee vremia," RGASPI, f. 17, op. 132, d. 224, ll. 48–52. This plan was all-inclusive and discussed measures to be taken in radio, public lectures, scientific publishing, political and economic studies, as well as in theater, film, and literature.

54. Along with *The Russian Question* and *Governor of the Provinces* (*Gubernator provintsii*, later filmed as *The Meeting on the Elbe*), *Ostrov mira* by E. Petrov, *Na toi storone* and *Serdtsa i dollary* by A. Levada were already playing in Moscow and Leningrad but also in some peripheral cities. From P. Lebedev, Chairman of the Arts Committee at the Soviet Council of Ministers, to Georgy Malenkov, 31 March 1949, RGASPI, f. 17, op. 132, d. 234, l. 26; and "Plan meropriiatii po provedniiu antiamerikanskoi propagandy uchrezhdeniiami iskusstva," ll. 27–28. During the 1940s, several American plays were adapted for the Soviet stage; for an overview see Washburn, *Soviet Theater*, 62.

55. Hellman, "Samuil Marshak," 229. For more on American images in children's literature, see Milla Fedorova, "The Pedagogy of Patriotism: America and Americans in Soviet Children's Literature," in *Russian/Soviet Studies in the United States, Amerikanistika in Russia: Mutual Representations in Academic Projects*, ed. Ivan Kurilla and Victoria I. Zhuravleva (Lanham, MD: Lexington Books, 2016), 121–36.

56. From P. Lebedev to Georgy Malenkov, 31 March 1949, RGASPI, f. 17, op. 132, d. 234, l. 26; and "Plan meropriiatii po provedniiu antiamerikanskoi propagandy uchrezhdeniiami iskusstva," RGASPI, f. 17, op. 132, d. 234, ll. 27–28.

57. Ibid., l. 26.

58. Boris Lavrenev to Stalin, February 6, 1950, RGASPI, f. 17, op. 132, d. 417, ll. 122–26; "Plan meropriiatii po provedniiu antiamerikanskoi propagandy uchrezhdeniiami iskusstva," RGASPI, f. 17, op. 132, d. 234, ll. 27–28.

59. Gorchakov, *Theater in Soviet Russia*, 385. See also Boris Lavrenev's play, *Golos Ameriki*, in Vsevolod Vishnevskii, Sergei Mikhalkov, Konstantin Simonov, and Boris Lavrenev, *Sovetskaia dramaturgiia 1949: P"esy* (Moscow: Iskusstvo, 1950).

60. Gorchakov, *Theater in Soviet Russia*, 385.

61. A. Anastas'ev, "V zashchitu demokratii," *Pravda*, May 16, 1950. Cited in Gorchakov, *Theater in Soviet Russia*, 386.

62. From V. Kruzhkov, deputy head of Agitprop, to M. A. Suslov, April 4, 1950, RGASPI, f. 17, op. 132, d. 417, l. 121.

63. Lavrenev to Stalin, February 6, 1950, RGASPI, f. 17, op. 132, d. 417, ll. 122–26.

64. Ibid., l. 123.

65. Ibid., ll. 122–26.

66. Ibid.

67. Ibid.

68. Gorchakov, *Theater in Soviet Russia*, 385.

69. Lavrenev to Stalin, February 6, 1950, RGASPI, f. 132, d. 417, l. 126.

70. Maria Zezina, "Crisis in the Union of Soviet Writers in the Early 1950s," *Europe-Asia Studies* 46, no. 4 (1994): 649–61.
71. Kenez, *Cinema and Soviet Society*, 201.
72. From Boris Lavrenev to Mikhail Suslov, February 25, 1950, RGASPI, f. 17, op. 132, d. 417, ll. 127–28.
73. Gorchakov, *Theater in Soviet Russia*, 386.
74. Shaw and Youngblood, *Cinematic Cold War*, 41.
75. "Plan meropriiatii po provedniiu antiamerikanskoi propagandy uchrezhdeniiami iskusstva," RGASPI, f. 17, op. 132, d. 234, ll. 27–28.
76. "Postanovlenie Sekretariata TsK VKP(b). O merakh usileniia antiamerikanskoi propagandy po linii iskusstva," RGASPI, f. 17, op. 132, d. 234, ll. 52–53.
77. Hasty and Fusso, *America through Russian Eyes*, 128; Holtzman, "A Mission That Failed," 234. See also Rougle, *Three Russians Consider America*; Poole, "Maxim Gorki in New York"; and Twain, "The Gorki Incident," 37–38.
78. Holtzman, "A Mission That Failed," 230 and 234.
79. Rougle, *Three Russians Consider America*, 143–44.
80. Ibid., 42.
81. From D. Shepilov to Stalin, July 19, 1949, RGASPI, f. 17, op. 132, d. 251, l. 54. Also in Nadzhafov, *Stalin i kosmopolitizm*, 452–53. For more on "The City of the Yellow Devil" by Maxim Gorky see Abbott Gleason's "Republic of Humbug: The Russian Nativist Critique of the United States, 1830–1930," *American Quarterly* 44, no. 1 (1992): 1–23.
82. I. Bol'shakov to Malenkov, March 30, 1949 (forwarded to Suslov March 31, 1949), RGASPI, f. 17, op. 132, d. 251, ll. 46–47; From D. Shepilov and L. Il'ichev to Malenkov, RGASPI, f. 17, op. 132, d. 251, l. 53; and from D. Shepilov to Stalin, July 19, 1949, RGASPI, f. 17, op. 132, d. 251, l. 54. The last document is also printed in Nadzhafov, *Stalin i kosmopolitizm*, 452–53.
83. Krystyna Pomorska, "A Vision of America in Early Soviet Literature," *Slavic and East European Journal* 11, no. 4 (1967): 389–97. Here p. 392.
84. Gleason, "Republic of Humbug," 17.
85. L. Il'ichev to Suslov, March 20, 1948, RGASPI, f. 17, op. 125, d. 610, l. 98.
86. "A.M. Gor'kii: Otvet na ankety amerikanskogo zhurnala," RGASPI, f. 17, op. 125, d. 610, ll. 101–4.
87. Ibid.
88. Alexei Yurchak, *Everything Was Forever, until It Was No More: The Last Soviet Generation* (Princeton, NJ: Princeton University Press, 2005), 48.
89. From Kruzhkov to Suslov, August 19, 1949, RGASPI, f. 17, op. 132, d. 133, l. 48.
90. Ibid., and Kruzhkov to Suslov, undated, RGASPI, f. 17, op. 132, d. 133, l. 49.
91. See E. S. Afanas'eva and V. Iu. Afiani, *Ideologicheskie komissii TsK KPSS 1958–1964: Dokumenty* (Moscow: Rosspen, 2000), 133; and Vladimir Mayakovsky, *My Discovery of America* (London: Hesperus Press, 2005).
92. Joshua Rubenstein, *Tangled Loyalties: The Life and Times of Ilya Ehrenburg* (London: I. B. Tauris, 1996), 238 and 241.

93. Rubenstein, *Tangled Loyalties*, 241. For more on Ehrenburg's experiences in the United States, see chapter 3. Ehrenburg also lectured on his 1946 experiences in the United States and in France. He was critical of both the United States and its people. He spent much energy talking about the unculturedness of Americans as opposed to the culturedness of the French people. For a transcript of a 1946 speech, see Rossiiskii gosudarstvennyi arkhiv literatury i iskusstva, hereafter RGALI, f. 631, op. 14, d. 56, ll. 2–36.
94. From Ehrenburg to Suslov, August 20, 1949, RGASPI, f. 17, op. 132, d. 233, l. 14.
95. Rubenstein, *Tangled Loyalties*, 241.
96. Slepov to Suslov, September 22, 1949, RGASPI, f. 17, op. 132, d. 233, ll. 15–16.
97. Rubenstein, *Tangled Loyalties*, 241.
98. In addition to Rubenstein's *Tangled Loyalties* see Julian L. Laychuk, *Ilya Ehrenburg: An Idealist in an Age of Realism* (Bern: Peter Lang, 1991), 216–39.
99. See *Kul'tura i zhizn'*, April 10 and 20, 1947.
100. Ehrenburg to Suslov, August 20, 1949, RGASPI, f. 17, op. 132, d. 233, l. 14.
101. Slepov to Suslov, September 22, 1949, RGASPI, f. 17, op. 132, d. 233, ll. 15–16.
102. Nikolai Krementsov, *The Cure: A Story of Cancer and Politics from the Annals of the Cold War* (Chicago: University of Chicago Press, 2002), 211.
103. "O sostoianii nauchnoi raboty v oblasti izucheniia Ameriki," From Kruzhkov and Yuri Zhdanov to Suslov, registered June 3, 1951, RGASPI, f. 17, op. 132, d. 452, ll. 37–39.
104. Ibid.
105. In 1952, 101 Soviet organizations received American periodical literature: 1,238 titles were of a scientific and technical nature, 238 of a socioeconomic nature, and 3 titles had to do with the arts. "Spravka ob amerikanskoi periodicheskoi literature, vypisannoi cherez Vsesoiuznoe Ob"edinenie 'Mezhdunarodnaia kniga' sovetskimi organizatsiiami v 1952 godu," Signed by deputy director of the Office of Import P. Konev, RGASPI, f. 17, op. 132, d. 561, l. 59.
106. "O sostoianii nauchnoi raboty v oblasti izucheniia Ameriki," RGASPI, f. 17, op. 132, d. 452, ll. 37–39.
107. Robert D. English, *Russia and the Idea of the West: Gorbachev, Intellectuals, and the End of the Cold War* (New York: Columbia University Press, 2000), 125. See also Kurilla and Zhuravleva, "Preface," in *Russian/Soviet Studies in the United States, Amerikanistika in Russia*, x.
108. For the creation of American Russian and Soviet area studies, see David C. Engerman, *Know Your Enemy: The Rise and Fall of America's Soviet Experts* (Oxford and New York: Oxford University Press, 2009).
109. "O merakh usileniia antiamerikanskoi propagandy po linii iskusstva," RGASPI, f. 17, op. 132, d. 234, ll. 52–53; "O meropriiatiiakh Soiuza sovetskikh pisatelei po usileniiu antiamerikanskoi propagandy," RGASPI, f. 17, op. 132, d. 234, ll. 54–55.

110. For an overview and biographies of several popular and accepted American writers such as Howard Fast, Sinclair Lewis, Upton Sinclair, and Langston Hughes, see RGALI, f. 631, op. 14, d. 1151.

111. Soviet propaganda authorities, however, encouraged Soviet literary scholars to write about the influence of, for example, Tolstoy and Gorky on American writers such as Theodore Dreiser, Upton Sinclair, and Jack London. See Struve, "Anti-Westernism in Recent Soviet Literature," 214.

112. Melville J. Ruggles, "American Books in Soviet Publishing," *Slavic Review* 20, no. 3 (1961): 419–35. Here p. 424.

113. David Caute, *The Fellow-Travellers: A Postscript to the Enlightenment* (New York: Macmillan, 1973), 12.

114. *American and Soviet Leaders Meet at the American Cultural and Scientific Conference for World Peace, New York, 1949. Addresses by Fadeyev, Shostakovich, Oparin* (San Fransisco: American Russian Institute, 1949), 6.

115. "Plan meropriiatii po usileniiu anti amerikanskoi propagandy na blizhaishee vremia," RGASPI, f. 17, op. 132, d. 224, ll. 48–52. Here l. 50.

116. Paul Hollander reminds us that the appeal of the Soviet Union remained widespread in the late 1920s and throughout the Second World War. Paul Hollander, *Political Pilgrims: Western Intellectuals in Search of the Good Society* (New Brunswick, NJ: Transaction, 1998), 103. For an outstanding account of this period, see David-Fox, *Showcasing the Great Experiment*.

117. Ruggles, "American Books in Soviet Publishing," 428. For more about the American literary canon in the Soviet Union, see Olga Yu. Antsyferova, "American Literary Canons in the Soviet Union and Post-Soviet Russia," in *Russian/Soviet Studies in the United States, Amerikanistika in Russia*, 137–54.

118. Ruggles, "American Books in Soviet Publishing," 431–32.

119. Valentin Kiparsky, *English and American Characters in Russian Fiction* (Berlin: In Kommission bei O. Harrassowitz Wiesbaden, 1964), 194–95.

120. Ruggles, "American Books in Soviet Publishing," 426.

121. Allison Blakely, *Russia and the Negro: Blacks in Russian History and Thought* (Washington, DC: Howard University Press, 1986), 105.

122. Ibid., 110.

123. For more on Paul Robeson's and W. E. B. Du Bois's outspoken criticism of American racial problems, see Mary L. Dudziak, "Josephine Baker, Racial Protest, and the Cold War," *Journal of American History* 81, no. 2 (1994): 546. Also see Tony Perucci, *Paul Robeson and the Cold War Performance Complex: Race, Madness, Activism* (Ann Arbor: University of Michigan Press, 2012).

124. We hear more about that in chapter 4.

125. When the US State Department and the Library of Congress requested Soviet journals in 1952, the Soviet Ministry of Foreign Trade decided that it was not urgent to answer such requests. From G. Koftov, December 27, 1952, RGASPI, f. 17, op. 132, d. 561, l. 57.

126. From Konstantin Simonov to Malenkov, April 1, 1949, RGASPI, f. 17, op. 132, d. 224, l. 55.

127. From A. Morozov, director of Gosinoizdat (the State Publishing House of Foreign Literature), to A. N. Poskrevyshev, August 30, 1948, RGASPI, f. 17, op. 132, d. 22, l. 9; L I'lichev to Malenkov et al., September 14, 1948, RGASPI, f. 17, op. 132, d. 22, l. 10 (direct quote). See also Lee Fryer, *The American Farmer: His Problems & His Prospects* (New York and London: Harper & Brothers, 1947).

128. For information on the politics of literature in the Soviet Union see Harold Swayze, *Political Control of Literature in the USSR, 1946–1959* (Cambridge, MA: Harvard University Press, 1962). Swayze does not deal directly with American topics but his study provides a very useful background for understanding the control the Soviet Communist Party exerted over literature. For a detailed analysis of America and Americans in Soviet literature in a more recent account, see Fedorova, *Yankees in Petrograd*. For older works, see Vera Alexandrova, "America and Americans in Soviet Literature," *Russian Review* 2, no. 2 (1943): 19–26; Kiparsky, *English and American Characters in Russian Fiction*; and Rougle, *Three Russians Consider America*.

129. Penny M. von Eschen, "'Satchmo Blows Up the World': Jazz, Race, and Empire During the Cold War," in *'Here, There, and Everywhere': The Foreign Politics of American Popular Culture*, ed. Reinhold Wagnleitner and Elaine Tyler May (Hanover, NH: University Press of New England, 2000), 163–78. Here p. 164.

CHAPTER 2

1. Cull, *The Cold War and the United States Information Agency*, 38.

2. Belmonte, *Selling the American Way*, 5 and 9.

3. Cull, *The Cold War and the United States Information Agency*, 34–35.

4. "Otchet o rabote lektorskoi gruppy Dnepropetrovskogo obkoma, gorkomov i raikomov KP(b) Ukrainy za 1950–1951 uchebnyi god," RGASPI, f. 17, op. 132, d. 467, ll. 18–30. Here l. 22.

5. Cull, *The Cold War and the United States Information Agency*, 29–30.

6. Belmonte, *Selling the American Way*, 15 and 21. Quotes on p. 15.

7. Ibid., 15. This is a matter of dispute. Kennan said in 1947 he was misunderstood, and he never wanted to inspire the policy of containment as it was implemented by Truman and Dulles. See John Lewis Gaddis, *George F. Kennan: An American Life* (New York: Penguin Books, 2011).

8. Cull, *The Cold War and the United States Information Agency*, 35.

9. Hixson, *Parting the Curtain*, 10–11.

10. Ibid., 10–11, 32.

11. See, for example, Cull, *The Cold War and the United States Information Agency*.

12. For example, Hixson, *Parting the Curtain*; and Yale Richmond, *Cultural Exchange and the Cold War: Raising the Iron Curtain* (University Park: Pennsylvania State University Press, 2003).

13. See, for example, Laura Belmonte, *Selling the American Way*, 11. Parts of Johnston's book *Being Soviet* touch upon this issue. Also see Juliane Fürst, *Stalin's Last Generation: Soviet Post-War Youth and the Emergence of Mature Socialism* (Oxford: Oxford University Press, 2010), 68–73; and Konstantin Valentinovich Avramov, "Soviet America: Popular Responses to the United States in Post-World War II Soviet Union" (Ph.D. diss., University of Kansas, 2012).

14. This of course builds on a tradition of Soviet censorship—see T. M. Goriaeva, *Politicheskaia tsenzura v SSSR, 1917–1991* (Moscow: Rosspen, 2002)—but the focus here is on the anti-American campaign, which was new.

15. From Ramsin, Ministry of Communications, to K. S. Kuzakov, deputy head of Agitprop, and K. V. Zinchenko, Press Department at the Ministry of Foreign Affairs (MID), August 15, 1946, RGASPI, f. 17, op. 125, d. 436, ll. 5–5ob.

16. Ibid.

17. From Ramsin to K. S. Kuzakov, August 26, 1946, RGASPI, f. 17, op. 125, d. 436, l. 6.

18. To Zhdanov, undated. RGASPI, f. 17, op. 125, d. 436, ll. 41–42. Also cited in Vladimir O. Pechatnov, "The Rise and Fall of Britansky Soyuznik: A Case Study in Soviet Response to British Propaganda of the Mid-1940s," *Historical Journal* 41, no. 1 (1998): 293–301. Here p. 300. Translation is my own. The Agitprop discussion often refers to both the American journal, *Amerika*, and the British publication, *Britanskii Soiuznik*.

19. Pechatnov, "The Rise and Fall of Britansky Soyuznik," 300.

20. "Razmeshenie tirazha ezhenedel'nika *Britanskii Soiuznik* s 1947 goda i ezhemesiachnogo zhurnala *Amerike* no 7," RGASPI, f. 17, op. 125, d. 436, l. 7.

21. From Psurtsev, Soiuzpechat' to Molotov, November 18, 1949, RGASPI, f. 82, op. 2, d. 982, ll. 27–29.

22. Andrey Vyshinsky replaced Molotov as foreign minister in March 1949. Fitzpatrick, *On Stalin's Team*, 205.

23. From Psurtsev, Soiuzpechat' to Molotov, RGASPI, f. 82, op. 2, d. 982, ll. 27–29.

24. From Molotov to Malenkov, Beria, Kaganovich, and Bulganin, November 18, 1949, RGASPI, f. 82, op. 2, d. 982, l. 32.

25. From Psurtsev to Molotov, November 18, 1949, RGASPI, f. 82, op. 2, d. 982, ll. 33–35.

26. Ramsin, November 1949, "Proekt peregovorov s press attashe posol'stva SShA ob usloviiakh raschetov za zhurnal *Amerika*," RGASPI, f. 82, op. 2, d. 982, ll. 49–52.

27. The whole case also involves the publications of *Britanskii Soiuznik* and *Britanskii Khronik*, not detailed here. Stalin, "Postanovlenie, 1949g. Moskva, Kreml', Ob izmenenii uslovii rasprostraneniia izdanii *Britanskii Soiuznik, Britanskaia Khronika, i Amerika*," RGASPI, f. 82, op. 2, d. 982, ll. 40–41.

28. Cull, *The Cold War and the United States Information Agency*, 38. According to Cull, the American embassy in Moscow saw these "developments as a testament to the effectiveness of US information work."

29. Foreign Relations of the United States, 1950, 4 (hereafter FRUS, year, vol): 1119–20.

30. FRUS, 1950, 4: 1103–4.

31. Ibid., 1119–20.

32. Ibid.

33. "Proekt peregovorov s press attashe posol'stva SShA ob usloviiakh raschetov za zhurnal *Amerika*," RGASPI, f. 82, op. 2, d. 982, ll. 49–52.

34. FRUS, 1950, 4: 1120.

35. From the American embassy in Moscow, July 14, 1952. Gosudarstvennyi arkhiv Rossiiskoi Federatsii, hereafter GARF, f. 5283, op. 22, d. 338, l. 113.

36. From A. Khan'kovskii to Malenkov, May 14, 1951, RGASPI, f. 17, op. 132, d. 486, ll. 131–32. The letter is also published in Nadzhafov, *Stalin i kosmopolitizm*, 621–22.

37. Ibid.

38. From A. Khan'kovskii to Malenkov and Suslov, October 29, 1951, RGASPI, f. 17, op. 132, d. 486, ll. 267–72.

39. Belmonte, *Selling the American Way*, 47.

40. Michael Nelson, *War of the Black Heavens: The Battles of Western Broadcasting in the Cold War* (Syracuse, NY: Syracuse University Press, 1997), 10.

41. "Nekotorye dannye po organizatsii i deiatel'nosti radioveshchaniia iz SShA na zagranitsu 'Golos Ameriki,'" RGASPI, f. 17, op. 132, d. 94, ll. 67–70. This document is a translation from the *Armed Forces Talk* bulletin. See also Ludmilla Alexeyeva, *US Broadcasting to the Soviet Union* (New York: US Helsinki Watch Committee, 1986).

42. Alexeyeva, *US Broadcasting to the Soviet Union*, 9 and 79. The languages are Russian, Ukrainian, Georgian, Armenian, Azeri, Uzbek, Estonian, Latvian, and Lithuanian. The Baltic countries were assigned to the VOA European division (because the United States did not recognize incorporation of the three Baltic republics into the USSR).

43. Nelson, *War of the Black Heavens*, 20. No English-language broadcasts of either the VOA or the BBC were jammed; see ibid., 24.

44. Maury Lisann, *Broadcasting to the Soviet Union: International Politics and Radio* (New York: Praeger Publishers, 1975), 8.

45. See, for example, Kristin Roth-Ey, *Moscow Prime Time: How the Soviet Union Built the Media Empire That Lost the Cultural Cold War* (Ithaca, NY, and London: Cornell University Press, 2011), 138–41.

46. Alex Inkeles, "The Soviet Attack on the Voice of America: A Case Study in Propaganda Warfare," *American Slavic and East European Review* 12, no. 3 (1953): 319.

47. Rubenstein, *Tangled Loyalties*, 240.

48. Nelson, *War of the Black Heavens*, 22.

49. The estimate on radio receivers in 1950 comes from a translation from *Armed Forces Talk* bulletin in RGASPI, f. 17, op. 132, d. 94, ll. 67–70. The estimate on 1955 comes from Lisann, *Broadcasting to the Soviet Union*, 4.

50. Roth-Ey, *Moscow Prime Time*, 132–33. See also Stephen Lovell, *Russia in the Microphone Age: A History of Soviet Radio, 1919–1970* (Oxford: Oxford University Press, 2015), 135.

51. Lisann, *Broadcasting to the Soviet Union*, 4. The study Lisann refers to is a 1967 dissertation by Rosemarie S. Rodgers, "The Soviet Audience: How It Uses the Mass Media" (Ph.D. diss., Massachusetts Institute of Technology, 1967).

52. "O navedenii poriadka v ispol'zovanii radiopriemnikov kollektivnogo sluzhaniia," August 30, 1950, RGASPI, f. 17, op. 88, d. 950, ll. 74–75.

53. "O transliatsiiakh antisvoetskoi radiostantsii 'Golos Ameriki' po Chukotskoi radioseti," RGASPI, f. 17, op. 88, d. 950, l. 50.

54. Sniečkus to Suslov, April 2, 1951, RGASPI, f. 17, op. 132, d. 491, l. 1.

55. Hixson, *Parting the Curtain*, 38–46. See also Alexander Rapoport, "The Russian Broadcasts of the Voice of America," *Russian Review* 16, no. 3 (1957): 3–14.

56. Hixson, *Parting the Curtain*, 40, 42–44.

57. *The Image of the Voice of America as Drawn in Soviet Media*. Prepared for the Office of Research and Intelligence at the United States Information Agency by the Department of Sociology (New Brunswick, NJ: Rutgers University, 1954).

58. Alex Inkeles, *Social Change in Soviet Russia* (Cambridge, MA: Harvard University Press, 1968), 346.

59. Nelson, *War of the Black Heavens*, 35–38.

60. For a good overview of this literature, see Mark Edele, "Strange Young Men in Stalin's Moscow: The Birth and Life of the Stiliagi, 1945–1953," *Jahrbücher für Geschichte Osteuropas* 50, no. 1 (2002): 37–61. Fürst, *Stalin's Last Generation*, also provides an excellent analysis of postwar Soviet youth; especially chapter 6 focuses on the role of *stiliagi* in terms of challenging Soviet identity.

61. Plamper, "Beyond Binaries: Popular Opinion in Stalinism," 66.

62. Sheila Fitzpatrick, "Popular Opinion in Russia under Pre-war Stalinism," in Corner, *Popular Opinion in Totalitarian Regimes*, 17–32. Here p. 20.

63. Brandenberger, *Propaganda State in Crisis*, 6.

64. Sheila Fitzpatrick, "Popular Opinion in Russia under Pre-war Stalinism," 20.

65. "Informatsiia o podgotovke k vyboram v Verkhovnyi Sovet SSSR po Novgorodskoi oblasti," January 11, 1946, RGASPI, f. 17, op. 125, d. 420, ll. 32–33.

66. "Spisok voprosov, zadavaemykh trudiashchimisia Novosibirskoi oblasti v poslednee vremia," June 2, 1945, RGASPI, f. 17, op. 125, d. 343, l. 97.

67. "Informatsiia ob otklikakh trudiashchikhsia Leningradskoi oblasti na sessiiu General'noi assamblei organizatsii Ob"edinennykh natsii," RGASPI, f. 17, op. 125, d. 510, ll. 16–19. Here l. 17.

68. Ibid. The sources usually use Angliia, or England, rather than the United Kingdom.

69. "Naibolee kharakternykh voprosov, zadannykh lektoram i dokladchikam Voronezhskogo Obkoma VKP(b) v dekabre 1945 goda," RGASPI, f. 17, op. 125, d. 420, ll. 21–24.

70. Ibid. See also "Perechen' voprosov zadannykh chlenam propgrupp Upravleniia propagandy v oktiabre s.g. [1947]," RGASPI, f. 17, op. 125, d. 515, l. 24.

71. "Informatsiia o podgotovke k vyboram v Verkhovnyi Sovet SSSR po Novgorodskoi oblasti," January 11, 1946, RGASPI, f. 17, op. 125, d. 420, ll. 32–33. Here l. 33.

72. Andrea Graziosi and Oleg Khlevniuk, eds., *Sovetskaia zhizn', 1945–1953* (Moscow: Rosspen, 2003), passim.

73. See for example David J. Dallin, *The Real Soviet Russia*, trans. Joseph Shaplen (New Haven: Yale University Press, 1947), 101.

74. See, for example, Johnston, *Being Soviet*, 162.

75. "Voprosy, kotorye interesuiut rabochikh, sluzhashchikh, domokhoziaek po mezhdunarodnomu i vnutrennemu polozheniiu pri provedenii dokladov, lektsii i besed na predpriiatiiakh, ucherezhdeniiakh, i sredi naseleniia Sokol'nicheskogo raiona," October 8, 1947, RGASPI, f. 17, op. 125, d. 510, l. 23–25.

76. Sheila Fitzpatrick, "Popular Opinion in Russia under Pre-war Stalinism," 20. Fitzpatrick is discussing Terry Martin's unpublished conclusions in term of how the latest research on the creation and role of the *svodki* suggests, that "by the end of the 1920s the political leaders had mainly lost interest in the information from *svodki*, being less interested in opinion in general than in warnings about where active unrest was likely to flare up."

77. "Spisok voprosov zadannykh lektoram i dokladchhikam po tekushchemu momentu (za oktiabr' 1947g)," RGASPI, f. 17, op. 125, d. 510, ll. 30–32. Here l. 31.

78. See, for example, Hugo S. Cunningham's English translation, "Article 58, Criminal Code of the RSFSR (1934)," retrieved from http://www.cyberussr.com/rus/uk58-e.html (Accessed on March 10, 2016).

79. The review files are cited by archival acronym, fond number, opis', and delo.

80. Radio broadcasting, as Maury Lisann has speculated, "may account for more communication between the Communist and non-Communist parts of the world than all forms of private and laboriously negotiated intergovernmental exchanges combined." Lisann, *Broadcasting to the Soviet Union*, v. See also Alexeyeva, *US Broadcasting to the Soviet Union*.

81. It should be noted that due to both published and unpublished databases at GARF, it was possible to search for files that addressed either Amerika or USA.

82. GARF, f. 8131, op. 31, d. 41583, l. 28. See A. Ia. Livshin and I.V. Orlov, eds. *Sovetskaia propaganda v gody Velikoi otechestvennoi voiny: 'Kommunikatsiia ubezhdeniia' i mobilizatsionnye mekhanizmy* (Moscow: Rosspen, 2007). In order to protect the identity of people accused of anti-Soviet behavior, I do not refer to individuals by their real names.

83. V. A. Kozlov and S. V. Mironenko, *58.10: nadzornye proizvodstva prokuratury SSSR po delam ob antisovetskoi agitatsii i propagande. Annotirovannyi katalog, mart 1953–1991* (Moscow: Mezhdunardnyi fond "Demokratiia"), 297.

84. GARF, f. 8131, op. 31, d. 43024, ll. 1–2.

85. Clearly this person fit many anti-Soviet categories and would obviously have been a surveillance target. For an analysis of the tensions inherent in the operation of Soviet control, see Cynthia Hooper, "Terror from Within: Participation and Coercion in Soviet Power, 1924–1964" (Ph.D. diss., Princeton University, 2003).

86. GARF, f. 8131, op. 31, d. 14162, ll. 1, 1ob. In 1957 when this woman appealed for rehabilitation, her appeal was declined. See ibid., l. 37: "Your guilt was confirmed by a number of witnesses and other materials in your file."

87. For more cases, see for example GARF, f. 8131, op. 31, d. 12854, ll. 1–4 and the emphasis on defeatist moods or ibid., d. 12917, l. 2, where "nice treatment of German occupants among the village population" is a main crime.

88. "O sostoianii politicheskoi raboty sredi naseleniia zapadnykh oblastei Belorusskoi SSR," RGASPI, f. 17, op. 125, d. 311, ll. 1–8.

89. GARF, f. 8131, op. 31, d. 44809, l. 11.

90. GARF, f. 8131, op. 36, d. 1052, l. 7.

91. GARF, f. 8131, op. 31, d. 14157, l. 1.

92. Ibid., l. 15.

93. Ibid.

94. Ibid., ll. 1–2.

95. Nikolaeva, "Obraz SShA v Sovetskom obshchestve v poslevoennye gody, 1945–1953," 246–47.

96. GARF, f. 8131, op. 31, d. 38230, l. 7.

97. GARF, f. 8131, op. 31, d. 40557, l. 8. Another international postwar issue much debated in the Soviet Union was the state of Israel. Soviet Jews were often prosecuted for their anti-Soviet (i.e., "nationalistic") behavior, and often their "crime" involved applauding Israel's orientation toward America.

98. GARF, f. 8131, op. 31, d. 38577, l. 62.

99. Ibid., l. 82.

100. GARF, f. 8131, op. 31, d. 78153, l. 4.

101. Ibid., l. 26.

102. GARF, f. A-461, op. 1, d. 131, ll. 16–20 and 29.

103. This is likely a play of words on the title of the famous article by Ilya Ehrenburg published in *Kul'tura i zhizn'* April 10, 1947, discussed in chapter 1. The article was entitled "A False Voice" and marked the opening of the Soviet attack on the Voice of America. In a quantitative study of the Soviet response to the Voice of America, Alex Inkeles considered the Soviet Press and Soviet radio broadcasts and the frequency of references to VOA in them. He claimed that most references to the VOA were made in passing, but in looking at how Soviet sources countered the impact of the VOA, he concluded that they did so almost solely "by presenting a negative picture of the United States, its policies and intentions, rather than by concentrating on redrawing the negative image of the Soviet Union which the VOA disseminates." See Alex Inkeles, "The Soviet Attack on the Voice of America," 333. See also his "Soviet Reactions to the Voice of America," *Public Opinion Quarterly* 16, no. 4 (1952–1953): 612–17.

104. GARF, f. A-461, op. 1, d. 131, l. 18.

105. GARF, f. A-461, op. 1, d. 1307, ll. 9–14. For a similar statement mentioning the Voice of America as a source of information, see GARF, f. 8131, op. 31, d. 40704, l. 6.

106. Hoffmann, *Stalinist Values*, 155.
107. Ibid. See also Jan Plamper, *The Stalin Cult: A Study in the Alchemy of Power* (New Haven: Yale University Press, 2012); and Brooks, *Thank You, Comrade Stalin!*
108. GARF, f. 8131, op. 31, d. 43064, l. 3.
109. Ibid., l. 4.
110. GARF, f. 8131, op. 31, d. 40557, l. 9.
111. Ibid.
112. Ibid., l. 7.
113. GARF, f. 8131, op. 31, d. 44809, l. 4.
114. Ibid., l. 6.
115. See, for example, Zubkova, *Russia after the War*; and Steven Lovell, *The Shadow of War: The Soviet Union and Russia, 1941 to the Present* (Malden, MA: Wiley-Blackwell, 2010).
116. Fitzpatrick, "Popular Opinion in Russia under Pre-war Stalinism," 24.
117. Roth-Ey, *Moscow Prime Time*, 133–34; and Simo Mikkonen, "Stealing the Monopoly of Knowledge? Soviet Reactions to US Cold War Broadcasting," *Kritika: Explorations in Russian and Eurasian History* 11, no. 4 (2010): 771–805.
118. On foreign radio broadcasts, see Roth-Ey, *Moscow Prime Time*, 133–34.
119. A summary of the 1944 agreement is available in RGASPI, f. 17, op. 125, d. 355, l. 102.

CHAPTER 3

1. "Otchet o rabote VOKS v SShA v 1946 godu," GARF, f. 5283, op. 22s, d. 581, ll. 25–77. Here l. 28. VOKS stands for Vsesoiuznoe obshchestvo kul'turnykh sviazei s zagranitsei.
2. Caroline S. Emmons, ed., *Cold War and McCarthy Era: People and Perspectives* (Santa Barbara, CA: ABC-CLIO, 2010), xx–xxii. Quote on p. xxii.
3. Department of State, *Cultural Relations between the United States and the Soviet Union: Efforts to Establish Cultural-Scientific Exchanges Blocked by USSR* (Washington, DC: United States Government Printing Office, 1949).
4. This was also true for the prewar years. See David-Fox, *Showcasing the Great Experiment*, 5.
5. Louis Nemzer, "The Soviet Friendship Societies," *Public Opinion Quarterly* 13, no. 2 (1949): 265–84. Here p. 271. Nemzer claims that VOKS was established on August 8, 1925, but April 5 is the official date. See S. V. Mironenko, *Fondy Gosudarstvennogo arkhiva Rossiiskoi Federatsii po istorii SSSR*, Vol. 3 (Moscow: Reaktsionno-izdatel'skii otdel federal'nykh arkhivov, 1997), 644. While the financial side of cultural relations is interesting, especially in terms of how much funding American front organizations got directly from Soviet sources, it is not a subject here.
6. Michael David-Fox, "From Illusory 'Society' to Intellectual 'Public': VOKS, International Travel, and Party-Intelligentsia Relations in the Interwar Period," *Contemporary European History* 11, no. 1 (2002): 7–32. Here p. 11.

7. Nemzer, "The Soviet Friendship Societies," 271–74. According to the VOKS organizational charts, its several departments dealt with anything from book exchanges, exhibits, printed materials, and the receiving of foreigners in the Soviet Union. The VOKS Moscow office had different geographical departments and issues of the United States were dealt with in the American department, which also included Canada and Latin America. Mironenko, *Fondy Gosudarstvennogo arkhiva*, 644.

8. See, for example, Ludmila Stern, "The All-Union Society for Cultural Relations with Foreign Countries and French Intellectuals, 1925–29," *Australian Journal of Politics & History* 45, no. 1 (1999): 99–109.

9. Nemzer, "The Soviet Friendship Societies," 273–74.

10. Ibid., 274. See also articles by Shawn Salmon and Anne E. Gorsuch in *Turizm: The Russian and East European Tourist under Capitalism and Socialism*, ed. Anne E. Gorsuch and Diane Koenker (Ithaca, NY: Cornell University Press, 2006).

11. David-Fox, *Showcasing the Great Experiment*, 60.

12. Ibid., 57.

13. David-Fox, "From Illusory 'Society,'" 10. Michael David-Fox emphasizes the role of the non-party intelligentsia in the early stages of Soviet cultural diplomacy and discusses the role of VOKS within what he calls the two "cultural fronts"—that is, a domestic as well as an international one.

14. Mironenko, *Fondy Gosudarstvennogo arkhiva*, 172. See also an Intourist organizational chart from 1948 in GARF, f. 9612, op. 1, d. 186, ll. 1–6.

15. Mironenko, *Fondy Gosudarstvennogo arkhiva*, 172. Intourist was meant to develop every aspect of foreign tourism in the USSR: it serviced foreign tourists, welcomed them in the USSR, and organized tourism from the USSR to other countries. In the 1960s, when tourism had become more of a common practice, Intourist worked closely with the friendship societies in order to set up contacts for foreigners with "likeminded" Soviet people. See "Spravka o rabote otdelov po turizmu so stranami i otdelov gidovperevodchikov Pravleniia po organizatsii vstrech inostrannykh turistov s sovetskimi liud'mi na baze kollektivnykh chlenov obshchestv druzhby SSOD v sezone 1963 goda," GARF, f. 9612, op. 1, d. 555, ll. 1–3.

16. Shawn Salmon, "Marketing Socialism: Inturist in the Late 1950s and Early 1960s," in *Turizm*, 186–204. Here p. 188–89.

17. Frederic Dimanche and Lidia Andrades, eds., *Tourism in Russia: A Management Handbook* (Bingley: Emerald Group, 2015), 24.

18. Rose, *The Soviet Propaganda Network*, 252.

19. Ibid., 253.

20. The National Council of American-Soviet Friendship and the American Russian Institute were the main public organizations (front groups) in the United States.

21. David-Fox, *Showcasing the Great Experiment*, passim.

22. Kemenov, "O rabote Vsesoiuznogo obshchestva kul'turnoi sviazi s zagranitsei," 1945, RGASPI, f. 17, op. 125, d. 371, ll. 138–144ob. See also similar appeals from the American department at VOKS in January 1946, citing repeated advances from the Americans, in GARF, f. 5283, op. 22, d. 14.

23. "O rabote Vsesoiuznogo obshchestva kul'turnoi sviazi s zagranitsei," 1945, RGASPI, f. 17, op. 125, d. 371, l. 143.
24. Cited in Pechatnov, "Exercise in Frustration," 1.
25. "Otchet o rabote VOKS v SShA v 1946 godu," GARF, f. 5283, op. 22s, d. 581, l. 27.
26. Ibid., ll. 25–26.
27. Ibid., ll. 27–28. Quote on l. 27.
28. Ibid., ll. 25–26.
29. From V. Kemenov to Molotov and Malenkov, June 25, 1945, RGASPI, f. 17, op. 125, d. 371, l. 127.
30. Department of State, *Cultural Relations*, 7.
31. "O sovetskikh radioperedachakh na SShA," received April 13, 1946, RGASPI, f. 17, op. 125, d. 470, ll. 126–27.
32. "Otchet o rabote VOKS v SShA v 1946 godu," GARF, f. 5283, op. 22s, d. 581, l. 28.
33. Ilya Ehrenburg and his traveling companions published a book with this title after their trip to the United States. See Ilya Ehrenburg, Mikhail Galaktinov, and Konstantin Simonov, *We Have Seen America* (New York: National Council of American-Soviet Friendship, 1946).
34. Caute, *The Dancer Defects*, 89.
35. Ibid., 89 and 91. Quote on p. 91. See also Ehrenburg et al., *We Have Seen America*.
36. Caute, *The Dancer Defects*, 89.
37. Rubenstein, *Tangled Loyalties*, 232–33.
38. Cited in ibid., 238.
39. Ehrenburg et al., *We Have Seen America*.
40. "Otchet o rabote VOKS v SShA v 1946 godu," GARF, f. 5283, op. 22s, d. 581, l. 28.
41. Ehrenburg et al., *We Have Seen America*, 13. This particular passage was written by Galaktinov.
42. "Ob"iasnitel'naia zapiska k planu amerikanskogo otdela VOKS na 1947 god," GARF, f. 5283, op. 22s, d. 590, ll. 2–3. Quote on l. 2.
43. Ibid., l. 2.
44. Ibid.
45. Ibid.
46. The American government supported a group of anti-Soviet American writers called "Americans for Intellectual Freedom" in its efforts to disrupt the meeting. Richard H. Pells, *Not Like Us: How Europeans Have Loved, Hated, and Transformed American Culture since World War II* (New York: Basic Books, 1997), 70. On the secret cultural activities of the American government in Western Europe, see Frances Stonor Saunders, *The Cultural Cold War: The CIA and the World of Arts and Letters* (New York: New Press, 2000).
47. Caute, *The Dancer Defects*, 420–21.
48. The Central Committee clearly controlled the themes the delegation was allowed to bring up in the United States. "V sviazi s predstoiashchei poezdkoi v SShA v sostave sovetskoi delegatsii na kongress 'Za mir' kompozitora Shostakovicha D.D.,

t. Paniushkin zaprazhivaet o vozmozhnosti ego vystupleniia v kontsertakh," March 10, 1949, RGASPI, f. 17, op. 132, d. 242, l. 27.

49. *American and Soviet Leaders Meet at the American Cultural and Scientific Conference for World Peace, New York, 1949. Addresses by Fadeyev, Shostakovich, Oparin* (San Francisco: American Russian Institute, 1949), 3.

50. J. D. Parks, *Culture, Conflict, and Coexistence: American-Soviet Cultural Relations, 1917–1958* (Jefferson, NC: McFarland, 1983), 127.

51. J. D. Parks recounts how a Soviet chess team of fifteen players visited the United States in May 1953. Parks, *Culture, Conflict, and Coexistence*, 138.

52. From the Soviet Embassy in Washington to VOKS, August 5, 1952, GARF, f. 5283, op. 22, d. 338, ll. 133–36.

53. Ibid., l. 133.

54. The other American was Peter Blackman, a radical poet, who was not listed in the VOKS document. Several other organizations could have invited him, most likely the Soviet Writers' Union. For more on the 1949 festivities see Olga Voronina, "'The Sun of World Poetry': Pushkin as a Cold War Writer," *Pushkin Review* 14 (2011): 63–95.

55. "Spisok delegatsii i deiatelei Amerikanskoi kul'tury i nauki, posetivshikh SSSR nachinaia s 1945 g," GARF, f. 5283, op. 14. d. 573, ll. 1–1a. The report lists American scientific and cultural delegations and visitors from 1945 to 1951.

56. Department of State, *Cultural Relations*, 10.

57. Anne E. Gorsuch, *All This Is Your World: Soviet Tourism at Home and Abroad after Stalin* (New York: Oxford University Press, 2011), 26–27. Quote on p. 27. See also Diane P. Koenker, *Club Red: Vacation Travel and the Soviet Dream* (Ithaca, NY: Cornell University Press, 2013), 128–66.

58. "Kon"iunkturnyi obzor po mezhdunarodnomu turizmu v poslevoennyi period," October 30, 1947, GARF, f. 9612, op. 1, d. 174, ll. 1–18. Quote l. 1.

59. In this context, it seemed to also be of some concern that Slavic countries aspired to good relations with the capitalist world.

60. See, for example, Brian A. McKenzie, "Creating a Tourist's Paradise: The Marshall Plan and France, 1948 to 1952," *French Politics, Culture & Society* 21, no. 1 (2003): 35–54; Kathleen Burk, "The Marshall Plan: Filling In Some of the Blanks," *Contemporary European History* 10, no. 2 (2001): 267–94. See also Christopher Endy, *Cold War Holidays: American Tourism in France* (Chapel Hill: University of North Carolina Press, 2004).

61. "Spisok delegatsii i deiatelei Amerikanskoi kul'tury i nauki, posetivshikh SSSR nachinaia s 1945 g," GARF, f. 5283, op. 14, d. 573, ll. 1–1a.

62. Steinbeck, *Russian Journal*, xxi–xxii.

63. GARF, f. 5283, op. 22, d. 25, passim.

64. "Iz dnevnika zampredsedatelia UOKS o noseshcheni Kieva Dzhonom Steinbek i fotoreporterom Kapa," July 7, 1947, GARF, f. 5283, op. 22, d. 26, ll. 176–77.

65. Ibid. Here l. 174. "Dokladnaia zapiska o prebyvanii v Kieve korrespondentov amerikanskoi gazety *New York Herald Tribune* amerikanskogo pisatelia Dzhona Steinbek i foto-reportera Roberta Kapa," GARF, f. 5283, op. 22, d. 26, ll. 216–21. Here l. 216. Also cited in Wolodymyr Stojko and Volodymyr Serhiychuk, "J. Steinbeck in Ukraine: What the Secret Soviet Archives Reveal," *Ukrainian Quarterly* 51, no. 1 (1995): 62–76. Here p. 64.

66. Steinbeck, *Russian Journal*, xii.

67. Steinbeck and Capa's "visual record" of their journey was first published early 1948 in the *New York Herald Tribune* and in the *Ladies' Home Journal*, but *A Russian Journal* was published in book form later that same year. Steinbeck, *Russian Journal*, xvii, xix. The coverage in the *New York Herald Tribune* started on January 14, 1948, and ran on p. 3 until January 31. *Ladies' Home Journal* published the accounts in February.

68. See, for example, Rósa Magnúsdóttir, "Cold War Correspondents and the Possibilities of Convergence: American Journalists in the Soviet Union, 1968–1979," *Soviet and Post-Soviet Review* 41, no. 1 (2014): 33–56.

69. Both John Steinbeck in *A Russian Journal* and the Soviet documents claim that his first visit took place in 1937. The introduction to *A Russian Journal* refers to his 1936 trip (xxi) but that date is incorrect.

70. Yuriy Sherekh, "Why Did You Not Want to See, Mr. Steinbeck?" *Ukrainian Quarterly* 4 (1948): 317–24.

71. Steinbeck, *Russian Journal*, 78.

72. Ibid., 74.

73. Ibid., 54–55.

74. These reports apparently came from Soviet journalists monitoring the American media and interpreting it in such a way that Americans were gearing up for another war. The rumor about a new war, this time between the United States and the Soviet Union, was nearly as old as victory in the Great Patriotic War.

75. Steinbeck, *A Russian Journal*, 55.

76. Ibid., 102.

77. Ibid., 56.

78. Ibid., 54.

79. Stojko and Serhiychuk, "J. Steinbeck in Ukraine," 64.

80. "Dokladnaia zapiska o prebyvanii v Kieve korrespondentov amerikanskoi gazety *New York Herald Tribune* amerikanskogo pisatelia Dzhona Steinbek i foto-reportera Roberta Kapa," GARF, f. 5283, op. 22, d. 26, ll. 216–21. Here l. 219. Also cited in Stojko and Serhiychuk, "J. Steinbeck in Ukraine," 67.

81. Khmarskii was careful enough to state that "the sense of any photo, of course, can lead to a critical opinion," GARF, f. 5283, op. 22, d. 26, l. 220. Stojko and Serhiychuk, "J. Steinbeck in Ukraine," 68 also cite this episode.

82. Ibid. See also discussion of Capa's photos in GARF, f. 5283, op. 22, d. 26, l. 221 and Stojko and Serhiychuk, "J. Steinbeck in Ukraine," 68.

83. GARF, f. 5283, op. 22, d. 26, ll. 219–20 and Stojko and Serhiychuk, "J. Steinbeck in Ukraine," 67.

84. Cited in Stojko and Serhiychuk, "J. Steinbeck in Ukraine," 66. See also GARF, f. 5283, op. 22, d. 26, l. 218.

85. From Khmarskii to V. Ermilov, main editor of *Literaturnaia gazeta*, March 27, 1948, GARF, f. 5283, op. 22, d. 81, ll. 190–91. Here l. 190.

86. "Spravka ob otzyvakh amerikanskoi pressy na knigu Steinbeka 'Russkii dnevnik,'" June 11, 1948, GARF, f. 5283, op. 22, d. 83, ll. 54–64. See also Caute, *The Dancer Defects*, 112. Steinbeck's *A Russian Journal* was controversial in the United States as well. People saw in it what they wanted to see: some saw it as pro-communist, while others saw it as anti-Soviet.

87. "Spravka ob otzyvakh amerikanskoi pressy na knigu Steinbeka 'Russkii dnevnik,'" June 11, 1948, GARF, f. 5283, op. 22, d. 82, l. 54 and "Spravka o kommentariiakh amerikanskoi pressy na knigu Dzhona Steinbeka 'Russkii dnevnik,'" GARF, f. 5283, op. 22, d. 83, ll. 56–64. Steinbeck went to the Soviet Union yet again in 1963 as part of the now official exchange programs. Although he had fallen out of favor after *A Russian Journal*, *The Winter of Our Discontent* put him back on the map as a "progressive writer" in the Soviet Union. In 1963, Steinbeck was prepared by the US State Department on which writers he should try to contact and talk to and his own personal mission was "raise as much fuss as possible about the Russian piracy of Western books." Jackson J. Benson, *The True Adventures of John Steinbeck, Writer* (New York: Viking Press, 1984), 926–33. Quote on p. 930.

88. "Iz dnevnika zampredsedatelia UOKS o noseshcheni Kieva Dzhonom Steinbek i fotoreporterom Kapa," July 7, 1947, GARF, f. 5283, op. 22, d. 26, ll. 176–77. Here l. 177.

89. See, for example, Gorsuch, *All This Is Your World*, 26.

90. Vladimir Shlapentokh, *Soviet Public Opinion and Ideology: Mythology and Pragmatism in Interaction* (New York: Praeger Publishers, 1986), xii.

CHAPTER 4

1. "Spravka o sostoianii kul'turnykh sviazei mezhdu Sovetskim Soiuzom i SShA," GARF, f. 5283, op. 14, d. 577, ll. 169–71. Here l. 169.

2. Interview with Eduard Ivanian, November, 27, 2002.

3. For more on the 1955 Geneva Summit, see Günther Bischof and Saki Dockdrill, eds., *Cold War Respite: The Geneva Summit of 1955* (Baton Rouge: Louisiana State University Press, 2000). With the Federal Republic of Germany admitted into NATO in May 1955, the German question was a major issue at the meeting. For a view on the summit and its cultural context see Parks, *Culture, Conflict, and Coexistence*, 146–55.

4. Zubok, *A Failed Empire*, 107.

5. "Spravka o sostoianii kul'turnykh sviazei mezhdu Sovetskim Soiuzom i SShA," GARF, f. 5283, op. 14, d. 577, ll. 169–71.

6. Gilburd, "The Revival of Soviet Internationalism in the Mid to Late 1950s"; Eleonory Gilburd, "Books and Borders: Sergei Obraztsov and Soviet Travels to London in the 1950s," *Turizm*, 227–47; and Mark B. Smith, "Peaceful Coexistence at All Costs: Cold War Exchanges between Britain and the Soviet Union in 1956," *Cold War History* 12, no. 3 (2012): 537–58.

7. Eleonory Gilburd has argued that the "French-Soviet program of exchanges became the prototype for the initial conversations with the Americans that same fall, 1957," Gilburd, "The Revival of Soviet Internationalism," 367. For more information about the agreement see Yale Richmond, *Cultural Exchange and the Cold War: Raising the Iron Curtain* (University Park: Pennsylvania State University Press, 2003), 15. See also GARF, f. 9518, op. 1, d. 346, ll. 54–60 for a transcript of an early meeting between Zarubin and Lacy, October 28, 1957.

8. "Spravka o sostoianii kul'turnykh sviazei mezhdu Sovetskim Soiuzom i SShA," GARF, f. 5283, op. 14, d. 577, ll. 169–71.

9. From Elizabeth Moos to VOKS, January 12, 1954, GARF, f. 5283, op. 14, d. 577, l. 7. Emphasis in original.

10. Ibid.

11. Ibid.

12. Also, American delegations of doctors, economists, legal professionals, and literature visited the Soviet Union and a delegation of Soviet professors visited Columbia University to celebrate its two hundredth anniversary, to give more examples. "Spravka o sostoianii kul'turnykh sviazei mezhdu Sovetskim Soiuzom i SShA," GARF, f. 5283, op. 14, d. 577, ll. 169–71. For more about Gilels and Oistrakh in the United States in 1955, see Kirill Tomoff, *Virtuosi Abroad: Soviet Music and Imperial Competition during the Early Cold War, 1945–1958* (Ithaca, NY: Cornell University Press, 2015), 119–29.

13. "Spravka o sostoianii kul'turnykh sviazei mezhdu Sovetskim Soiuzom i SShA," GARF, f. 5283, op. 14, d. 577, ll. 169–71. Here l. 169.

14. Ibid.

15. Ibid., l. 170.

16. Ibid., ll. 169–71.

17. Ibid., l. 170. Henry Shapiro had a long career as United Press International's chief Moscow correspondent and bureau manager. He was hired in 1937, appointed manager of the Moscow bureau in 1939, and remained in that position until retirement in 1973. In 1954, Shapiro published the book *L'U.R.S.S. après Staline* (Paris: Gallimard, 1954). For Soviet treatment of American journalists in this period, see Fainberg, "Unmasking the Wolf in Sheep's Clothing." For Khrushchev's focus on housing see Steven E. Harris, *Communism on Tomorrow Street: Mass Housing and Everyday Life after Stalin* (Washington, DC: Woodrow Wilson Center Press, 2013).

18. Isaiah Berlin, *The Soviet Mind: Russian Culture under Communism*, ed. Henry Hardy (Washington, DC: Brookings Institution Press, 2004), 120.

19. Ibid., 121–22.

20. The mainstream medium for performance arts also changed from theater to films, and, with the rise of mass culture in the Soviet Union, it became more difficult to promote pure propaganda as entertainment. For the rise of mass culture in the Soviet Union see Roth-Ey, *Moscow Prime Time*. In the 1960s and 1970s, the theater became a medium for progressive ideas that did not make it to the media. Anatoly Smeliansky, *The Russian Theatre after Stalin* (Cambridge: Cambridge University Press, 1999), xvi.

21. Zubok, *A Failed Empire*, 172.

22. Ibid., 172–73.

23. See, for example, Lowell H. Schwartz, *Political Warfare against the Kremlin: US and British Propaganda Policy at the Beginning of the Cold War* (New York: Palgrave Macmillan, 2009), 192–93. For more on Van Cliburn see Nigel Cliff, *Moscow Nights: The Van Cliburn Story—How One Man and His Piano Transformed the Cold War* (New York: Harper Perennial, 2016).

24. Blakely, *Russia and the Negro*, 118–19.

25. Ibid.

26. In April 1946, the State Academic Opera Theater (Gosudarstvennyi Akademicheskii Malyi Opernyi Teatr) in Leningrad had asked for VOKS's assistance in acquiring the music sheets for George Gershwin's *Porgy and Bess*. The United States Information Office in Moscow announced that in order to protect the copyright of the author, the score could not be released. From Kemenov to M. B. Khrapchenko, Chairman of the Arts Committee at the Soviet Council of Ministers, April 6, 1946, GARF, f. 5283, op. 22, d. 14, l. 157.

27. Ellen Noonan, *The Strange Career of* Porgy and Bess: *Race, Culture, and America's Most Famous Opera* (Chapel Hill: University of North Carolina Press, 2012), 192.

28. Ibid.

29. Ibid., 196. This is supported in Parks, *Culture, Conflict, and Coexistence*, 162.

30. Parks, *Culture, Conflict, and Coexistence*, 162.

31. Hollis Alpert, *The Life and Times of* Porgy and Bess: *The Story of an American Classic* (New York: Knopf, 1990), 217.

32. Noonan, *The Strange Career of* Porgy and Bess, 188–89, 203–7.

33. Ibid., 188–89.

34. Ibid., 221.

35. "Stenogramma soveshchaniia s predstaviteliami zarubezhnykh bratskikh partii stran Latinskoi Ameriki, USA, Avstralii, Kanady, i Portugalii, Sostoiavshegosia 27-go Fevralia 1956 goda," GARF, f. 5283, op. 22, d. 532, ll. 1–33. Here l. 28. See also David Monod, "Disguise, Containment, and the *Porgy and Bess* Revival of 1952–1956," *Journal of American Studies* 35, no. 2 (2001): 275–312; also David Monod, "'He Is a Cripple and Needs My Love': *Porgy and Bess* as Cold War Propaganda," in

The Cultural Cold War in Western Europe, 300–12; J. H. Taylor, "From Catfish Row to Red Square: *Porgy and Bess* and the Politics of the Cold War," *Theatre InSight* 7, no. 1 (1996): 29–35.

36. Alpert, *The Life and Times of* Porgy and Bess, 237.
37. Noonan, *The Strange Career of* Porgy and Bess, 188.
38. "Spravka o sostoianii kul'turnykh sviazei mezhdu Sovetskim Soiuzom i SShA," GARF, f. 5283, op. 14, d. 577, l. 169.
39. J. D. Parks also notes that the year 1955 was "pivotal" in American-Soviet cultural relations because it saw growing numbers of Americans traveling to Moscow. Parks, *Culture, Conflict, and Coexistence*, 139.
40. "Spravka o sostoianii kul'turnykh sviazei mezhdu Sovetskim Soiuzom i SShA," GARF, f. 5283, op. 14, d. 577, l. 169.
41. Ibid., ll. 169–71.
42. V. Matskevich, *Chto my videli v SShA i Kanade* (Moscow: Gosudarstvennoe izdatel'stvo politicheskoi literatury, 1956), 3. The book was originally published in 200,000 copies.
43. "Spravka o sostoianii kul'turnykh sviazei mezhdu Sovetskim Soiuzom i SShA," GARF, f. 5283, op. 14, d. 577, l. 169.
44. An American agricultural delegation visited the USSR at the same time, and both reported that their delegations had been met with much goodwill on the other side. Matskevich, *Chto my videli*, 3.
45. Ibid., 4.
46. Quoted from an interview with William Randolph Hearst in Moscow, November 2, 1957. GARF, f. 5283, op. 14, d. 622, l. 253.
47. Matskevich, *Chto my videli*, 4.
48. Ibid.
49. Ibid., 228.
50. Ibid., 227 and 228.
51. Ibid., 239.
52. Ibid.
53. Ibid., 236.
54. Matskevich recounted a few "mistakes" that American journalists made in their coverage and treatment of the delegation, but overall he was pleased by the good welcome the delegation received.
55. Matskevich, *Chto my videli*, 233.
56. The stenographic record (stenogramma) of the October 4, 1955 meeting is in RGANI, f. 5, op. 30, d. 107, ll. 1–11.
57. V. I. Zhuravleva, "Amerikanskaia kukuruza v Rossii: uroki narodnoi diplomatii i kapitalizma," *Vestnik RGGU* 21, no. 122 (2013): 121–46.
58. See Adlai E. Stevenson, *Friends and Enemies: What I Learned in Russia* (New York: Harper, 1958), 14.

59. Polevoi's book was originally published in 30,000 copies in 1956. In 1957, it was published again in a series for middle school children called *Shkolnaia biblioteka* (School Library). This edition was printed in 50,000 copies.

60. Boris Polevoi, "Otchet o poezdke delegatsii sovetskikh zhurnalistov po SShA," RGANI, f. 5, op. 16, d. 734, ll. 131–45. See Frederick C. Barghoorn, *The Soviet Cultural Offensive: The Role of Cultural Diplomacy in Soviet Foreign Policy* (Princeton, NJ: Princeton University Press, 1960), 296.

61. Barghoorn, *The Soviet Cultural Offensive*, 294.

62. Ibid.

63. RGANI, f. 5, op. 16, d. 734, ll. 131–32.

64. Ibid., l. 132.

65. Ibid., ll. 132–33.

66. Ibid., l. 133.

67. Ibid., l. 137.

68. Ibid., ll. 131–34. Quote l. 134.

69. The delegation also met with progressive cultural activists such as Paul Robeson, Howard Fast, and others. Ibid., l. 134 and 137. Quotes l. 134.

70. Ibid., l. 134.

71. See, for example, Belmonte, *Selling the American Way*, 148–49.

72. RGANI, f. 5, op. 16, d. 734, l. 134

73. Ibid., l. 135.

74. Ibid.

75. Ibid.

76. Afanas'eva and Afiani, eds., *Ideologicheskie komissii TsK KPSS*, 127–35. Nikolai M. Gribachev, *Avgustovskie zvezdy* (Moscow: Sovetskii pisatel', 1958) is cited in the editor's footnotes to this published document, but I think it is more likely that the original report was referring to Gribachev's nonfictional account of the delegations' travels in the United States, *Semero v Amerike: Zapiski korrespondenta "Literaturnoi gazety" o poezdke v SShA gruppy sovetskikh zhurnalistov v oktiabre-noiabre 1955g.* (Moscow: Sovetskii pisatel', 1956). The theme of America seems to have continued to occupy Gribachev, who also published a poem about the United States in 1961. See his *Amerika, Amerika . . . poema* (Moscow: Sovetskii pisatel', 1961).

77. Afanas'eva and Afiani, eds., *Ideologicheskie komissii TsK KPSS*, 127–35.

78. RGANI, f. 5, op. 16, d. 734, l. 137. Emphasis in original.

79. Ibid.

80. Barghoorn, *The Soviet Cultural Offensive*, 298.

81. Ibid., 298–99.

82. RGANI, f. 5, op. 16, d. 734, l. 138.

83. Ibid., l. 138.

84. Ibid.

85. Ibid., ll. 140–41.

86. Ibid., l. 143.

87. Ibid., l. 144.

88. According to the report, John Jacobs had been to the Soviet Union and written a few reports and about ten articles that all stressed the spirit of friendship and mutual understanding. Ibid., l. 142.

89. Here Polevoi is referring to the aircrafts designed by the famous Soviet aircraft designer, Sergei Vladimirovich Iliushin, who had designed attack aircrafts before and during the war and passenger planes after the war ended.

90. RGANI, f. 5, op. 16, d. 734, ll. 142–43.

91. Ibid. Emphasis in original.

92. Ibid.

93. Afanas'eva and Afiani, *Ideologicheskie komissii TsK KPSS*, 133. M. Kol'tsov and L. Reisner are also mentioned as good representatives.

94. Ibid. The document in question is B. Iarustovskii and I. Chernoutsan, "Postanovlenie Komissii TsK KPSS 'O neverno mizobrazhenii burzhuazno ideistvitel'nosti v sovremennom sovetskom iskusstvei literature' 26 dekabria 1958 g. Prilozhenie No. 2: Zapiska otdela kul'tury TsK KPSS. 18 noiabria 1958 g," 127–35.

95. Ibid., 128.

96. Ibid., 134.

97. Ibid., 128.

98. Ibid.

99. RGANI, f. 5, op. 16, d. 734, l. 134.

100. Barghooorn, *The Soviet Cultural Offensive*, 298.

101. Boris Polevoi, *Amerikanskie dnevniki* (Moscow: Sovetskii pisatel', 1956), 6.

102. Polevoi, *Amerikanskie dnevniki*, 65, 80, and 169. Also discussed in Barghoorn, *The Soviet Cultural Offensive*, 298.

103. Polevoi, *Amerikanskie dnevniki*, 384–85.

104. Scott, *Yanks Meet Reds*, 11.

105. Ibid., 10.

106. From Joseph Polowsky to Konstantin Chugunov, head of the American department at VOKS, December 5, 1957, GARF, f. 9576, op. 8, d. 18, ll. 2–4. Here l. 3.

107. "Russians Bar US Trip," *New York Times*, April 18, 1956, 7. For Soviet discussions on Polowsky's invitation, see a letter from Yuri (Georgii) Zhukov to D. Shepilov, January 27, 1956, RGANI, op. 30, d. 161, ll. 64–66.

108. "Russians Cancel a Reunion in US," *New York Times*, April 24, 1955, 53; "Ceremonies Mark Elbe Link-Up Day: Veterans Differ on Sincerity of Russian Reunion Plans—Embassy Fetes Some," *New York Times*, April 26, 1955, 9; "12 GI's Cleared for Visit to Soviet," *New York Times*, April 30, 1955, 18; "US Elbe Veterans Greeted in Moscow," *New York Times*, May 9, 1955, 2; "Solovsky Sends Eisenhower 'Friendly Greetings' at Elbe Fete," *New York Times*, May 13, 1955, 1.

109. Ibid.
110. From G. Zhukov and A. Zheltov to the Central Committee of the Soviet Communist Party, May 21, 1955, RGANI, f. 5, op. 30, d. 118, ll. 28–31.
111. Ibid., 30.
112. Mitrokhin, "The Rise of Political Clans in the Era of Nikita Khrushchev," 31.
113. From Zhukov and Zheltov to the Central Committee, May 21, 1955, RGANI, f. 5, op. 30, d. 118, ll. 28–31.
114. Ibid.
115. For Zhukov's relationship with Eisenhower see the cover article of *Time* magazine on Victory Day 1955: "Russia: Dragoon's Day," *Time*, May 9, 1955.
116. From Polowsky to Chugunov, December 5, 1957, GARF, f. 9576, op. 8, d. 18, ll. 2–4.
117. Ibid.
118. From Zhukov and Zheltov to the Central Committee, May 21, 1955, RGANI, f. 5, op. 30, d. 118, ll. 28–31.
119. "US-Soviet Reunion," *New York Times*, April 10, 1958, 22; "Elbe Veterans to Meet," *New York Times*, April 19, 1958, 2; "5 Russian Veterans Here for Elbe Fete," *New York Times*, April 21, 1958, 44.
120. See, for example, Zubok, *Zhivago's Children*.
121. Caute, *The Dancer Defects*, 30. Direct quote is from Polowsky's letter in GARF, f. 9576, op. 8, d. 18, ll. 2–4.
122. Kirill Tomoff reached a similar conclusion in his *Virtuosi Abroad*.
123. See, for example, Richmond, *Cultural Exchange and the Cold War*.

CHAPTER 5

1. William Taubman, *Khrushchev: The Man and His Era* (New York: W. W. Norton, 2003), 270. The Party Congress was scheduled to end on February 25, and foreign delegates and guests were therefore not present when the Soviet delegates arrived for the unscheduled secret session on February 26.
2. Ibid., 271. See the opening paragraphs of the Secret Speech in *Doklad N. S. Khrushcheva o kul'te lichnosti Stalina na XX s'ezde KPSS: Dokumenty*, ed. K. Aimermakher et al. (Moscow: Rosspen, 2002), 51.
3. Benjamin Tromly, *Making the Soviet Intelligentsia: Universities and Intellectual Life under Stalin and Khrushchev* (Cambridge: Cambridge University Press, 2014), 20.
4. Tromly, *Making the Soviet Intelligentsia*; and Robert Hornsby, *Protest, Reform and Repression in Khrushchev's Soviet Union* (Cambridge: Cambridge University Press, 2013).
5. Denis Kozlov and Eleonory Gilburd, "The Thaw as an Event in Russian History," in *The Thaw*, 18–81. Here p. 32.
6. Hixson, *Parting the Curtain*, 117.

7. Barghoorn, *The Soviet Cultural Offensive*, 24–25. See also Pia Koivunen, "The 1957 Moscow Youth Festival: Propagating a New, Peaceful Image of the Soviet Union," in *Soviet Society under Nikita Khrushchev*, ed. Melanie Ilic and Jeremy Smith (London and New York: Routledge, 2009), 46–65.

8. Zubok and Pleshakov, *Inside the Kremlin's Cold War*, 174.

9. Zubkova, *Russia after the War*, 198. On the failed experiment in information policy following the Secret Speech, see Susanne Schattenberg's "'Democracy' or 'Despotism'? How the Secret Speech was Translated into Everyday Life," in *The Dilemmas of De-Stalinization: Negotiating Cultural and Social Change in the Khrushchev Era*, ed. Polly Jones (London: Routledge-Curzon, 2006), 64–79. See also "Zapiska otdela kul'tury TsK KPSS s soglasiem sekretarei TsK o neobkhodimosti publikatsii redaktsionnykh statei v gazetakh po dokladam N. S. Khrushcheva o literature i iskusstve, 24 avgusta 1957g," in *Apparat TsK KPSS i kul'tura, 1953–1957: Dokumenty*, ed. E. S. Afanas'eva and V. Iu. Afiani (Moscow: Rosspen, 2001), 697–98.

10. Hornsby, *Protest, Reform, and Repression*, 108.

11. Tromly, *Making the Soviet Intelligentsia*, 20

12. Elena Papovian, "Primenenie stat'i 58–10 UK RSFSR v 1957–1958 gg. Po materialam Verkhovnogo suda SSSR i Prokuratury SSSR v GARF," in *Korni travy: Sbornik statei molodykh istorikov*, ed. L. S. Ereminaia and E. B. Zhemkova (Moscow: Zvenia, 1996), 73–87. Here p. 73.

13. Miriam Dobson, *Khrushchev's Cold Summer: Gulag Returnees, Crime, and the Fate of Reform after Stalin* (Ithaca, NY: Cornell University Press, 2009).

14. Papovian, "Primenenie stat'i 58–10," 83.

15. Karl E. Loewenstein, "Re-Emergence of Public Opinion in the Soviet Union: Khrushchev and Responses to the Secret Speech," *Europe-Asia Studies* 58, no. 8 (2006): 1329–45; here p. 1330. See also Hornsby, *Protest, Reform, and Repression*, 111; Papovian, "Primenenie stat'i 58–10"; and V. A. Kozlov and S. V. Mironenko, eds., *Kramola: Inakomyslie v SSSR pri Khrushcheve i Brezhneve 1953–1982gg. Rassekrechennye dokumenty Verkhovnogo suda i Prokuratury SSSR* (Moscow: Materik, 2005).

16. Loewenstein, "Re-Emergence of Public Opinion in the Soviet Union," 1341–42.

17. For the Khrushchev period, Robert Hornsby and Benjamin Tromly have also reached similar conclusions. See, for example, Hornsby, *Protest, Reform, and Repression*, 155 and Tromly, *Making the Soviet Intelligentsia*, 202–10.

18. GARF, f. 8131, op. 31, d. 77481, l. 3.

19. GARF, f. 8131, op. 31, d. 83258, ll. 1–2.

20. Ibid., l. 3.

21. GARF, f. 8131, op. 31, d. 82753, l. 7.

22. GARF, f. 8131, op. 31, d. 84264, l. 28.

23. Ibid.

24. GARF, f. 8131, op. 31, d. 43336, l. 11.

25. GARF, f. 8131, op. 31, d. 83367, l. 8.

26. Hornsby, *Protest, Reform, and Repression*, 54. See also Loewenstein, "Re-Emergence of Public Opinion in the Soviet Union"; Tromly, *Making the Soviet Intelligentsia*; Fürst, *Stalin's Last Generation*; and Vladimir A. Kozlov, *Mass Uprisings in the USSR: Protest and Rebellion in the Post-Stalin Years*, trans. and ed. Elaine McClarnand MacKinnon (Armonk, NY, and London: M. E. Sharpe, 2002).

27. Kozlov, *Mass Uprisings in the USSR*, 12.

28. Ibid.

29. From K. Sergeichuk to the Ministry of Communication, October 10, 1956, RGANI, f. 5, op. 33, d. 16, l. 72.

30. From A. Romanov and K. Bogoliubov, December 24, 1956, RGANI, f. 5, op. 33, d. 16, l. 73.

31. Viktor Mikhailovich Lukhin's unpublished memoir is available in the Memorial' archive. It was without a title and not cataloged. I am indebted to the archivists at Memorial' for allowing me to read the manuscript.

32. GARF, f. 8131, op. 31, d. 84691, l. 1.

33. Ibid., l. 3.

34. Ibid.

35. He wrote about having listened to the Voice of America in his memoir but his Procuracy review file does not mention it.

36. For an account that emphasizes "Soviet agency over American cultural penetration" in the Khrushchev era, see Anne E. Gorsuch, "From Iron Curtain to Silver Screen: Imagining the West in the Khrushchev Era," in *Imagining the West in Eastern Europe and the Soviet Union*, ed. György Péteri (Pittsburgh, PA: University of Pittsburgh Press, 2010), 153–71.

37. Hixson, *Parting the Curtain*, 114.

38. Roth-Ey, *Moscow Prime Time*, 133.

39. "Zapis' besedy s direktorom Agentstvo Informatsii SShA Dzhordzhem Allenom," December 10, 1957, RGANI, f. 5, op. 33, d. 72, ll. 2–4. In 1958, the Voice of America broadcast in Russian to the Soviet Union for twenty-two hours a week. F. Konstantinov and G. Zhukov, February 14, 1958, RGANI, f. 5, op. 33, d. 75, l. 94.

40. From the Soviet Embassy in Washington, "O poseshchenii redaktsii i studii 'Golosa Ameriki,'" December 23, 1957, GARF, f. 9518, op. 1, d. 346, ll. 124–25.

41. Roth-Ey, *Moscow Prime Time*, 138.

42. "O zaglushenii inostrannykh radiostantsii," August 6, 1958, RGANI, f. 5, op. 33, d. 75, ll. 163–67. Here l. 165.

43. Various writings between the KGB and the Central Committee about the radio program "Life in America," January and February 1958, RGANI, f. 5, op. 33, d. 75, ll. 2–23.

44. A. Romanov and G. Kaganov, March 8, 1958, RGANI, f. 5, op. 33, d. 75, l. 97.

45. F. Konstantinov and G. Zhukov, February 14, 1958, RGANI, f. 5, op. 33, d. 75, l. 94.

46. A. Romanov and G. Kaganov, March 8, 1958, RGANI, f. 5, op. 33, d. 75, l. 97.

47. G. Zhukov, February 21, 1958, RGANI, f. 5, op. 33, d. 75, l. 95.

48. "O zaglushenii inostrannykh radiostantsii," August 6, 1958, RGANI, f. 5, op. 33, d. 75, ll. 163–67. Here l. 165.

49. Ibid., l. 164.

50. Nevertheless, Soviet cultural organizations continued to monitor and analyze the contents of the programs. See, for example, a description of VOA programs from January 26–February 1, 1959. GARF, f. 9518, op. 1, d. 592, ll. 52–59.

51. E. Mamedov, May 8, 1956, RGANI, f. 5, op. 30, d. 20, ll. 16–17.

52. "Vstrecha s amerikanskimi chitateliami zhurnala *SSSR*, kratkii otchet," April 17, 1957, GARF, f. 9518, op. 1, d. 346, ll. 8–12.

53. Ibid.

54. Ibid.

55. Ibid.

56. Barghoorn, *The Soviet Cultural Offensive*, 24.

57. Susan E. Reid, "Cold War in the Kitchen: Gender and the De-Stalinization of Consumer Taste in the Soviet Union under Khrushchev," *Slavic Review* 61, no. 2 (2002): 211–52. Here p. 224. She is citing Khrushchev's election address to the Supreme Council: "Rech' tovarishcha N. S. Khrushcheva," *Pravda*, 15 March 1958.

58. From Aleksandr Shelepin, first secretary of Komsomol's Central Committee, to the Central Committee of the Communist Party, March 13, 1957, RGANI, f. 5, op. 33, d. 31, ll. 18–22.

59. Margaret Peacock, "The Perils of Building Cold War Consensus at the 1957 Moscow World Festival of Youth and Students," *Cold War History* 12, no. 3 (2012): 515–35. Here p. 516.

60. The Soviet organizers worried about the "reactionary circles" above all in the United States, who would send their "agents" to the festival with provocative goals in mind. The Central Committee focused on the "necessity" for Soviet people, especially youth, to watch out for these kinds of influences. RGASPI, f. m-3, op. 15, d. 1, ll. 35–40.

61. "Ob organizatsii raboty s inostrannymi delegatsiiami na festivale," April 1957, RGASPI, f. m-3, op. 15, d. 186, ll. 34–35.

62. See Zubok, *Zhivago's Children*, 100–11.

63. O. Bordarin, G. Grigoryan, V. Popov, R. Saakov, R. Vishinsky, I. Yefremova, and V. Zolotov, eds. and compilers, *Sixth World Youth and Students Festival* (Moscow: Prepared by the Committee of Youth Organizations of the USSR, 1958), 22.

64. "Moscow Denounces Youth Fete Critics," *New York Times*, Wednesday, July 24, 1957, D2; and O. Bordarin et al., *Sixth World Youth and Students Festival*, 23.

65. John Hoberman, in his *The Olympic Crisis: Sport, Politics, and the Moral Order* (New Rochelle, NY: Aristide O. Caratz, 1986) claims that the World Youth Festivals were Stalin's counter Olympics. That view has been contested (see Hugh Murray's review of Hoberman's book in *Journal of Sport History* 16, no. 1 [1989]: 104–8),

but it is interesting to compare the propaganda effects of the two events, especially in relation to the fact that it was the Soviet Olympic Committee that organized the festival sports program and it was dubbed "Festival Olympics." The Soviets, of course, sent professional sportsmen and women while others sent mostly amateurs. Understandably, this caused considerable frustration among participants. About reaction to sports events, see *Courtship of Young Minds: A Case Study of the Moscow Youth Festival* (New York: East European Student and Youth Service, 1959), 21.

66. O. Bordarin et al., *Sixth World Youth and Students Festival*, 22–27.

67. Karen Petrone, *Life Has Become More Joyous, Comrades: Celebrations in the Time of Stalin* (Bloomington: Indiana University Press, 2000); Malte Rolf, "Feste der Einheit und Schauspiele der Partizipation: Die Inszenierung von Öffentlichkeit in der Sowjetunion um 1930," *Jahrbücher für Geschichte Osteuropas* 50, no. 2 (2002): 163–71.

68. Zubok, *Zhivago's Children*, 103.

69. Darrell P. Hammer, "Law Enforcement, Social Control, and the Withering of the State: Recent Soviet Experience," *Soviet Studies* 14, no. 4 (1963): 379–97. Here p. 379.

70. In the case of the youth festival, the Komsomol took care of the day-to-day planning and organization.

71. Summary from the Ministry of Internal Affairs, July 8, 1957, GARF, f. 9401, op. 2, d. 491, ll. 150–55.

72. Ibid.

73. "Spravka ob organizatsii raboty s zarubezhnymi delegatsiiami festivalia v puti sledovaniia ot pogranichnykh punktov SSSR do g. Moskvy," RGASPI, f. m-3, op. 15, d. 186, ll. 30–34. Here one can find information on how to decorate trains and ships, and stock them with games (such as chess) and movies for the youth's entertainment. Train stations en route were also to see major facelifts. A station where the trains would stop for longer than ten minutes would sell periodical literature, a 15–20 minute stop would give opportunities for some meetings with local youth, and stations where a stop of 25–40 minutes would be made would see organized meetings of youth. The Komsomol was also involved in training the people who were to work with the foreigners, see "Ob otvetstvennykh za rabotu s inostrannymi delegatsiiami," RGASPI, f. m-3, op. 15, d. 186, ll. 1–11.

74. In 1956, 40 million rubles had already been earmarked for the festival, out of which 22 million rubles were earmarked for construction and assembling work. The All-Union Agricultural Exhibit was supposed to be accessible to foreign delegates and tourists in Moscow from June 1 to September 1, 1957. See Directive No. 1487 of the Council of Ministers from November 17, 1956: "O podgotovke k VI VFMS v g. Moskve," RGASPI, f. m-3, op. 15, d. 1, ll. 23–25ob. This document also addressed issues of transporting delegates on sea and land, souvenir sales during the festival, and various other organizational matters and how they were to be taken care of by the various ministries in the Soviet Union. The organization of such an event took the collaborated effort of the complete state structure.

75. Zubok, *Zhivago's Children*, 102.
76. "Ob organizatsii raboty s inostrannymi delegatsiiami na festivale," RGASPI, f. m-3, op. 15, d. 186, ll. 34–35.
77. Pia Koivunen, "Performing Peace and Friendship: The World Youth Festival as a Tool of Soviet Cultural Diplomacy, 1947–1957" (Ph.D. diss., University of Tampere, 2013), 173.
78. "Zamechaniia po proekty lozungov k VI Vsemirnomu festivaliu molodezhi i studentov," June 18, 1957, GARF, f. 5446, op. 91, d. 299, l. 22.
79. "Proekt lozungy k VI Vsemirnomu festivaliu molodezhi i studentov dlia oformleniia g. Moskvy, pogranichnykh stantsii i stantsii v puti sledovaniia," GARF, f. 5446, op. 91, d. 299, ll. 18–20.
80. "Svodka ob ygolovnykh prestupleniiakh i proisshestviiakh, imevshikh mesto v gorode Moskve s 8 chasov 30 iiulia do 8 chasov 31 iiulia s.g.," GARF, f. 9401, op. 2, d. 491, ll. 289–91. The woman then posed with two of the men and the rest took photographs.
81. Koivunen, *Performing Peace and Friendship*, 289–95.
82. "Svodka o proisshestviiakh, imevshikh mesto s 8 chasov 1 do 8 chasov 2 avgusta 1957 goda," GARF, f. 9401, op. 2, d. 491, ll. 309–13. Here l. 312.
83. Ibid.
84. Jan S. Prybyla concluded in 1961 that while living standards had risen since 1955, there were wide "deficiency areas, especially in housing and consumer services." See his "The Soviet Consumer in Khrushchev's Russia," *Russian Review* 20, no. 3 (1961): 194–205. Here p. 205. See also Mark B. Smith, *Property of Communists: Urban Housing Program from Stalin to Khrushchev* (DeKalb: Northern Illinois University Press, 2010).
85. "Svodka ob ugolovnyk prestupleniiakh i proisshestviiakh, imevshikh mesto v gorode Moskve s 8 chasov 30 iiulia do 8 chasov 31 iiulia s.g.," GARF, f. 9401, op. 2, d. 491, ll. 289–91.
86. Summary from the Ministry of Internal Affairs (MVD), July 1957, GARF, f. 9401, op. 2, d. 491, ll. 250–51.
87. Summary from MVD, August 3, 1957, GARF, f. 9401, op. 2, d. 491, ll. 314–15.
88. Summary from MVD, August 16, 1957, GARF, f. 9401, op. 2, d. 491, ll. 425–34. Here l. 431.
89. Interview with Eduard Ivanian, November, 27, 2002.
90. "Svodka o proisshestviiakh, sviazannykh s provedeniem festivalia," GARF, f. 9401, op. 2, d. 491, ll. 376–79.
91. Kristin Joy Roth-Ey, "Mass Media and the Remaking of Soviet Culture, 1950s–1960s" (Ph.D. diss., Princeton University, 2003), 74–75.
92. See, for example, Valur Ingimundarson, "Immunizing against the American Other: Racism, Nationalism, and Gender in US-Icelandic Military Relations during the Cold War," *Journal of Cold War Studies* 6, no. 4 (2004): 65–88.

93. It is also interesting to note the changed attitude in the Soviet Union; in 1906, the Soviet people were outraged to learn about the cold welcome Gorky and his mistress got in the United States, blaming it on American prudery. In 1957, however, Soviet principles had become remarkably similar to American turn-of-the-century morality. See Holtzman, "A Mission That Failed."

94. "Spravka o sostoianii agitatsionno-propagandistskoi raboty na predpriiatiiakh i v uchrezhdeniiakh g. Moskvy v sviazi s podgotovkoi k VI Vsemirnomu festivaliu molodezhi i studentov," March 1957, Tsentral'nyi arkhiv obshchestvennykh dvizhenii Moskvy, hereafter TsAODM, f. 4, op. 113, d. 23, ll. 1–8. Here l. 5.

95. Ibid. For more on youth clubs and youth culture in this period see Gleb Tsipursky, *Socialist Fun: Youth, Consumption, and State Sponsored Popular Culture in the Soviet Union, 1945–1970* (Pittsburgh, PA: University of Pittsburgh Press, 2016).

96. Gleb Tsipursky, "Coercion and Consumption: The Khrushchev Leadership's Ruling Style in the Campaign against 'Westernized' Youth, 1954–1964," in *Youth and Rock in the Soviet Bloc: Youth Cultures, Music, and the State in Russia and Eastern Europe*, ed. William Jay Risch (Lanham, MD: Lexington Books, 2015), 55–79.

97. Tanya Frisby, "Soviet Youth Culture," in *Soviet Youth Culture*, ed. Jim Riordan (Bloomington: Indiana University Press, 1989), 1–15. Here p. 2. This followed trends in the United States and Europe, where youth as such was becoming a much more visual and present group with its own ideas and culture. See also Fürst, *Stalin's Last Generation*.

98. Edele, "Strange Young Men in Stalin's Moscow," 43.

99. Summary from the Ministry of Internal Affairs, August 4–5 1957, GARF, f. 9401, op. 2, d. 491, ll. 319–24.

100. Summary from MVD, July 24, 1957, GARF, f. 9401, op. 2, d. 491, ll. 221–22a.

101. Ibid.

102. Summary from MVD, August 10, 1957, GARF, f. 9401, op. 2, d. 491, ll. 373–75.

103. From Episode 14 of the CNN Cold War Series: "Red Spring: The Sixties."

104. Koivunen, *Performing Peace and Friendship*, 290. She notes fifteen convictions for political dissent related to Moscow Youth Festival.

105. Summary from MVD, July 8, 1957, GARF, f. 9401, op. 2, d. 491, ll. 150–55. The police "resolved a number of practical issues of how to prevent the machinations of speculators, currency dealers, peculators, and other individuals, who intended to use festival events and the arrival of foreigners for their criminal intentions." Ibid., l. 152

106. Summary from MVD, GARF, f. 9401, op. 2, d. 491, l. 268.

107. "Svodka ob ugolovnykh prestupleniiakh i proisshestviiakh, imevshikh mesto s 8 chasov 31 iiulia do 8 chasov 1 avgusta 1957 goda," GARF, f. 9401, op. 2, d. 491, ll. 296–99.

108. Ibid., l. 299.

109. Summary from MVD, August 15, 1957, GARF, f. 9401, op. 2, d. 491, ll. 427–34. Here l. 432. See also Koivunen, *Performing Peace and Friendship*, 268–72. As an indicator of the purchasing power of the ruble at the time, a typical men's suit cost roughly 1,500 rubles and a dress from about 375–700 rubles in 1956. Cited in Roth-Ey, "Mass Media and the Remaking of Soviet Culture," 66.

110. "Svodka ob ugolovnykh proiavleniiakh i proisshestviiakh, sviazannykh s provedeniem festivalia," GARF, f. 9401, op. 2, d. 491, ll. 343–48.

111. "Svodka o proisshestviiakh, sviazannykh s provedeniem festivalia," August 6, 1957, GARF, f. 9401, op. 2, d. 491, ll. 355–62. Here ll. 361–62.

112. "Svodka o proisshestviiakh, sviazannykh s provedeniem festivalia," August 9, 1957, GARF, f. 9401, op. 2, d. 491, ll. 376–79.

113. Summary from MVD, August 8, 1957, GARF, f. 9401, op. 2, d. 491, ll. 364–65. Here l. 364.

114. Flora Lewis, "Youth from 102 Lands Swarms Over Moscow," *Life* 43, no. 7, August 12, 1957, 22.

115. "V otnoshenii regional'nykh vstrech," RGASPI, f. m-3, op. 15, d. 191, l. 17 (in Russian) and "Concerning the Regional Meetings," l. 18 (in English).

116. This is apparent in Aleksei Kozlov's biography, *Kozel na sakse—i tak vsiu zhizn'* (Moscow: Vagrius, 1998) and some of the works of Vasilii Aksenov, especially his *V poiskakh grustnogo bebi: Kniga ob Amerike* (New York: Liberty Publishing House, 1987).

117. "Nekotorye predlozeniia po organizatsii raboty s krupnymi delegatsiiami molodezhi i studentov iz kapitalisticheskikh stran na festivale v Moskve," RGASPI, f. m-3, op. 15, d. 186, ll. 36–39. Here l. 37.

118. "Predlozheniia," July 27, 1957, RGASPI, f. m-3, op. 15, d. 191, ll. 11–13.

119. Flora Lewis, "Youth from 102 Lands Swarms Over Moscow," 26.

120. Twenty questions were listed. "Spisok osnovnykh voprosov, zadannykh uchastnikami festivalia," TsAODM, f. 4, op. 113, d. 23, l. 120.

121. See, for example, Susan E. Reid, "Cold War in the Kitchen."

122. Barghoorn, *The Soviet Cultural Offensive*, 310.

CHAPTER 6

1. Zubok and Pleshakov, *Inside the Kremlin's Cold War*, 184.
2. Hixson, *Parting the Curtain*, 109.
3. "Otchet otdela stran Ameriki po razvitiiu kul'turnykh sviazei s USA v 1959g," GARF, f. 9576, op. 8, d. 27, ll. 158–74.
4. Hans Rogger, "Amerikanizm and the Economic Development of Russia," *Comparative Studies in Society and History* 23, no. 3 (1981): 382–420. Here p. 386.
5. Hixson, *Parting the Curtain*, 151.
6. Reid, "Cold War in the Kitchen," 224.

7. Formal discussions between the United States and the Soviet Union started on October 28, 1957. The agreement is often called the "Zarubin-Lacy agreement" after its negotiators Soviet Ambassador to the US Georgi Zarubin and William S. B. Lacy, head of the new State Department section called the East-West contact desk. Richmond, *Cultural Exchange and the Cold War*, 15; Barghoorn, *The Soviet Cultural Offensive*, 7; and Hixson, *Parting the Curtain*, 155.

8. Richmond, *Cultural Exchange and the Cold War*, 15 and 17.

9. Gould-Davies, "The Logic of Soviet Cultural Diplomacy," 203.

10. Gilburd, "The Revival of Soviet Internationalism in the Mid to Late 1950s," 373.

11. Mironenko, *Fondy Gosudarstvennogo arkhiva*, 653. This was how the organizational structure remained on the Soviet side until the end of 1991 when there were ninety-eight friendship societies with peoples of foreign countries. The highest organ of SSOD was the All-Union Conference, which gathered every five years with a presidium in charge in between. VOKS and SSOD were referred to as "Public Organisations" (obshchestvennye organizatsii) although they were, of course, party-controlled. See Rose, *The Soviet Propaganda Network*, 257. SSOD stands for Soiuz sovetskikh obshsestv druzhby i kul'turnoi sviazei s zarubezhnymi stranami.

12. Gilburd, "The Revival of Soviet Internationalism in the Mid to Late 1950s," 374.

13. Ibid., 374–75. For pen pal requests, see, for example, GARF, f. 9576, op. 8, d. 46, passim.

14. Its full name was Komitet po kul'turnym sviaziam s zarubezhnymi stranami pri sovete Ministrov SSSR. See Gould-Davies, "The Logic of Soviet Cultural Diplomacy," 206. See also Barghoorn, *The Soviet Cultural Offensive*, 159.

15. Mironenko, *Fondy Gosudarstvennogo arkhiva*, 221. The committee was in charge of the Soviet Commission on UNESCO matters and was engaged in international relations at the state level in the areas of education, public health, culture, literature, art, and sports and had missions at Soviet embassies abroad.

16. Barghoorn, *The Soviet Cultural Offensive*, 159–60.

17. Gould-Davies, "The Logic of Soviet Cultural Diplomacy," 206–8.

18. Naima Prevots, *Dance for Export: Cultural Diplomacy and the Cold War* (Middletown, CT: Wesleyan University Press, 1998), 70.

19. A letter to Rockwell Kent and a summary of the Pushkin Museum of Fine Arts about his exhibition in Moscow, GARF, f. 9576, op. 8, d. 18, ll. 193–95. For more on art exchanges see Simo Mikkonen, "Soviet-American Art Exchanges during the Thaw: From Bold Openings to Hasty Retreats," in *Art and Political Reality*, ed. Merike Kurisoo (Tallinn: Art Museum of Estonia–Kumu Kunstimuseum, 2013), 57–76; and Julia Emily Tatiana Bailey, "The Spectre of Communist Art: American Modernism and the Challenge of Socialist Realism, 1923–1960" (Ph.D. diss., University College London, 2015).

20. Jonathan Rosenberg, "Fighting the Cold War with Violins and Trumpets: American Symphony Orchestras Abroad in the 1950s," in *Winter Kept Us Warm: Cold War Interactions Reconsidered*, ed. Sari Autio-Sarasmo and Brendan Humphreys (Helsinki: Aleksanteri Cold War Series, 2010), 23–43.

21. Barghoorn, *The Soviet Cultural Offensive*, 317.

22. See, for example, Harlow Robinson, *The Last Impresario: The Life, Times, and Legacy of Sol Hurok* (New York: Penguin Books, 1994).
23. From N. Popova to the Central Committee, April 30, 1959, GARF, f. 9576, op. 18, d. 16, ll. 49–50.
24. From L. Kislova to R. Kent, Chairman of the NCASF, April 19, 1958, GARF, f. 9576, op. 8, d. 18, ll. 127.
25. From Zhukov to the Central Committee, September 27, 1957, RGANI, f. 5, op. 33, d. 31, l. 72. See also "Stat'ia Vill'iama Bentona izdatelia 'Entsiklopediia Britannika,' opublikovannaia v voskresnom prilozhenii k gazeta Vashington Post za 25 avgusta 1957: Chto dumaet o nas Ivan," RGANI, f. 5, op. 33, d. 31, ll. 73–78. For information about William Benton, see Biographical Note in his Papers, Special Collections Research Center, University of Chicago Library, https://www.lib.uchicago.edu/e/scrc/findingaids/view.php?eadid=ICU.SPCL.BENTON (Accessed on February 2, 2018).
26. "O vnutrennei antisovetskoi propagande, vedushcheisia v SShA," July 20, 1958, GARF, f. 9518, op. 1, d. 347, ll. 133–53. Here l. 133.
27. Ibid.
28. Ibid. This was apparently from the *New York Times*.
29. Ibid., l. 137.
30. Ibid., ll. 144–47.
31. Polevoi, "Otchet o poezdke delegatsii sovetskikh zhurnalistov po SShA," RGANI f. 5, op. 16, d. 734, l. 140. For more on Soviet-American film negotiations see Marsha Siefert, "Meeting at a Far Meridian: US-Soviet Cultural Diplomacy on Film in the Early Cold War," in *Cold War Crossings*, 166–209; and Andrei Kozovoi, "A Foot in the Door: The Lacy-Zarubin Agreement and Soviet-American Film Diplomacy during the Khrushchev Era, 1953–1963," *Historical Journal of Film, Radio and Television* 36, no. 1 (2016): 21–39.
32. "O vnutrennei antisovetskoi propagande, vedushcheisia v SShA," July 20, 1958, GARF, f. 9518, op. 1, d. 347, l. 148.
33. Ibid., l. 151.
34. Polevoi, "Otchet o poezdke delegatsii sovetskikh zhurnalistov po SShA," RGANI, f. 5, op. 16, d. 734, ll. 131–45.
35. Allan P. Cramer, "International Copyright and the Soviet Union," *Duke Law Journal* 3 (1965): 531–45.
36. "O vnutrennei antisovetskoi propagande, vedushcheisia v SShA," July 20, 1958, GARF, f. 9518, op. 1, d. 347, ll. 144–47. Polevoi also recommended increased exchanges of journalists after visiting the journalism faculty at Columbia University. RGANI, f. 5, op. 16, d. 734, l. 141.
37. "O vnutrennei antisovetskoi propagande, vedushcheisia v SShA," July 20, 1958, GARF, f. 9518, op. 1, d. 347, l. 152.
38. Cadra Peterson McDaniel, *American-Soviet Cultural Diplomacy: The Bolshoi Ballet's American Premiere* (Lanham, MD: Lexington Books, 2015), 83. See also

Christina Ezrabi, *Swans of the Kremlin: Ballet and Soviet Power in Soviet Russia* (Pittsburgh, PA: University of Pittsburgh Press, 2012).

39. "O vnutrennei antisovetskoi propagande, vedushcheisia v SShA," July 20, 1958, GARF, f. 9518, op. 1, d. 347, l. 151.

40. Stevenson had visited the USSR in 1926.

41. The newly established State Committee for Cultural Relations with Foreign Countries at the Council of Ministers reported on Stevenson's trip, while in 1947 VOKS had been responsible for monitoring Steinbeck's visit.

42. Stevenson, *Friends and Enemies*, xi.

43. Ibid., xi–xii.

44. GARF, f. 9518, op. 1, d. 347, passim.

45. "Spravka o prebyvanii E. Stivensona v SSSR 23–23 iiulia s.g. (g. Rubtsovsk, Altaiskii krai)," July 24, 1958, GARF, f. 9518, op. 1, d. 347, ll. 22–24. The report repeatedly claims that his wishes were granted.

46. Steinbeck, *A Russian Journal*, 16.

47. Stevenson, *Friends and Enemies*, 15.

48. Wesley Andrew Fisher, *The Soviet Marriage Market: Mate-Selection in Russia and the USSR* (New York: Praeger Publishers, 1980), 257.

49. "Spravka o prebyvanii v SSSR E. Stivensona 24–25 iiulia s.g. (g.g. Rubtsovsk, Novosibirsk)," July 25, 1958, GARF, f. 9518, op. 1, d. 347, ll. 25–29. Here l. 25.

50. From G. Zhukov to the Central Committee, July 31, 1958, RGANI, f. 5, op. 33, d. 68, l. 177.

51. "Spravka o prebyvanii v SSSR E. Stivensona 28–30 iiulia s.g. (g.g. Kazan', Gor'kii), July 30, 1958, GARF, f. 9518, op. 1, d. 347, ll. 96–98.

52. Stevenson, *Friends and Enemies*, 46.

53. Ibid.

54. Ibid.

55. Ibid., 48.

56. Ibid., 40–41.

57. Ibid., 40 and 42.

58. Ibid., 40.

59. G. Zhukov, "Zapis' besedy s E. Stivensonom 31 iiulia 1958 g.," GARF, f. 9518, op. 1, d. 347, ll. 92–95. Here l. 93.

60. Stevenson, *Friends and Enemies*, 41.

61. Ibid., 92.

62. Ibid., 97.

63. Steinbeck, *A Russian Journal*, 212.

64. Stevenson, *Friends and Enemies*, 101–2.

65. Iurii Aksiutin, *Khrushchevskaia "ottepel'" i obshchestvennye nastroeniia v SSSR v 1953–1964 gg.* (Moscow: Rosspen, 2004), 350. For a further discussion of the slogan, see "Dokladyvaem o plane vypuska literatury sviazy s resheniiami iiunskogo plenuma TsK KPSS," July 27, 1957, RGANI, f. 5, op. 33, d. 38, l. 120.

66. A protocol agreement from September 10, 1958, called for the reciprocal exhibits. "Facts about the American National Exhibition in Moscow 1959," revised on April 1, 1959, GARF, f. 9518, op. 1, d. 595, ll. 127–32. Here l. 131. The American exhibition was a "joint endeavor of the US government, American industry, and other private groups and organizations. Government participation centers in the Department of State, the Department of Commerce, and the US Information Agency, with the Director of USIA, George V. Allen, serving as coordinator."

67. For literature on the American National Exhibition, consult Hixson, *Parting the Curtain*, and Amanda Wood Aucoin, "Deconstructing the American Way of Life: Soviet Responses to Cultural Exchange and American Information Activity during the Khrushchev Years" (Ph.D. diss., University of Arkansas, 2001).

68. The US organizers used many features from their successful display at the 1958 Brussels World Fair. The Soviets showed great skepticism of American declarations that the exhibit would not have a propagandistic character. See also "Spravka," April 1959, RGANI, f. 5, op. 33, d. 95, ll. 5–7. Soviet authorities also distributed materials about America to Soviet journals and newspapers for them to publish in the months leading up to and during the exhibit. See from A. Romanov and K. Bogoliubov to the Central Committee, June 22, 1959, RGANI, f. 5, op. 33, d. 95, l. 12. Finally, they planned a "major political and cultural information campaign among the population during the American Exhibition in Moscow," Zhukov to the Central Committee, June 1959, RGANI, f. 5, op. 33, d. 95, ll. 13–18 and "Plan meropriiatii MGK KPSS po organizatsii massovo-politicheskoi i kul'turno-prosvetitel'noi raboty sredi naseleniia na period deistviia gosud. vystavki SShA v Moskve," RGANI, f. 5, op. 33, ll. 23–32.

69. Hixson, *Parting the Curtain*, 187. On the new pavilions, see Victor Rosenberg, *Soviet-American Relations, 1953–1960: Diplomacy and Cultural Exchange during the Eisenhower Presidency* (Jefferson, NC, and London: McFarland, 2005), 210.

70. Hixson, *Parting the Curtain*, 188.

71. G. Mamrykin, "Nekotorye nabliudeniia na amerikanskoi vystavke 22 iiulia 1959 goda," GARF, f. 9518, op. 1, d. 594, ll. 222–24. Here l. 224.

72. A list of films and documentaries is in a report from G. Zhukov to the Central Committee, July 23, 1959, GARF, f. 9518, op. 1, d. 594, ll. 225–28.

73. "O khudozhestvennom otdele amerikanskoi natsional'noi vystavki v Moskve," July 14, 1959, GARF, f. 9518, op. 1, d. 594, ll. 255–57.

74. There is much documentation on the book display. "Pamiatnaia Zapiska," July 23, 1959, GARF, f. 9518, op. 1, d. 594, l. 217–20 contains a list of twenty-one books considered anti-Soviet propaganda. Among the books were Leopold Haimson's *The Russian Marxists and the Origins of Bolshevism*; George Vernadsky's *A History of Russia*; and Frederick Barghoorn's *The Soviet Image of the United States*. See also ibid., ll. 232–34.

75. GARF, f. 9518, op. 1, d. 594, passim.

76. Hixson, *Parting the Curtain*, 190.

77. Timur Timofeevich Timofeev, *Negry SShA v bor'be za svobodu* (Moscow: Gos. izd-vo polit. lit-ry, 1957).

78. Three Central Committee representatives went to New York for two weeks (June 19–July 2, 1959) to check on the preparation for the Soviet exhibition and wrote a report upon returning, RGANI, f. 5, op. 36, d. 88, ll. 234–41.

79. "Guides Outdraw Soviet Exhibits: Although Difficult to Find, They Face Many Queries on Personal Matters," *New York Times*, August 9, 1959, 9.

80. Summary from the Ministry of Internal Affairs, July 29, 1959, GARF, f. 9401, op. 2, d. 506, ll. 263–64.

81. "Spravka," May 4, 1959, GARF, f. 9518, op. 1, d. 593, ll. 121–22. See also Hixson, *Parting the Curtain*, 189.

82. "Zapis' besedy s direktorom amerikanskoi natsional'noi vystavki v Moskve Maklelanom 11 avgusta 1959g," GARF, f. 9518, op. 1, d. 593, ll. 247–48.

83. Larissa Zakharova, "Dior in Moscow: A Taste for Luxury in Soviet Fashion under Khrushchev," in *Pleasures in Socialism: Leisure and Luxury in the Eastern Bloc*, ed. David Crowley and Susan E. Reid (Evanston, IL: Northwestern University Press, 2010), 95–119.

84. Reid, "Cold War in the Kitchen," 239.

85. GARF, f. 5446, op. 93, d. 1311, ll. 87–102.

86. Ibid.

87. Taubman, *Khrushchev*, 409.

88. For more on Nixon's trip to the Soviet Union see chapter 11 in Rosenberg, *Soviet-American Relations*.

89. "Otchet otdela stran Ameriki po razvitiiu kul'turnykh sviazei s USA v 1959g," GARF, f. 9576, op. 8, d. 27, ll. 158–74.

90. Ibid., l. 158.

91. Ibid.

92. In late August, a delegation of Soviet writers and journalists to the United States, August 11–23, 1959, reported that Americans were very much looking forward to receiving the Soviet leader. From A. Chakovskii to the Central Committee, GARF, f. 9518, op. 1, d. 349, ll. 209–12.

93. GARF, f. 5446, op. 93, d. 1321 is devoted to letters from abroad.

94. Taubman, *Khrushchev*, 415–16.

95. Dmitrii Bobyshev, *Ia zdes' (Chelovekotekst)* (Moscow: Vagrius, 2003), 210.

96. My analysis has benefited from Sheila Fitzpatrick's article "Supplicants and Citizens: Public Letter-Writing in Soviet Russia in the 1930s," *Slavic Review* 55, no. 1 (1996): 78–105. Fitzpatrick analyzed several genres of public letter writing in the 1930s, and while some of her analyses only apply to the period, many can be applied to the letter collection at hand.

97. The Soviet version of the book, *Litsom k litsu s Amerikoi. Rasskaz o poezdke N. S. Khrushcheva v SShA.15–27 sentiabria 1959 goda* (Moscow: Gosudarstvennoe izdatel'stvo politicheskoi literatury, 1959).

98. *Face to Face with America: The Story of N. S. Khrushchov's Visit to the USA September 15–27, 1959* (Moscow: Foreign Languages Publishing House, 1960), 474. The unpublished letters discussed here are all found in the archives of the Council of Ministers, where at least eleven *dela* (files) comprise letters and telegrams "concerning the reciprocal visits of Khrushchev to the USA and Eisenhower to the USSR." The letters were sent either to the Central Committee of the Communist Party or to the Council of Ministers.

99. Judging from the number preserved in the archives of the Council of Ministers.

100. This is borrowed from Sheila Fitzpatrick, "Supplicants and Citizens," 81. It is also worth noting that comparing the concerns and topics to those discussed by Fitzpatrick's letter writers, new themes are prevalent in 1959. This is mostly due to the occasion of the letter writing (Khrushchev's visit to America) but also because since the 1930s, World War II had replaced the Civil War as a major traumatic experience that people referred to when discussing their lives, support, and sacrifices for the regime.

101. *Face to Face with America*, 529–30.

102. Ibid., 522–23.

103. *Pravda*, August 6, 1959, 1–3.

104. *Face to Face with America*, 533. Early public opinion surveys in the Soviet Union, conducted in the late 1950s, support my argument that peaceful coexistence struck a chord with the Soviet people who expressed enthusiastic support for it from the outset. See Boris A. Grushin, *Chetyre zhizni Rossii v zerkale oproso v obshchestvennogo mneniia: ocherki massovogo soznaniia rossiian vremen Khrushcheva, Brezhneva, Gorbacheva, i El'tsina v 4-kh knigakh.* Vol. 1. *Zhizn 1-aia. Epokha Khrushcheva* (Moscow: Progress-Traditsiia, 2001).

105. *Face to Face with America*, 500.

106. Ibid., 504.

107. Ibid., 544.

108. *Pravda*, September 13, 1959, 1 and 3.

109. *Face to Face with America*, 492.

110. Ibid., 498.

111. Ibid.

112. Ibid., 538.

113. Ibid., 525 and passim.

114. Ibid., 531 and passim.

115. Ibid., 528.

116. Ibid.

117. GARF, f. 5446, op. 93, d. 1320, l. 106.

118. Ibid., d. 1316, ll. 96–97.

119. Nixon claimed that fifty million American families had a private car, and that fifty million television sets and 143 million radios were in circulation. *Pravda,* July 27, 1959. For Soviet counterpropaganda see, for example, *Pravda*, July 28, 1959, 4: "O

chem govoriat fakty: Po stranitsam sbornika faktov o trude v SShA" by V. Zhukov. Also *Pravda*, July 30, 1959, 4: " 'My s etim ne soglasny.' Pis'ma iz Ameriki."

120. *Face to Face with America*, 541.

121. Ibid., 495.

122. Ibid., 483.

123. Ibid., 478.

124. On the failed experiment in information policy following the Secret Speech, see Schattenberg, " 'Democracy' or 'Despotism'?" About the renewed intensity in political purges after the 1956 Secret Speech and the invasion of Hungary, see Papovian, "Primenenie stat'i 58–10 UK RSFSR v 1957–1958 gg."

125. See chapter 2 of this book.

126. GARF, f. 5446, op. 93, d. 1313, ll. 126–28. The United States withheld diplomatic recognition of the Soviet Union until 1933. Increased trade between the two nations expedited the recognition process.

127. Khrushchev's biographer, William Taubman, recounted the following story that happened during the visit to America: "When Khrushchev encountered Governor Nelson Rockefeller in New York City in 1959, Rockefeller needled him by saying that half a million Russians had emigrated to New York at the turn of the century seeking freedom and opportunity. 'Don't give me that stuff,' Khrushchev replied. 'They only came to get higher wages. I was almost one of them. I gave very serious consideration to coming.'" Taubman, *Khrushchev*, 40. His source is Joseph E. Persico, *The Imperial Rockefeller: A Biography of Nelson Rockefeller* (New York: Simon and Schuster, 1982), 86.

128. GARF, f. 5446, op. 93, d. 1309, ll. 137–39.

129. See Albert Rhys Williams, *The Bolsheviks and the Soviets* (New York: Rand School of Social Science, 1919).

130. GARF, f. 5446, op. 93, d. 1309, ll. 137–39.

131. Ibid., ll. 148–49.

132. Ibid., d. 1316, ll. 98–99.

133. Ibid., d. 1314, ll. 136, 136ob. The photograph is not in the file, but that is no indication that it was returned. About half the letters are originals with the rest copies from the originals. Sometimes both the original and a typed copy is on file.

134. Zubok and Pleshakov, *Inside the Kremlin's Cold War*, 184–5. Quote on p. 185.

135. GARF, f. 5446, op. 93, d. 1309, l. 110.

136. Ibid.

137. Ibid., ll. 182–83.

138. Ibid., d. 1319, ll. 50–54.

139. Ibid., d. 1311, ll. 33–34.

140. Ibid.

141. Like Jochen Hellbeck's diarists, the letter writers "situated their personal, and particular, existence with respect to the general public interest," 357. Jochen Hellbeck,

"Working, Struggling, Becoming: Stalin-Era Autobiographical Texts," *Russian Review* 60, no. 3 (2001): 340–59.

142. See Kevin A. Stein, "Apologia, Antapologia, and the 1960 Soviet U-2 Incident," *Communication Studies* 59, no. 1 (2008): 19–34.

EPILOGUE

1. Steven L. B. Jensen, *The Making of International Human Rights: The 1960s, Decolonization, and the Reconstruction of Global Values* (Cambridge: Cambridge University Press, 2016), 214–16.

2. Petr Vail and Aleksandr Genis, *60e—mir sovetskogo cheloveka* (Moscow: Novoe literaturnoe obozrenie, 1996).

3. See Sergei Zhuk, *Rock and Roll in the Rocket City: The West, Identity, and Ideology in Soviet Dniepropetrovsk, 1960–1985* (Baltimore: Johns Hopkins University Press, 2010).

4. Yurchak, *Everything Was Forever*, 288–89.

5. For a good overview of Soviet cultural perceptions of the United States see Marsha Siefert, "From Cold War to Wary Peace: American Culture in the USSR and Russia," in *The Americanization of Europe: Culture, Diplomacy, and Anti-Americanism after 1945*, ed. Alexander Stephan (New York: Berghahn, 2006), 185–217.

6. Vladimir Voinovich's *Antisovetskii Sovetskii Soiuz: Dokumental'naia fantastagoriia v 4-kh chastiakh* (Moscow: Izdatel'stvo "Materik," 2002), 37.

7. Algis Ruksenas, *Is That You Laughing Comrade? The World's Best Russian (Underground) Jokes* (Secaucus, NJ: Citadel Press, 1986), 150. For an account of the continued ambivalence of attitudes during the late Cold War, see Andreï Kozovoï, *Par-delà le Mur: la culture de guerre froide soviétique entre deux détentes* (Bruxelles: Éditions Complexe, 2009).

8. Eric Shiraev, "Russia's Views of America in a Historic Perspective," in *America: Sovereign Defender or Cowboy Nation*, ed. Vladimir Shlapentokh, Joshua Woods, and Eric Shiraev (Burlington, VT: Ashgate, 2005), 45–52. Here p. 46.

9. Ibid., 46–47. See also Donald J. Raleigh, *Soviet Baby Boomers: An Oral History of Russia's Cold War Generation* (New York: Oxford University Press, 2012).

10. Eric Shiraev, "'Sorry, but . . .': Russia's Responses in the Wake of 9/11," in *America: Sovereign Defender or Cowboy Nation*, 53–68. Here p. 66.

11. Ariel Cohen and Helle C. Dale, "Russian Anti-Americanism: A Priority Target for US Public Diplomacy," *Backgrounder* 2373 (Washington: Heritage Foundation, 2010), 1–10. Here 5–7.

12. Vladimir Shlapentokh, "The Puzzle of Russian Anti-Americanism: From 'Below' or From 'Above'," *Europe-Asia Studies* 63, no. 5 (2011): 875.

13. Sarah E. Mendelson and Theodore P. Gerber, "Us and Them: Anti-American Views of the Putin Generation," *Washington Quarterly* 31, no. 2 (2008): 131–50.

14. Ibid., 133.

15. The White House. Office of the Press Secretary, "Statement on Visit of Russian President Medvedev to White House: Obama Looks Forward to Discussing Bilateral Relations with Russia," http://www.america.gov/st/texttrans-english/2010/June/20100611162555ptellivremos0.1076624.html?CP.rss=true (Accessed on November 4, 2011). The White House. Office of the Press Secretary, "Remarks by President Obama and President Medvedev of Russia at Joint Press Conference. June 24, 2010," http://www.whitehouse.gov/the-press-office/remarks-president-obama-and-president-medvedev-russia-joint-press-conference (Accessed on December 20, 2016).

16. "Spravka o sostoianii kul'turnykh sviazei mezhdu Sovetskim Soiuzom i SShA," GARF, f. 5283, op. 14, d. 577, l. 169.

17. The White House. Office of the Press Secretary, "Joint Statement by the Presidents of the United States of America and the Russian Federation Commemorating the 65th Anniversary of the Meeting of Soviet and American Troops at the Elbe River." April 25, 2010, http://www.whitehouse.gov/the-press-office/joint-statement-presidents-united-states-america-and-russian-federation-commemorati (Accessed on December 20, 2016).

18. "Vladimir Putin Snubs Britain and US over VE Day Celebrations," May 7, 2010, http://www.guardian.co.uk/world/2010/may/07/putin-snub-west-war-celebrations?INTCMP=ILCNETTXT3487 (Accessed on December 20, 2016).

19. For a thorough discussion of this, see Stephen M. Norris, "Memory for Sale: Victory Day 2010 and Russian Remembrance," *Soviet and Post-Soviet Review* 38, no. 2 (2011): 201–29. Here pp. 210–15.

20. "'Victory Day Parade Is a Sign of Russia Opening to the West'—Expat," *Russia Today*, May 14, 2010, http://rt.com/news/prime-time/victory-day-parade-expats/ (Accessed on November 11, 2011).

21. From Reuters, see, for example, "Russia Offers Olive Branch as NATO Joins Parade," http://www.stabroeknews.com/2010/news/world/05/10/russia-offers-olive-branch-as-nato-joins-parade/ (Accessed on December 20, 2016).

22. Ibid.

23. "Three monuments to Stalin to Be Unveiled in Russia and Ukraine," January 1, 2005, http://english.pravda.ru/history/20-01-2005/7629-stalin-0/ (Accessed on December 20, 2016). A sand sculpture of the "Big Three" was also on display in VDNKh in Moscow in 2010.

24. Nataliya Danilova, *The Politics of War Commemoration in the UK and Russia* (New York: Palgrave Macmillan, 2015), 194.

25. "Mira Todorovskaia zakanchivaet rabotu nad 'Vstrechei na El'be," January 1, 2015, http://tvkultura.ru/article/show/article_id/126343/ (Accessed on March 14, 2016).

26. "'Spoi ty mne pro voinu . . .'.'V dalekom 45-m. Vstrecha na El'be' rezhissery Mira Todorovskaia, Petro Aleksoovskii," May 5, 2015, *Iskusstvo Kino*, http://www.kinoart.ru/archive/2015/05/spoj-ty-mne-pro-vojnu-v-dalekom-45-m-vstrecha-na-elbe-rezhissery-mira-todorovskaya-petro-aleksovskij (Accessed on March 14, 2016).

27. Ibid.

28. "The Russian Military-Historical Society," *Rossiskoe voenno-istoricheskoe obshchestvo*, http://histrf.ru/ru/rvio/rvio/English (Accessed on March 17, 2016).

29. "The Cooperation of the Anti-Hitler Coalition," *Rossiskoe voenno-istoricheskoe obshchestvo*, http://histrf.ru/ru/rvio/activities/projects/publication (Accessed on March 17, 2016).

30. "USRBC-American-Russian Cultural Cooperation Foundation (ARCCF) Private Screening at MPAA: 'Meetings on the Elbe River: Love on the Ashes of War,'" https://www.usrbc.org/index.php/calendar/event/2503 (Accessed on March 17, 2016).

GLOSSARY

Agitprop Upravlenie propagandy i agitatsii TsK (1939–1948), Otdel propagandy i agitatsii TsK (1948–1956), Otdel propagandy i agitatsii TsK KPSS po soiuznym respublikam (1956–1965); Agitprop Commission of the Central Committee

AN Akademiia nauk; Academy of Sciences

ARCCF American-Russian Cultural Cooperation Foundation

Comintern Kommunisticheskii internatsional (Komintern); Communist International (Comintern)

CPUSA Communist Party of the United States of America

GKKS Komitet po kul'turnym sviaziam s zarubezhnymi stranami pri Sovete Ministrov SSSR (1957–1967); State Committee for Cultural Relations with Foreign Countries at the Council of Ministers

Glavpur Glavnoe politicheskoe upravlenie Ministerstva oborony SSSR (1953–1958); Main Political Administration of the Ministry of Defense

Glavrepertkom Glavnyi komitet po kontroliu za repertuarom; the State Repertoire Commission

Gosinoizdat Gosudarstvennoe izdatel'stvo inostrannoi literatury; State Publishing House of Foreign Literature

IMLI Institut mirovoi literatury; Institute for Global Literature

Intourist Vsesoiuznoe aktsionernoe obshchestvo po inostrannomu turizmu v SSSR; Ministerstva vneshnei torgovli SSSR (1946–1964); State Joint-Stock Company for Foreign Tourism

KGB Komitet gosudarstvennoi bezopasnosti (1954–1991); Committee for State Security

Komsomol Kommunisticheskii soiuz molodezhi (1918–1991); Communist Youth League

KPSS Kommunisticheskaia partiia sovetskogo soiuza (1952–1991); Communist Party of the Soviet Union

Mezhkniga Mezhdunarodnaia kniga; International Book (publishing house)

MGK Moskovskii gorodskoi komitet; Moscow City Committee

MID Ministerstvo inostrannykh del; Ministry of Foreign Affairs

MVD Ministerstvo vnutrennykh del; Ministry of the Interior

NCASF National Council for American-Soviet Friendship

Prokuratura The Procuracy

RVIO Rossiiskoe voenno-istoricheskoe obshchestvo; The Russian Military-History Society

Soiuzpechat' Union Print (e.g., administration and distribution of periodicals)

Sovetskii pisatel' Soviet Writer (publishing house)

Sovinformbiuro Sovetskoe informatsionnoe biuro; The Soviet Information Bureau

Sputnik Biuro mezhdunarodnogo molodezhnogo turizma Sputnik (1958–1991); Bureau of International Youth Tourism

SSOD Soiuz sovetskikh obshsestv druzhby i kul'turnoi sviazei s zarubezhnymi stranami; The Union of Soviet Societies for Friendship and Cultural Relations with Foreign Countries

SSSR Soiuz sovetskikh sotsialisticheskikh respublik; Union of Soviet Socialist Republics

TASS Telegrafnoe agentstvo Sovetskogo Soiuza; Telegraph Agency of the Soviet Union

TsK Tsentral'nyi komitet; Central Committee

UOKS Ukrainskoe obshchestvo kul'turnoi sviazi s zagranitsei; Ukrainian Society for Cultural Relations with Foreign Countries

USIA United States Information Agency

USRBC The US-Russia Business Council

VDNKh Vystavka dostizhenii narodnogo khoziaistva (1959–1991); Exhibition of the Achievements of the National Economy

VKP(b) Vsesoiuznaia kommunisticheskaia partiia (bolshevikov) (1925–1952); All-Union Communist Party (Bolsheviks)

VOKS Vsesoiuznoe obshsestvo kul'turrnykh sviazei s zagranitsei; All-Union Society for Cultural Relations with Foreign Countries

VSKhV Vsesoiuznaia sel'sko-khoziaistvennaia vystavka (1935–1959); All-Union Agricultural Exhibition

BIBLIOGRAPHY

ARCHIVAL MATERIALS

Gosudarstvennyi arkhiv Rossiiskoi Federatsii (State Archive of the Russian Federation)

f. A-461   State Prosecutor of the Russian Federation
f. R-5283   Soviet All-Union Society for Cultural Relations with Foreign Countries (VOKS)
f. R-5446   Council of People's Commissars/Council of Ministers
f. R-8131   State Prosecutor of the Soviet Union
f. R-9401   Special Files (*osobye papki*) of Stalin and Molotov
f. R-9415   Main Police Administration of the Ministry of Internal Affairs
f. R-9518   The Council of Ministers' State Committee for Cultural Relations with Foreign Countries
f. R-9576   Union of Soviet Societies for Friendship and Cultural Relations with Foreign Countries (SSOD)
f. R-9612   Intourist

Obshchestvennoe dvizhenie Memorial' (Archives of Memorial)

Viktor Mikhailovich Lukin's memoir in manuscript

Rossiiskii gosudarstvennyi arkhiv literatury i iskusstva (Russian State Archive of Literature and Art)

f. 631   Soviet Writers' Union
   op. 14   Foreign Commission
   op. 26   Foreign Commission (1951–56)

Rossiiskii gosudarstvennyi arkhiv noveishei istorii (Russian State Archive of Contemporary History)

f. 5   Apparat of the Central Committee of the Communist Party of the
           Soviet Union
  op. 30   General Department
  op. 33   Department of Propaganda and Agitation in the Soviet Republics
  op. 36   Department of Culture

Rossiiskii gosudarstvennyi arkhiv sotsial'no-politicheskoi istorii (Russian State Archive of Socio-Political History)

f. 17   Central Committee of the Communist Party of the Soviet Union
  op. 88   Information Sector of the Organizational-Instructional Section
  op. 125 Agitation and Propaganda (1939–48)
  op. 132 Agitation and Propaganda (1948–56)
f. 82   Viacheslav Mikhailovich Molotov

Rossiiskii gosudarstvennyi arkhiv sotsial'no-politicheskoi istorii-m (Russian State Archive of Socio-Political History-Komsomol Archive)

f. m-3   Committee of Youth Organizations (1956–91)
  op. 15   Festival of Youth and Students in Moscow, 1957

Tsentral'nyi arkhiv obshchestvennykh dvizhenii Moskvy (State Archive of Social Movements of Moscow)

f. 4   Moscow City Committee of the Soviet Communist Party
  op. 113 Propaganda and Agitation (1955–58)

DOCUMENT COLLECTIONS AND FINDING AIDS

Afanas'eva, E. S., and V. Iu. Afiani, eds. *Apparat TsK KPSS i kul'tura, 1953–1957: Dokumenty*. Moscow: Rosspen, 2001.
———, eds. *Ideologicheskie komissii TsK KPSS 1958–1964: Dokumenty*. Moscow: Rosspen, 2000.
Aimermakher, K., et al., eds., *Doklad N. S. Khrushcheva o Kul'te Lichnosti Stalina na XX s"ezde KPSS: Dokumenty*. Moscow: Rosspen, 2002.
Foreign Relations of the United States, 1950, 4.
Graziosi, Andrea, and O. V. Khlevniuk, eds. *Sovetskaia zhizn', 1945–1953*. Moscow: Rosspen, 2003.

Kozlov, V. A., and S. V. Mironenko. *58.10: nadzornye proizvodstva prokuratury SSSR po delam ob antisovetskoi agitatsii i propagande. Annotirovannyi katalog, mart, 1953– 1991.* Moscow: Mezhdunarodnyi fond "Demokratiia," 1999.

Livshin, A. Ia., and I. V. Orlov, eds. *Sovetskaia propaganda v gody Velikoi otechestvennoi voiny: 'Kommunikatsiia ubezhdeniia' i mobilizatsionnye mekhanizmy.* Moscow: Rosspen, 2007.

Mironenko, S. V. *Fondy Gosudarstvennogo arkhiva Rossiiskoi Federatsii po istorii SSSR.* Vol. 3. Moscow: Reaktsionno-izdatel'skii otdel federal'nykh arkhivov, 1997.

Nadzhafov, D. G. *Stalin i kosmopolitizm: Dokumenty Agitpropa TsK KPSS, 1945–1953.* Moscow: Materik, 2005.

INTERVIEW

Eduard Ivanian, historian at the Institute for US and Canada Studies in Moscow, 27 November 2002.

NEWSPAPERS AND JOURNALS

Kul'tura i zhizn'
Life
New York Times
Pravda
Time

MEMOIRS AND OTHER PERSONAL ACCOUNTS

Aksenov, Vasilii. *V poiskakh grustnogo bebi: Kniga ob Amerike.* New York: Liberty Publishing House, 1987.

Alekseeva, Liudmila, and Paul Goldberg. *The Thaw Generation: Coming of Age in the Post-Stalin Era.* Boston: Little Brown, 1990.

American and Soviet Leaders Meet at the American Cultural and Scientific Conference for World Peace, New York, 1949. Addresses by Fadeyev, Shostakovich, Oparin. San Francisco: American Russian Institute, 1949.

Amerikantsy ob amerikanskom obraze zhizni. Moscow: Izdatel'stvo Znanie, 1959.

Amerikantsy ob Amerike. Moscow: Izdatel'stvo sotsial'no-ekonomicheskoi literatury, 1959.

Bobyshev, Dmitrii. *Ia zdes' (Chelovekotekst).* Moscow: Vagrius, 2003.

Bordarin, O., et al., eds. and compilers. *Sixth World Youth and Students Festival.* Moscow: Prepared by the Committee of Youth Organizations of the USSR, 1958.

Courtship of Young Minds: A Case Study of the Moscow Youth Festival. New York: East European Student and Youth Service, 1959.

Ehrenburg, Ilya, et al. *We Have Seen America.* New York: National Council of American-Soviet Friendship, 1946.

Face to Face with America: The Story of N. S. Khrushchov's Visit to the U.S.A. September 15–27, 1959. Moscow: Foreign Languages Publishing House, 1960.

Gribachev, Nikolai M. *Semero v Amerike: Zapiski korrespondenta "Literaturnoi gazety" o poezdke v SShA gruppy sovetskikh zhurnalistov v oktiabre–noiabre 1955g*. Moscow: Sovetskii pisatel', 1956.

Grushin, Boris A. *Chetyre zhizni Rossii v zerkale oprosov obshchestvennogo mneniia: Ocherki massovogo soznaniia rossiian vremen Khrushcheva, Brezhneva, Gorbacheva i El'tsina v 4-kh knigakh. Vol 1. Zhizn' 1-aia. Epokha Khrushcheva*. Moscow: Progress-Traditsiia, 2001.

Il'f, Il'ia, and Evgenii Petrov. *Odnoetazhnaia Amerika*. Moscow: Khudozh. lit-ra, 1937.

Koslov, Aleksei. *"Kozel na sakse" i tak vsiu zhizn'*. Moscow: Vagrius, 1998.

Litsom k litsu s Amerikoi. Rasskaz o poezdke N. S. Khrushcheva v SShA. 15–27 sentiabria 1959 goda. Moscow: Gosudarstvennoe izdatel'stvo politicheskoi literatury, 1959.

Matskevich, V. *Chto my videli v SShA i Kanade*. Moscow: Gosudarstvennoe izdatel'stvo politicheskoi literatury, 1956.

Mayakovsky, Vladimir. *My Discovery of America, Modern Voices*. London: Hesperus Press, 2005.

Mikoian, A. I. *Tak bylo: Razmyshleniia o minuvshem, moi 20. vek*. Moscow: Vagrius, 1999.

Polevoi, Boris. *Amerikanskie dnevniki*. Moscow: Sovetskii pisatel', 1956.

Roosevelt, Elliott. *As He Saw It*. New York: Duell, Sloan, and Pearce, 1946.

Shapiro, Henry. *L'U.R.S.S. après Staline*. Paris: Gallimard, 1954.

Steinbeck, John. *A Russian Journal, Penguin Twentieth-Century Classics*. New York: Penguin Books, 1999.

Stevenson, Adlai E. *Friends and Enemies: What I Learned in Russia*. New York: Harper, 1958.

Vishnevskii, Vsevolod, Sergei Mikhalkov, Konstantin Simonov, and Boris Lavrenev. *Sovetskaia dramaturgiia 1949: P'esy*. Moscow: Iskusstvo, 1950.

Voinovich, Vladimir. *Antisovetskii Sovetskii Soiuz: Dokumental'naia fantastagoriia v 4-kh chastiakh*. Moscow: Izdatel'stvo "Materik," 2002.

———. *The Anti-Soviet Soviet Union*. Translated by Richard Lourie. San Diego: Harcourt Brace Jovanovich, 1986.

UNPUBLISHED DISSERTATIONS AND THESES

Aucoin, Amanda Wood. "Deconstructing the American Way of Life: Soviet Responses to Cultural Exchange." Ph.D. diss., University of Arkansas, 2001.

Avramov, Konstantin Valentinovich. "Soviet America: Popular Responses to the United States in Post–World War II Soviet Union." Ph.D. diss., University of Kansas, 2012.

Bailey, Julia Emily Tatiana. "The Spectre of Communist Art: American Modernism and the Challenge of Socialist Realism, 1923–1960." Ph.D. diss., University College London, 2015.

Hooper, Cynthia. "Terror from Within: Participation and Coercion in Soviet Power, 1924–1964." Ph.D. diss., Princeton University, 2003.

Iwasaki, Kathy M. "The Memoir as Text: Impressions of American Engineers in the Soviet Union, 1928–1932." M.A. Thesis, UNC–Chapel Hill, 1990.

Koivunen, Pia. "Performing Peace and Friendship: The World Youth Festival as a Tool of Soviet Cultural Diplomacy, 1947–1957." Ph.D. diss., University of Tampere, 2013.

Rodgers, Rosemarie S. "The Soviet Audience: How It Uses the Mass Media." Ph.D. diss., Massachusetts Institute of Technology, 1967.

Roth-Ey, Kristin Joy. "Mass Media and the Remaking of Soviet Culture, 1950s–1960s." Ph.D. diss., Princeton University, 2003.

BOOKS AND ARTICLES

Aksiutin, Iurii. *Khrushchevskaia "ottepel'" i obshchestvennye nastroeniia v SSSR v 1953–1964 gg.* Moscow: Rosspen, 2004.

Alexandrova, Vera. "America and Americans in Soviet Literature." *Russian Review* 2, no. 2 (1943): 19–26.

Alexeyeva, Ludmilla. *U.S. Broadcasting to the Soviet Union.* New York: U.S. Helsinki Watch Committee, 1986.

Alpert, Hollis. *The Life and Times of Porgy and Bess: The Story of an American Classic.* 1st ed. New York: Knopf, 1990.

Althaus, Frank, and Mark Sutcliffe, *Drawing the Curtain: The Cold War in Cartoons.* London: Fontanka, 2012.

Anisimov, Oleg. "The Attitude of the Soviet People toward the West." *Russian Review* 13, no. 2 (1954): 79–90.

Antsyferova, Olga Yu. "American Literary Canons in the Soviet Union and Post-Soviet Russia." In *Russian/Soviet Studies in the United States, Amerikanistika in Russia: Mutual Representations in Academic Projects*, edited by Ivan Kurilla and Victoria I. Zhuravleva, 137–54. Lanham, MD: Lexington Books, 2016.

Autio-Sarasmo, Sari, and Katalin Miklóssy. *Reassessing Cold War Europe.* London: Routledge, 2011.

Azadovskii, Konstantin, and Boris Egorov. "From Anti-Westernism to Anti-Semitism: Stalin and the Impact of the 'Anti-Cosmopolitan' Campaigns on Soviet Culture." *Journal of Cold War Studies* 4, no. 1 (2002): 66–80.

Ball, Alan M. *Imagining America: Influence and Images in Twentieth-Century Russia.* Lanham, MD: Rowman & Littlefield, 2003.

Barghoorn, Frederick C. "The Image of Russia in Soviet Propaganda." In *Soviet Imperialism: Its Origins and Tactics*, edited by Waldemar Gurian, 137–65. Notre Dame, IN: University of Notre Dame Press, 1953.

———. *The Soviet Cultural Offensive: The Role of Cultural Diplomacy in Soviet Foreign Policy.* Princeton, NJ: Princeton University Press, 1960.

———. *The Soviet Image of the United States: A Study in Distortion.* New York: Harcourt, Brace, 1950.

Bauer, Raymond Augustine. *How the Soviet System Works: Cultural, Psychological, and Social Themes.* Cambridge, MA: Harvard University Press, 1956.

Becker, Jonathan A. *Soviet and Russian Press Coverage of the United States: Press, Politics, and Identity in Transition.* New York: Palgrave Macmillan 2002.

Beda, A. M. *Sovetskaia politicheskaia kul'tura cherez prizmu MVD: Ot "moskovskogo patriotizma" k idee "Bol'shogo Otechestva" (1946–1958).* Moscow: Izdatel'stvo ob"edineniia Mosgorarkhiv, 2002.

Belmonte, Laura. *Selling America: Propaganda, National Identity, and the Cold War, 1945–1959.* Philadelphia: University of Pennsylvania Press, 2008.

Benson, Jackson J. *The True Adventures of John Steinbeck, Writer.* New York: Viking Press, 1984.

Berlin, Isaiah. *The Soviet Mind: Russian Culture under Communism.* Edited by Henry Hardy. Washington, DC: Brookings Institution Press, 2004.

Bischof, Günther, and Saki Dockdrill, eds. *Cold War Respite: The Geneva Summit of 1955.* Baton Rouge: Louisiana State University Press, 2000.

Blakely, Allison. *Russia and the Negro: Blacks in Russian History and Thought.* Washington, DC: Howard University Press, 1986.

Boterbloem, Kees. *The Life and Times of Andrei Zhdanov, 1896–1948.* Montreal and Kingston: McGill–Queen's University Press, 2004.

Brandenberger, David. *National Bolshevism: Stalinist Mass Culture and the Formation of Modern Russian National Identity, 1931–1956.* Cambridge, MA: Harvard University Press, 2002.

———. *Propaganda State in Crisis: Soviet Ideology, Indoctrination, and Terror under Stalin, 1927–1941.* New Haven and London: Yale University Press, 2011.

———. "Stalin's Last Crime? Recent Scholarship on Postwar Soviet Antisemitism and the Doctor's Plot." *Kritika: Explorations in Russian and Eurasian History* 6, no. 1 (2005): 187–204.

Brooks, Jeffrey. "The Press and Its Message: Images of America in the 1920s and 1930s." In *Russia in the Era of NEP: Explorations in Soviet Society and Culture,* edited by Sheila Fitzpatrick, Alexander Rabinowitch, and Richard Stites, 231–52. Bloomington: Indiana University Press, 1991.

———. *Thank You, Comrade Stalin! Soviet Public Culture from Revolution to Cold War.* Princeton, NJ: Princeton University Press, 2000.

Burk, Kathleen. "The Marshall Plan: Filling in Some of the Blanks." *Contemporary European History* 10, no. 2 (2001): 267–94.

Caute, David. *The Dancer Defects: The Struggle for Cultural Supremacy during the Cold War.* Oxford and New York: Oxford University Press, 2003.

———. *The Fellow-Travellers: A Postscript to the Enlightenment.* New York: Macmillan, 1973.

Chatterjee, Choi, Lisa A. Kirschenbaum, and Deborah A. Field, *Russia's Long Twentieth Century: Voices, Memories, Contested Perspectives.* London and New York: Routledge, 2016.

Chernyshova, Natalya. *Soviet Consumer Culture in the Brezhnev Era*. New York: Routledge, 2013.

Cliff, Nigel. *Moscow Nights: The Van Cliburn Story—How One Man and His Piano Transformed the Cold War*. New York: Harper Perennial, 2016.

Cohen, Ariel, and Helle C. Dale. "Russian Anti-Americanism: A Priority Target for US Public Diplomacy." *Backgrounder* 2373. Washington: Heritage Foundation, 2010, 1–10.

Cramer, Allan P. "International Copyright and the Soviet Union." *Duke Law Journal* 3 (1965): 531–45.

Cull, Nicholas J. *The Cold War and the United States Information Agency: American Propaganda and Public Diplomacy, 1945–1989*. Cambridge: Cambridge University Press, 2009.

Dallin, David J. *The Real Soviet Russia*. Translated by Joseph Shaplen. New Haven: Yale University Press, 1947.

Danilova, Nataliya. *The Politics of War Commemoration in the UK and Russia*. New York: Palgrave Macmillan, 2015,

Davenport, Lisa E. *Jazz Diplomacy: Promoting America in the Cold War Era*. Jackson: University Press of Mississippi, 2009.

David-Fox, Michael. *Crossing Borders: Modernity, Ideology, and Culture in Russia and the Soviet Union*. Pittsburgh, PA: University of Pittsburgh Press, 2015.

———. "The Fellow Travelers Revisited: The 'Cultured West' through Soviet Eyes." *Journal of Modern History* 75, no. 2 (2003): 300–35.

———. "From Illusory 'Society' to Intellectual 'Public': VOKS, International Travel, and Party-Intelligentsia Relations." *Contemporary European History* 2, no. 1 (2002): 7–32.

———. "The Iron Curtain as Semipermeable Membrane: Origins and Demise of the Stalinist Superiority Complex." In *Cold War Crossings: International Travel and Exchange across the Soviet Bloc, 1940s–1960s*, edited by Patryk Babiracki and Kenyon Zimmer, 14–39. College Station: Texas A&M University Press, 2014.

———. *Showcasing the Great Experiment: Cultural Diplomacy and Western Visitors to the Soviet Union, 1921–1941*. New York: Oxford University Press, 2012.

de Keghel, Isabelle. "Meeting on the Elbe (Vstrecha na El'be): A Visual Representation of the Incipient Cold War from a Soviet Perspective." *Cold War History* 9, no. 4 (2009): 455–67.

Department of State. *Cultural Relations between the United States and the Soviet Union: Efforts to Establish Cultural-Scientific Exchanges Blocked by U.S.S.R.* Washington, DC: United States Government Printing Office, 1949.

Dimanche, Frederic, and Lidia Andrades, eds. *Tourism in Russia: A Management Handbook*. Bingley: Emerald Group, 2015.

Dobrenko, Evgeny. "Late Stalinist Cinema and the Cold War: An Equation without Unknowns." *Modern Language Review* 98, no. 4 (2003): 929–44.

Dobson, Miriam. *Khrushchev's Cold Summer: Gulag Returnees, Crime, and the Fate of Reform after Stalin*. Ithaca, NY: Cornell University Press, 2009.

Dudziak, Mary L. "Josephine Baker, Racial Protest, and the Cold War." *Journal of American History* 81, no. 2 (1994): 543–70.

Edele, Mark. "Strange Young Men in Stalin's Moscow: The Birth and Life of the Stiliagi, 1945–1953." *Jahrbücher für Geschichte Osteuropas* 50, no. 1 (2002): 37–61.

Emmons, Caroline S, ed. *Cold War and McCarthy Era: People and Perspectives*. Santa Barbara, CA: ABC-CLIO, 2010.

Endy, Christopher. *Cold War Holidays: American Tourism in France*. Chapel Hill: University of North Carolina Press, 2004.

Engerman, David C. *Know Your Enemy: The Rise and Fall of America's Soviet Experts*. Oxford and New York: Oxford University Press, 2009.

English, Robert D. *Russia and the Idea of the West: Gorbachev, Intellectuals, and the End of the Cold War*. New York: Columbia University Press, 2000.

Ezrabi, Christina. *Swans of the Kremlin: Ballet and Soviet Power in Soviet Russia*. Pittsburgh, PA: University of Pittsburgh Press, 2012.

Fainberg, Dina. "Unmasking the Wolf in Sheep's Clothing: Soviet and American Campaigns against the Enemy's Journalists, 1946–1953." *Cold War History* 15, no. 2 (2015): 155–78.

Fedorova, Milla. "The Pedagogy of Patriotism: America and Americans in Soviet Children's Literature." In *Russian/Soviet Studies in the United States, Amerikanistika in Russia: Mutual Representations in Academic Projects*, edited by Ivan Kurilla and Victoria I. Zhuravleva, 121–36. Lanham, MD: Lexington Books, 2016.

———. *Yankees in Petrograd, Bolsheviks in New York: America and Americans in Russian Literary Perception*. DeKalb: Northern Illinois Press, 2013.

Fisher, Wesley Andrew. *The Soviet Marriage Market: Mate-Selection in Russia and the USSR*. New York: Praeger Publishers, 1980.

Fitzpatrick, Sheila. *On Stalin's Team: The Years of Living Dangerously in Soviet Politics*. Princeton, NJ: Princeton University Press, 2015.

———. "Popular Opinion in Russia under Pre-war Stalinism." In *Popular Opinion in Totalitarian Regimes: Fascism, Nazism, Communism*, edited by Paul Corner, 17–32. Oxford: Oxford University Press, 2009.

———. "Supplicants and Citizens: Public Letter-Writing in Soviet Russia in the 1930s." *Slavic Review* 55, no. 1 (1996): 78–105.

Frisby, Tanya. "Soviet Youth Culture." In *Soviet Youth Culture*, edited by Jim Riordan, 1–15. Bloomington: Indiana University Press, 1989.

Fryer, Lee. *The American Farmer: His Problems & His Prospects*. New York and London: Harper & Brothers, 1947.

Fürst, Juliane. *Stalin's Last Generation: Soviet Post-War Youth and the Emergence of Mature Socialism*. Oxford: Oxford University Press, 2010.

Gaddis, John Lewis. *George F. Kennan: An American Life*. New York: Penguin Books, 2011.

Gienow-Hecht, Jessica C. E. "'How Good Are We?' Culture and the Cold War." In *The Cultural Cold War in Western Europe, 1945–1960*, edited by Giles Scott-Smith and Hans Krabbendam, 269–82. London: Frank Cass, 2003.

Gilburd, Eleonory. "Books and Borders: Sergei Obraztsov and Soviet Travels to London in the 1950s." In *Turizm: The Russian and East European Tourist under Capitalism and Socialism*, edited by Anne E. Gorsuch and Diane P. Koenker, 227–47. Ithaca, NY: Cornell University Press, 2006.

———. "The Revival of Soviet Internationalism in the Mid to Late 1950s." In *The Thaw: Soviet Society and Culture during the 1950s and 1960s*, edited by Denis Kozlov and Eleonory Gilburd, 362–401. Toronto: University of Toronto Press, 2013.

Gleason, Abbott. "Republic of Humbug: The Russian Nativist Critique of the United States, 1830–1930." *American Quarterly* 44, no. 1 (1992): 1–23.

Good, Jane E. "'I'd Rather Live in Siberia': V. G. Korolenko's Critique of America, 1893." *Historian* 44, no. 2 (1982): 190–206.

Gorchakov, Nikolai A. *The Theater in Soviet Russia*. Translated by Edgar Lehrman. New York: Columbia University Press, 1957.

Gordey, Michel. *Visa to Moscow*. 1st American ed. New York: Knopf, 1952.

Goriaeva, T. M. *Politicheskaia tsenzura v SSSR, 1917–1991*. Moscow: Rosspen, 2002.

Gorlizki, Yoram, and Oleg Khlevniuk. *Cold Peace: Stalin and the Soviet Ruling Circle, 1945–1953*. New York: Oxford University Press, 2004.

Gorsuch, Anne E. *All This Is Your World: Soviet Tourism at Home and Abroad after Stalin*. New York: Oxford University Press, 2011.

———. "From Iron Curtain to Silver Screen: Imagining the West in the Khrushchev Era." In *Imagining the West in Eastern Europe and the Soviet Union*, edited by György Péteri, 153–71. Pittsburgh, PA: University of Pittsburgh Press, 2010.

Gould-Davies, Nigel. "The Logic of Soviet Cultural Diplomacy." *Diplomatic History* 27, no. 2 (2003): 193–214.

Gribachev, Nikolai M. *Amerika, Amerika . . . poema*. Moscow: Sovetskii pisatel', 1961.

———. *Avgustovskie zvezdy*. Moscow: Sovetskii pisatel', 1958.

Gudkov, L., ed. *Obraz vraga*. Moscow: OGI, 2005.

Gudkov, Lev. "Ideologema 'vraga': 'vragi' kak massovyi sindrom i mekhanizm sotsiokul'turnoi integratsii." In *Obraz vraga*, edited by L. Gudkov, 7–79. Moscow: OGI, 2005.

Hahn, Werner G. *Postwar Soviet Politics: The Fall of Zhdanov and the Defeat of Moderation, 1946–53*. Ithaca, NY: Cornell University Press, 1982.

Hammer, Darrell P. "Law Enforcement, Social Control, and the Withering of the State: Recent Soviet Experience." *Soviet Studies* 14, no. 4 (1963): 379–97.

Harris, Steven E. *Communism on Tomorrow Street: Mass Housing and Everyday Life after Stalin*. Washington, DC: Woodrow Wilson Center Press, 2013.

Hasty, Olga Peters, and Susanne Fusso. *America through Russian Eyes, 1874–1926*. New Haven: Yale University Press, 1988.

Hellbeck, Jochen. "Working, Struggling, Becoming: Stalin-Era Autobiographical Texts." *Russian Review* 60, no. 3 (2001): 340–59.

Hellman, Ben. "Samuil Marshak: Yesterday and Today." In *Russian Children's Literature and Culture*, edited by Marina Balina and Larissa Rudova, 217–39. New York and London: Routledge, 2008.

Hixson, Walter L. *Parting the Curtain: Propaganda, Culture, and the Cold War, 1945–1961*. New York: St. Martin's Press, 1998.

Hoberman, John. *The Olympic Crisis: Sport, Politics, and the Moral Order*. New Rochelle, NY: Aristide O. Carataz, 1986.

Hoffmann, David L. *Stalinist Values: The Cultural Norms of Soviet Modernity, 1917–1941*. Ithaca, NY: Cornell University Press, 2003.

Hollander, Paul. *Political Pilgrims: Western Intellectuals in Search of the Good Society*. New Brunswick, NJ Transaction, 1998.

Holtzman, Filia. "A Mission That Failed: Gor'kij in America." *Slavic and East European Journal* 6, no. 3 (1962): 227–35.

Hornsby, Robert. *Protest, Reform, and Repression in Khrushchev's Soviet Union*. Cambridge: Cambridge University Press, 2013.

The Image of the Voice of America as Drawn in Soviet Media. Prepared for the Office of Research and Intelligence at the United States Information Agency by the Department of Sociology. New Brunswick, NJ: Rutgers University, June 1954.

Ingimundarson, Valur. "Immunizing against the American Other: Racism, Nationalism, and Gender in US-Icelandic Military Relations during the Cold War." *Journal of Cold War Studies* 6, no. 4 (2004): 65–88.

Inkeles, Alex. *Social Change in Soviet Russia*. Cambridge, MA: Harvard University Press, 1968.

———. "The Soviet Attack on the Voice of America: A Case Study in Propaganda Warfare." *American Slavic and East European Review* 12, no. 3 (1953): 319–42.

———. "Soviet Reactions to the Voice of America." *Public Opinion Quarterly* 16, no. 4 (Winter 1952–1953): 612–17.

Iriye, Akira. "Culture." *Journal of American History* 77, no. 1 (1990): 99–107.

———. "Culture and Power: International Relations and Intercultural Relations." *Diplomatic History* 3, no. 2 (1979): 115–28.

Jensen, Steven L. B. *The Making of International Human Rights: The 1960s, Decolonization, and the Reconstruction of Global Values*. Cambridge: Cambridge University Press, 2016.

Johnston, Timothy. *Being Soviet: Identity, Rumour, and Everyday Life under Stalin, 1939–1953*. Oxford: Oxford University Press, 2011.

Jones, Robert Huhn. *The Roads to Russia: United States Lend-Lease to the Soviet Union*. Norman: University of Oklahoma Press, 1969.

Kenez, Peter. *The Birth of the Propaganda State: Soviet Methods of Mass Mobilization, 1917–1929*. Cambridge and New York: Cambridge University Press, 1985.

———. *Cinema and Soviet Society: From the Revolution to the Death of Stalin*. London, New York: I. B. Tauris, 2001.

Kiparsky, Valentin. *English and American Characters in Russian Fiction*. Berlin: In Kommission bei O. Harrassowitz Wiesbaden, 1964.

Koenker, Diane P. *Club Red: Vacation Travel and the Soviet Dream*. Ithaca, NY: Cornell University Press, 2013.

Koivunen, Pia. "The 1957 Moscow Youth Festival: Propagating a New, Peaceful Image of the Soviet Union." In *Soviet Society under Nikita Khrushchev*, edited by Melanie Ilic and Jeremy Smith, 46–65. London and New York: Routledge, 2009.

Korolenko, Vladimir. *In a Strange Land.* New York: Bernard G. Richards, 1925.

———. *Puteshestvie v Ameriku.* Moscow: Zadruga, 1923.

Kozlov, Denis and Eleonory Gilburd. "The Thaw as an Event in Russian History." In *The Thaw: Soviet Society and Culture during the 1950s and 1960s*, edited by Denis Kozlov and Eleonory Gilburd, 18–81. Toronto: University of Toronto Press, 2013.

Kozlov, Vladimir A. *Mass Uprisings in the USSR: Protest and Rebellion in the Post-Stalin Years.* Translated and edited by Elaine McClarnand MacKinnon. Armonk, NY, and London, England: M. E. Sharpe, 2002.

Kozlov, V. A., and S. V. Mironenko, eds. *Kramola: Inakomyslie v SSSR pri Khrushcheve i Brezhneve 1953–1982 gg. Rassekrechennye dokumenty Verkhovnogo suda i Prokuratury SSSR.* Moscow: Materik, 2005.

Kozovoï, Andreï. "The Cold War and Film." In *The Routledge Handbook of the Cold War*, edited by Artemy M. Kalinovsky and Craig Daigle, 340–50. Oxford and New York: Routledge, 2014.

———. "A Foot in the Door: The Lacy-Zarubin Agreement and Soviet-American Film Diplomacy during the Khrushchev Era, 1953–1963." *Historical Journal of Film, Radio, and Television* 36, no. 1 (2016): 21–39.

———. *Par-delà le Mur: la culture de guerre froide soviétique entre deux détentes.* Bruxelles: Éditions Complexe, 2009.

———. "'This Film Is Harmful': Resizing America for the Soviet Screen." In *Winter Kept Us Warm: Cold War Interactions Reconsidered*, edited by Sari Autio-Sarasmo and Brendan Humphreys, 137–53. Helsinki: Aleksanteri Cold War Series, 2010.

Krementsov, Nikolai. *The Cure: A Story of Cancer and Politics from the Annals of the Cold War.* Chicago: University of Chicago Press, 2002.

Laychuk, Julian L. *Ilya Ehrenburg: An Idealist in an Age of Realism.* Bern: Peter Lang, 1991.

Leffler, Melvyn P. *For the Soul of Mankind: The United States, the Soviet Union, and the Cold War.* New York: Hill and Wang, 2007.

Leonhard, Wolfang. *The Kremlin since Stalin.* Translated by Elizabeth Wiskemann and Marian Jackson. New York: Frederick A. Praeger, 1962.

Lewis, Flora. "Youth from 102 Lands Swarms over Moscow." *Life* 43, no. 7, August 12, 1957.

Lisann, Maury. *Broadcasting to the Soviet Union: International Politics and Radio.* New York: Praeger Publishers, 1975.

Loewenstein, Karl E. "Re-Emergence of Public Opinion in the Soviet Union: Khrushchev and Responses to the Secret Speech." *Europe-Asia Studies* 58, no. 8 (2006): 1329–45.

Lovell, Stephen. *Russia in the Microphone Age: A History of Soviet Radio, 1919–1970.* Oxford: Oxford University Press, 2015.

———. *The Shadow of War: The Soviet Union and Russia, 1941 to the Present*. Malden, MA: Wiley-Blackwell, 2010.

Magnúsdóttir, Rósa. "Cold War Correspondents and the Possibilities of Convergence: American Journalists in the Soviet Union, 1968–1979." *Soviet and Post-Soviet Review* 41, no. 1 (2014): 33–56.

McDaniel, Cadra Peterson. *American-Soviet Cultural Diplomacy: The Bolshoi Ballet's American Premiere*. Lanham, MD: Lexington Books, 2015.

McKenna, Kevin J. *All the Views Fit to Print: Changing Images of the US in Pravda Political Cartoons, 1917–1991*. New York: Peter Lang, 2001.

McKenzie, Brian A. "Creating a Tourist's Paradise: The Marshall Plan and France, 1948 to 1952." *French Politics, Culture & Society* 21, no. 1 (2003): 35–54.

Mehnert, Klaus. *The Russians & Their Favorite Books*. Stanford, CA: Hoover Institution Press Stanford University, 1983.

Mendelson, Sarah E., and Theodore P. Gerber. "Us and Them: Anti-American Views of the Putin Generation." *Washington Quarterly* 31, no. 2 (2008): 131–50.

Mikkonen, Simo. "Soviet-American Art Exchanges during the Thaw: From Bold Openings to Hasty Retreats." In *Art and Political Reality*, edited by Merike Kurisoo, 57–76. Tallinn: Art Museum of Estonia–Kumu Kunstimuseum, 2013.

———. "Stealing the Monopoly of Knowledge? Soviet Reactions to US Cold War Broadcasting." *Kritika: Explorations in Russian and Eurasian History* 11, no. 4 (2010): 771–805.

Mitrokhin, Nikolai. "The Rise of Political Clans in the Era of Nikita Khrushchev." In *Khrushchev in the Kremlin: Policy and Government in the Soviet Union, 1953–1964*, edited by Jeremy Smith and Melanie Ilic, 26–40. London and New York: Routledge, 2011.

Monod, David. "Disguise, Containment, and the *Porgy and Bess* Revival of 1952–1956." *Journal of American Studies* 35, no. 2 (2001): 275–312.

———. "'He Is a Cripple and Needs My Love'": *Porgy and Bess* as Cold War Propaganda." In *The Cultural Cold War in Western Europe, 1945–1960*, edited by Giles Scott-Smith and Hans Krabbendam, 300–12. London: Frank Cass Publishers, 2003.

Moser, Charles A. "Korolenko and America." *Russian Review* 28, no. 3 (1969): 303–14.

———. "Mayakovsky and America." *Russian Review* 25, no. 3 (1966): 242–56.

———. "Mayakovsky's Unsentimental Journeys." *American Slavic and East European Review* 19, no. 1 (1960): 85–100.

Nelson, Michael. *War of the Black Heavens: The Battles of Western Broadcasting in the Cold War*. Syracuse, NY: Syracuse University Press, 1997.

Nemzer, Louis. "The Soviet Friendship Societies." *Public Opinion Quarterly* 13, no. 2 (1949): 265–84.

Nikolaeva, N. I. "Obraz SShA v Sovetskom obshchestve v poslevoennye gody, 1945–1953." In *Amerikanskii ezhegodnik*, edited by Nikolai N. Bolkhovitinov, 244–70. Moscow: Izd-vo Nauka, 2002.

Noonan, Ellen. *The Strange Career of* Porgy and Bess: *Race, Culture, and America's Most Famous Opera*. Chapel Hill: University of North Carolina Press, 2012.

Norris, Stephen M. "Memory for Sale: Victory Day 2010 and Russian Remembrance." *Soviet and Post-Soviet Review* 38, no. 2 (2011): 201–29.

Osgood, Kenneth. *Total Cold War: Eisenhower's Secret Propaganda Battle at Home and Abroad*. Lawrence: University Press of Kansas, 2006.

Papovian, Elena. "Primenenie stat'i 58-10 UK RSFSR v 1957–1958 gg. Po materialam Verkhovnogo suda SSSR i Prokuratury SSSR v GARF." In *Korni travy: Sbornik statei molodykh istorikov*, edited by L. S. Ereminaia and E. B. Zhemkova, 73–87. Moscow: Zvenia, 1996.

Parks, J. D. *Culture, Conflict, and Coexistence: American-Soviet Cultural Relations, 1917–1958*. Jefferson, NC: McFarland, 1983.

Peacock, Margaret. "The Perils of Building Cold War Consensus at the 1957 Moscow World Festival of Youth and Students." *Cold War History* 12, no. 3 (2012): 515–35.

Pechatnov, Vladimir. "Exercise in Frustration: Soviet Foreign Propaganda in the Early Cold War, 1945–47." *Cold War History* 1, no. 2 (2001): 1–27.

Pechatnov, Vladimir O. "The Rise and Fall of *Britansky Soyuznik*: A Case Study in Soviet Response to British Propaganda of the Mid-1940s." *Historical Journal* 41, no. 1 (1998): 293–301.

Pells, Richard H. *Not Like Us: How Europeans Have Loved, Hated, and Transformed American Culture since World War II*. New York: Basic Books, 1997.

Persico, Joseph E. *The Imperial Rockefeller: A Biography of Nelson Rockefeller*. New York: Simon and Schuster, 1982.

Perucci, Tony. *Paul Robeson and the Cold War Performance Complex: Race, Madness, Activism*. Ann Arbor: University of Michigan Press, 2012.

Petrone, Karen. *Life Has Become More Joyous, Comrades: Celebrations in the Time of Stalin*. Bloomington: Indiana University Press, 2000.

Philpott, Delbert E., and Donna Philpott. *Hands across the Elbe: The Soviet-American Linkup*. Paducah, KY: Turner Publications, 1995.

Plamper, Jan. "Beyond Binaries: Popular Opinion in Stalinism." In *Popular Opinion in Totalitarian Regimes: Fascism, Nazism, Communism*, edited by Paul Corner, 64–80. Oxford: Oxford University Press, 2009.

———. *The Stalin Cult: A Study in the Alchemy of Power*. New Haven: Yale University Press, 2012.

Pomorska, Krystyna. "A Vision of America in Early Soviet Literature." *Slavic and East European Journal* 11, no. 4 (1967): 389–97.

Poole, Ernest. "Maxim Gorki in New York." *Slavonic and East European Review American Series* 3, no. 1 (1944): 77–83.

Prybyla, Jan S. "The Soviet Consumer in Khrushchev's Russia." *Russian Review* 20, no. 3 (1961): 194–205.

Raleigh, Donald J. *Soviet Baby Boomers: An Oral History of Russia's Cold War Generation*. Oxford and New York: Oxford University Press, 2012.

Rapoport, Alexander. "The Russian Broadcasts of the Voice of America." *Russian Review* 16, no. 3 (1957), 3–14.

Reid, Susan E. "Cold War in the Kitchen: Gender and the De-Stalinization of Consumer Taste in the Soviet Union under Khrushchev." *Slavic Review* 61, no. 2 (2002): 211–52.

Richmond, Yale. *Cultural Exchange and the Cold War: Raising the Iron Curtain*. University Park, PA: Pennsylvania State University Press, 2003.

Robinson, Harlow. *The Last Impresario: The Life, Times, and Legacy of Sol Hurok*. New York: Penguin Books, 1994.

Rogger, Hans. "Amerikanizm and the Economic Development of Russia." *Comparative Studies in Society and History* 23, no. 3 (1981): 382–420.

Rolf, Malte. "Feste der Einheit und Schauspiele der Partizipation: Die Inszenierung von Öffentlichkeit in der Sowjetunion um 1930." *Jahrbücher für Geschichte Osteuropas* 50, no. 2 (2002): 163–71.

Rose, Clive. *The Soviet Propaganda Network: A Directory of Organisations Serving Soviet Foreign Policy*. London: Pinter Publishers, 1988.

Rosenberg, Jonathan. "Fighting the Cold War with Violins and Trumpets: American Symphony Orchestras Abroad in the 1950s." In *Winter Kept Us Warm: Cold War Interactions Reconsidered*, edited by Sari Autio-Sarasmo and Brendan Humphreys, 23–43. Helsinki: Aleksanteri Cold War Series, 2010.

Rosenberg, Victor. *Soviet-American Relations, 1953–1960: Diplomacy and Cultural Exchange during the Eisenhower Presidency*. Jefferson, NC, and London: McFarland, 2005.

Roth-Ey, Kristin. *Moscow Prime Time: How the Soviet Union Built the Media Empire That Lost the Cultural Cold War*. Ithaca, NY: Cornell University Press, 2011.

Rougle, Charles. *Three Russians Consider America: America in the Works of Maksim Gor'kij, Aleksandr Blok, and Vladimir Majakovskij*. Stockholm: Almqvist & Wiksell International, 1976.

Rubenstein, Joshua. *Tangled Loyalties: The Life and Times of Ilya Ehrenburg*. London: I. B. Tauris, 1996.

Ruggles, Melville J. "American Books in Soviet Publishing." *Slavic Review* 20, no. 3 (1961): 419–35.

Ruksenas, Algis. *Is That You Laughing Comrade? The World's Best Russian (Underground) Jokes*. Secaucus, NJ: Citadel Press, 1986.

Salmon, Shawn. "Marketing Socialism: Inturist in the Late 1950s and Early 1960s." In *Turizm: The Russian and East European Tourist under Capitalism and Socialism*, edited by Anne E. Gorsuch and Diane Koenker, 186–204. Ithaca, NY: Cornell University Press, 2006.

Satjukow, Silke, and Rainer Gries, eds., *Unsere Feinde: Konstruktionen des Anderen im Sozialismus*. Leipzig: Leipziger Universitätsverlag, 2004.

Saunders, Frances Stonor. *The Cultural Cold War: The CIA and the World of Arts and Letters*. New York: New Press, 1999.

Schattenberg, Susanne. "'Democracy' or 'Despotism'? How the Secret Speech Was Translated into Everyday Life." In *The Dilemmas of De-Stalinization: Negotiating Cultural and Social Change in the Khrushchev Era*, edited by Polly Jones, 64–79. London: Routledge-Curzon, 2006.

Schwartz, Lowell H. *Political Warfare against the Kremlin: US and British Propaganda Policy at the Beginning of the Cold War*. New York: Palgrave Macmillan, 2009.

Scott, Mark. *Yanks Meet Reds: Recollections of US and Soviet Vets from the Linkup in World War II*. Santa Barbara, CA: Capra Press, 1988.

Sharp, Paul. "Revolutionary States, Outlaw Regimes, and the Techniques of Public Diplomacy." In *The New Public Diplomacy: Soft Power in International Relations*, edited by Jan Melissen, 106–23. New York: Palgrave Macmillan, 2005.

Shaw, Tony, and Denise J. Youngblood. *Cinematic Cold War: The American and Soviet Struggle for Hearts and Minds*. Lawrence: University Press of Kansas, 2010.

Shearer, David R. *Policing Stalin's Socialism: Repression and Social Order in the Soviet Union, 1924–1953*. New Haven: Yale University Press, 2009.

Shepilov, Dmitrii. *The Kremlin's Scholar: A Memoir of Soviet Politics under Stalin and Khrushchev*. Edited by Stephen V. Bittner, translated by Anthony Austin. New Haven: Yale University Press, 2007.

Shiraev, Eric. "Russia's Views of America in a Historic Perspective." In *America: Sovereign Defender or Cowboy Nation*, edited by Vladimir Shlapentokh, Joshua Woods, and Eric Shiraev, 45–52. Burlington, VT: Ashgate, 2005.

———. "'Sorry, but . . .': Russia's Responses in the Wake of 9/11." In *America: Sovereign Defender or Cowboy Nation*, edited by Vladimir Shlapentokh, Joshua Woods, and Eric Shiraev, 53–68. Burlington, VT: Ashgate, 2005.

Shiraev, Eric, and Vladislav Zubok. *Anti-Americanism in Russia: From Stalin to Putin*. New York: Palgrave, 2000.

Shlapentokh, Dmitry, and Vladimir Shlapentokh. *Soviet Cinematography, 1918–1991: Ideological Conflict and Social Reality, Communication and Social Order*. New York: A. de Gruyter, 1993.

Shlapentokh, Vladimir. "The Puzzle of Russian Anti-Americanism: From 'Below' or From 'Above.'" *Europe-Asia Studies* 63, no. 5 (2011): 875–89.

———. *Soviet Public Opinion and Ideology: Mythology and Pragmatism in Interaction*. New York: Praeger Publishers, 1986.

Shvedov, S. "Obraz Genri Forda v sovetskoi publitsistike 1920–1930-kh godov: vospriiatie i transformatsiia tsennostei chuzhoi kul'tury." In *Vzaimodeistvie kul'tur SSSR i SShA XVIII–XX vv.*, edited by O. E. Tuganova, 133–42. Moscow: Nauka, 1987.

Siefert, Marsha. "From Cold War to Wary Peace: American Culture in the USSR and Russia." In *The Americanization of Europe: Culture, Diplomacy, and Anti-Americanism after 1945*, edited by Alexander Stephan, 185–217. New York: Berghahn Books, 2006.

———. "Meeting at a Far Meridian: US-Soviet Cultural Diplomacy on Film in the Early Cold War." In *Cold War Crossings: International Travel and Exchange across the Soviet Bloc, 1940s–1960s*, edited by Patryk Babiracki and Kenyon Zimmer, 166–209. College Station: Texas A&M University Press, 2014.

Smeliansky, Anatoly. *The Russian Theatre after Stalin*. Cambridge Studies in Modern Theatre. Cambridge: Cambridge University Press, 1999.

Smith, Mark B. "Peaceful Coexistence at All Costs: Cold War Exchanges between Britain and the Soviet Union in 1956." *Cold War History* 12, no. 3 (2012): 537–58.

———. *Property of Communists: Urban Housing Program from Stalin to Khrushchev*. DeKalb: Northern Illinois University Press, 2010.

Stein, Kevin A. "Apologia, Antapologia, and the 1960 Soviet U-2 Incident." *Communication Studies* 59, no. 1 (2008): 19–34.

Stephan, Alexander. *The Americanization of Europe: Culture, Diplomacy, and Anti-Americanism after 1945*. New York: Berghahn Books, 2006.

Stern, Ludmila. "The All-Union Society for Cultural Relations with Foreign Countries and French Intellectuals, 1925–29." *Australian Journal of Politics and History*, vol. 45, no. 1 (1999): 99–109.

Stites, Richard. "Frontline Entertainment." In *Culture and Entertainment in Wartime Russia*, edited by Richard Stites, 126–40. Bloomington: Indiana University Press, 1995.

———. *Revolutionary Dreams: Utopian Vision and Experimental Life in the Russian Revolution*. New York: Oxford University Press, 1989.

———. *Russian Popular Culture: Entertainment and Society since 1900*. Cambridge: Cambridge University Press, 1992.

Stojko, Wolodymyr, and Volodymyr Serhiychuk. "J. Steinbeck in Ukraine: What the Secret Soviet Archives Reveal." *Ukrainian Quarterly* 51, no. 1 (1995): 62–76.

Struve, Gleb. "Anti-Westernism in Recent Soviet Literature." *Yale Review* 39, no. 2 (1949): 209–24.

Swayze, Harold. *Political Control of Literature in the USSR, 1946–1959*. Cambridge, MA: Harvard University Press, 1962.

Taubman, William. *Khrushchev: The Man and His Era*. New York, London: Norton, 2003.

Taylor, J. H. "From Catfish Row to Red Square: *Porgy and Bess* and the Politics of the Cold War." *Theatre InSight* 7, no. 1 (1996): 29–35.

Timofeev, Timur Timofeevich. *Negry SShA v bor'be za svobodu*. Moscow: Gos. izd-vo polit. lit-ry, 1957.

Tomoff, Kirill. *Virtuosi Abroad: Soviet Music and Imperial Competition during the Early Cold War, 1945–1958*. Ithaca, NY: Cornell University Press, 2015.

Tromly, Benjamin. *Making the Soviet Intelligentsia: Universities and Intellectual Life under Stalin and Khrushchev*. Cambridge: Cambridge University Press, 2014.

Tsipursky, Gleb. "Coercion and Consumption: The Khrushchev Leadership's Ruling Style in the Campaign against 'Westernized' Youth, 1954–1964." In *Youth and Rock in the Soviet Bloc: Youth Cultures, Music, and the State in Russia and Eastern Europe*, edited by William Jay Risch, 55–79. Lanham, MD: Lexington Books, 2015.

———. *Socialist Fun: Youth, Consumption, and State-Sponsored Popular Culture in the Soviet Union, 1945–1970*. Pittsburgh, PA: University of Pittsburgh Press, 2016.

Tucker, Robert C. "The Cold War in Stalin's Time: What the New Sources Reveal." *Diplomatic History* 21, no. 2 (1997): 273–81.

Tuganova, O. E. *Vzaimodeistvie Kul'tur SSSR i SShA XVIII–XX vv.* Moscow: Nauka, 1987.

Turovskaya, Maya. "Soviet Films of the Cold War." In *Stalinism and Soviet Cinema*, edited by Richard Taylor and Derek Spring, 131–41. London and New York: Routledge, 1993.

Twain, Mark. "The Gorki Incident: An Unpublished Fragment (1906)." *Slavonic and East European Review American Series* 3, no. 2 (1944): 37–38.

Vail, Petr, and Aleksandr Genis. *60e—mir sovetskogo cheloveka*. Moscow: Novoe literaturnoe obozrenie, 1996.

Volkov, Vadim. "The Concept of *Kul'turnost'*: Notes on the Stalinist Civilizing Process." In *Stalinism: New Directions*, edited by Sheila Fitzpatrick, 210–30. London: Routledge, 2000.

von Eschen, Penny M. "'Satchmo Blows Up the World': Jazz, Race, and Empire during the Cold War." In *'Here, There, and Everywhere': The Foreign Politics of American Popular Culture*, edited by Reinhold Wagnleitner and Elaine Tyler May, 163–78. Hanover, NH: University Press of New England, 2000.

Voronina, Olga. "'The Sun of World Poetry': Pushkin as a Cold War Writer." *Pushkin Review* 14 (2011): 63–95.

Wagnleitner, Reinhold, and Elaine Tyler May. *Here, There, and Everywhere: The Foreign Politics of American Popular Culture*. Hanover, NH: University Press of New England, 2000.

Washburn, John N. *Soviet Theater: Its Distortion of America's Image, 1921 to 1973*. Chicago: American Bar Association, 1973.

Weiner, Amir. "The Making of a Dominant Myth: The Second World War and the Construction of Political Identities within the Soviet Polity." *Russian Review* 55, no. 4 (1996): 638–60.

Whitfield, Stephen J. *The Culture of the Cold War*. 2nd ed. Baltimore: Johns Hopkins University Press, 1996.

Williams, Albert Rhys. *The Bolsheviks and the Soviets*. New York: Rand School of Social Science, 1919.

Yurchak, Alexei. *Everything Was Forever, Until It Was No More: The Last Soviet Generation, In-Formation Series*. Princeton, NJ: Princeton University Press, 2005.

Zakharova, Larissa. "Dior in Moscow: A Taste for Luxury in Soviet Fashion under Khrushchev." In *Pleasures in Socialism: Leisure and Luxury in the Eastern Bloc*, edited by David Crowley and Susan E. Reid, 95–119. Evanston, IL: Northwestern University Press, 2010.

Zezina, Maria. "Crisis in the Union of Soviet Writers in the Early 1950s." *Europe-Asia Studies* 46, no. 4 (1994): 649–61.

Zhuk, Sergei. *Rock and Roll in the Rocket City: The West, Identity, and Ideology in Soviet Dniepropetrovsk, 1960–1985*. Baltimore: Johns Hopkins University Press, 2010.

Zhuravleva, Victoria I. "Amerikanskaia kukuruza v Rossii: uroki narodnoi diplomatii i kapitalizma." *Vestnik RGGU* 21, no. 122 (2013): 121–46.

———. *Ponimanie Rossii v SShA: obrazy i mify 1881–1914*. Moscow: RGGU, 2012.

Zubkova, Elena. *Russia after the War: Hopes, Illusions, and Disappointments, 1945–1957*. Translated and edited by Hugh Ragsdale. Armonk, NY and London, England: M. E. Sharpe, 1998.

Zubok, Vladislav M. *A Failed Empire: The Soviet Union in the Cold War from Stalin to Gorbachev*. Chapel Hill: University of North Carolina Press, 2007.

———. "Introduction." In *Cold War Crossings: International Travel and Exchange across the Soviet Bloc, 1940s–1960s*, edited by Patryk Babiracki and Kenyon Zimmer, 1–13. College Station: Texas A&M University Press, 2014.

———. *Zhivago's Children: The Last Russian Intelligentsia*. Cambridge, MA: Belknap Press of Harvard University Press, 2009.

Zubok, Vladislav, and Constantine Pleshakov. *Inside the Kremlin's Cold War: From Stalin to Khrushchev*. Cambridge, MA: Harvard University Press, 1996.

INDEX